✳ CELEBRATION FOR – JOURNEY OF *THE GREAT CIRCLE* ✳

This unique, heartfelt, and visionary book penetrates to the deepest questions of the human journey, and offers touching and inspiring poetic images to guide us. Oman Ken brings the wealth of his experience and deep insights as a welcome roadmap to awakening. I recommend Journey of *The Great Circle* to anyone dedicated to fathom the mysteries of life and advance on your own healing journey.

— *Alan Cohen, bestselling author of* **A Course in Miracles Made Easy**

In his book, **Journey of *The Great Circle***, Oman brings forth "pearls" of wisdom - and has strung those pearls together in a compelling narrative and practice. Bottom line: If you find yourself going around in circles in life, go around THIS circle, and you will spiral to a higher and brighter view.

— *Steve Bhaerman, aka Swami Beyondananda "cosmic comic" and co-author with Bruce Lipton of* **Spontaneous Evolution: Our Positive Future and a Way to Get There From Here.**

Oman's book inspires us to embark on a sacred journey and exploration of what life is truly about - and what really matters. Here is a book that can be utilized every day to polish the Diamond of our Souls.

— *Rama Jyoti Vernon, co-founder of* **The Yoga Journal** *and author of* **Yoga: The Practice of Myth & Sacred Geometry**

With the poetry of a passionate artist - and the perspectives of an intuitive scientist, Oman Ken has written a visionary book. Utilizing his unique system of daily practices, he lays out the vision and pathway for a more peaceful and compassionate world.

— *Reverend Max Lafser, Unity minister and former chairman of* **The Center For International Dialogue**

I know first-hand the power and beauty of a 365 daily transformation practice. Oman's deep reflection and soul searching has devoutly created this profound and poetic work. Use this book as a daily practice to soar into the heights of your soul. You will forever be transformed.

—*José R. Fuentes, Co-Founder and Facilitator of the Sedona Integral Group*

Oman's book, Journey of *The Great Circle,* is too rich with meaningful poetic and creative thinking not to be experienced. Through his 365 contemplative exercises, he brings a great gift to the human family for our next leap in wholeness. I celebrate this new work, for I know the reader will be assisted in their spiritual unfoldment.

— *Bruce Kellogg, Unity minister*

Journey of *The Great Circle* is Oman Ken's epic masterpiece to passionately hone and master the best in us. Four seasonal volumes of brilliant creativity weaving consciousness, science, art, history, and evolutionary spirituality. Stunningly written and organized. You will be blessed.

— *Enocha Ranjita Ryan, Transformational Healing Artist*

As a minister, I would highly recommend Oman's book to inspire other ministers with meaningful themes for Sunday talks. Each of the 365 contemplative narratives is rich with powerful ideas and inspiration. Oman's book is such a meaningful gift for humanity as well as a practical pathway to a better world at this crucial moment in human development.

— *Marshall Norman, former Unity minister of Madison, Wisconsin*

JOURNEY OF
THE GREAT CIRCLE

DAILY CONTEMPLATIONS FOR CULTIVATING INNER FREEDOM
AND LIVING YOUR LIFE AS A MASTER OF FREEDOM

SPRING VOLUME

OMAN KEN

BALBOA.PRESS
A DIVISION OF HAY HOUSE

Balboa Press books may be ordered through booksellers or by contacting:

Balboa Press
A Division of Hay House
1663 Liberty Drive
Bloomington, IN 47403
www.balboapress.com
844-682-1282

Cover art designed by Oman Ken – and created by Mark Gelotte.
Graphic art designed by Oman Ken – and created by Mark Gelotte.
Photography of Oman Ken by Charles Ruscher

ISBN: 978-1-9822-7862-5 (sc)
ISBN: 978-1-9822-7861-8 (e)

Print information available on the last page.

Balboa Press rev. date: 03/22/2022

✳ CONTENTS ✳
Themes and Metaphors of Spring

March 19	Gifts of Spring	Composing a New Version of a Universe
March 20	Qualities Within the Seasons of Life	The Journey of the Great Wheel of Life
March 21	The Great Story of Awakening	Four Horse-drawn Chariots
March 22	Journey of Awakening	Ascending the Mountain Summit
March 23	Transformation	Snakes Shed Their Old Skins
March 24	Transformative Practice	The Tuner Within a Radio or Television
March 25	Faith	The Hidden Fuel of Mighty Steamships
March 26	Innocence	Lessons from the Film, "Forrest Gump"
March 27	Polarities of Existence	The Story of Noah and the Great Flood

March 28	The Great Circle	Life Contains Many Paradoxes
March 29	The Great Circle of Heart Wisdom and Compassion	History Related to a Person's Life Cycle
March 30	The Great Circle of the Star of David	The Many Symbols of Everyday Life

✳ DEDICATION ✳

This book is dedicated to the scientists of the world
who help point all of us toward finding the truth of what is,

those devoted people who use the natural gifts of science
to attempt to improve life for everyone,

and those who use science as a vehicle
to understand how we are all intimately connected
as one global family.

The evolutionary perspective helps us make a transformation
from a limited self-oriented view of seeing our lives
solely within an individual context,
and invites us to cultivate a more expanded collective context
where we can truly understand how we are all intimately connected
with every other person
- and with all creatures on the planet.

✳ WHAT IS – JOURNEY OF *THE GREAT CIRCLE* ✳

JOURNEY OF *THE GREAT CIRCLE* is a collection of 365 contemplative narratives designed as a daily transformative practice for the purpose of personal transformation. The annual collection of narratives is divided into four volumes, Winter, Spring, Summer, and Autumn each beginning on either the solstice or equinox. Each of the 365 narratives has a specific spiritual theme to help you gain a more expansive understanding of what really matters - and points you to how to live a life with peace of mind and inner freedom.

The various themes of the narratives involve insights from spirituality, quantum physics, the evolutionary perspective, the study of visionary archetypes, healing, and transformative practice. **Journey of *The Great Circle*** can be thought of as "a spiritual map of an awakening life".

A life of inner freedom is when one consciously realizes the perfection that's always unfolding within - and within all of life. Living with this awareness allows the natural states of peace, happiness, joy and harmony to effortlessly arise. It is a life of one who has devotedly learned to love others and all of life unconditionally - and who has gained the joyful awareness of serving the wellbeing of others. In these writings, one who attains this level of mastery is referred to as a **Master of Freedom**.

We are all natural-born storytellers with a mandate from *Life* to generate the most fulfilling and creative story of life we can imagine. Every day is a new opportunity to make our life story a little more glorious, a little more fulfilling, a little more creative. We are the authors of this story in every moment of our lives based on the intentions we choose, either consciously or unconsciously. For most people, in order to have the most glorious, fulfilling, creative, and peaceful life requires some form of spiritual practice necessitating conscious attention each day.

Journey of *The Great Circle* utilizes a transformative system of daily practices that can help you:

1) Experience a life of peace, happiness, joy, harmony, and fulfilling creative expression.

2) Prepare for the day's activities and surprises that await you so you can meet each situation from the "sanctuary" of heart wisdom, gratitude, and centeredness.

3) Connect to the inner guidance of the heart so you may live you life with ease and grace.

4) Learn to love every expression of life unconditionally.

5) Maintain a conscious alignment with *a Greater Power*. *A Greater Power* has been called myriad names, including but not limited to, *the Source of Life, the Infinite Presence of Love, God, the Great Spirit,* and *the Infinite Intelligence of the Universe.*

When **Journey of *The Great Circle*** is used on a daily basis it will help cultivate inner freedom and assist you in fulfilling your sacred destiny of an awakened life as a **Master of Freedom**.

Like a "magnet from the future" magically pulling each of us towards it,
awakening is the natural process of shifting our awareness
from the imprisoning bondage of our habitual egoic needs
oriented around self-centered power, control, and fear-based concerns,
to the freedom and liberation of aligning with *the Source of Life*
and being in service to the wellbeing of others.

✳ PREFACE – THE GENESIS ✳

I WAS STANDING ALONE on a large wooden stage in front of a thousand people performing my original songs with my two dear companions - my acoustic guitar and my lyrical voice. I had also created a photographic slide show to visually animate the poetic images of my songs, which projected on a large screen behind me.

As the strings of my guitar rang out, I was offering the last song of a two-week concert tour where I had traveled through the lush Northwest in late spring. As the musical notes of this final composition came to an end, I felt something was very wrong. I could feel a turbulent energy within my ailing body crashing through every cell. My physical form was in some kind of crisis, and from that moment on, my life would never be the same.

The Story of How This Book Came To Be

Life seems to lead each of us on an adventurous journey in which we must ultimately make important choices based on the many possible roads and different turns that come before us along the way. When we were young, most of us conjured up some sort of future vision about how our life would unfold when we grew older. Yet usually for most of us, there was a plethora of surprises and unpredictable twists along life's journey. This book is the surprising result of one of those twists.

In 2005, after numerous years of steadily declining health, a mysterious illness had become a major challenge, and I became deeply frustrated and depressed. I lost most of my physical energy and was very fatigued and exhausted. A heat sensation would rush up into my head each day accompanied by reddish flushing of my chest, neck, and head. At times I felt an internal shaking in my body that was strange, frightening, and uncomfortable. Because of these curious symptoms, I had to adjust my entire life. My musical career came to a halt, and I had to adapt to a new expression of who I was and what I did. I was no longer able to tour around the country performing concerts and retreats with my music. I lost all motivation and energy to record music in my home studio as I did in previous years. And I was barely able to perform at short local events - such as conferences and weddings in order to pay monthly bills.

Because of these increasing physical challenges, I spent many years and lots of money seeing numerous doctors, naturopaths, nutritionists, chiropractors, hypnotherapists, spiritual counselors, health wizards, and a "host of pretty cosmic characters" to find a resolution to my situation. I did get a little help here and there, but for the most part, nothing seemed to work ongoing. My health kept declining slowly. I got very angry at life. At God. At the *Infinite Intelligence* that was supposed to be good and fair. What was happening to me did not feel fair.

I thought of myself as "a spiritual person" because I did a host of "spiritual things". I meditated every day, read spiritual books, attended self-help workshops, exercised regularly, ate a fantastic array of organic food, projected what I thought was a positive attitude toward life, served people with my uplifting music, donated money to environmental organizations - and therefore in my mind, I did everything "right". Why would someone like me, who is "spiritual" and is doing everything "right", suffer from a physical condition that felt so "wrong"? Over time, I was getting more and more depressed, even suicidal. After a long period of feeling this way, I got very tired of living a depressed life and decided to take more responsibility for my healing.

When I made this shift in awareness, one of the ways I chose to responsibly deal with my ongoing depression was to re-dedicate my life to my spiritual practice. I did this by spending more time in Nature, so I could deeply contemplate my personal situation. I wanted to find out what, if anything, I was supposed to learn about myself from this challenging opportunity I was dealing with.

At that time I had been living in Sedona, Arizona for eighteen years. I received the inner guidance to spend one day a week out in Nature alongside a beautiful wooded creek called Oak Creek and use this time to explore my inner spiritual quest. Each week at the water's edge I would spend five to seven hours in contemplation and inquiry, and then wrote down any insights or realizations. I wanted to use this time in Nature to gain insights about what I could discover about myself from my increasing health challenges and how they might relate to my life-long quest of spiritual awakening, however I understood it.

Thus this weekly ritual of sitting beside the creek, quieting my mind, and waiting began. And then insights started to come. And they continued to emerge each week with different spiritual themes and different life perspectives for me to consider. The thought came to me that it would be easier to remember these insights at a later time if I could find a simpler form to record them, rather than writing long paragraphs of prose as in a spiritual journal. Previously, I had done a lot of journal writing, but I noticed I had a tendency to not go back and read my journals very often. Therefore, I wanted to devise another way to record my thoughts.

I decided to use the basic circular form of the Native American medicine wheel with its four cardinal points and a center point. I picked four primary concepts of each theme or idea I was exploring during my contemplations and wrote them down in four short phrases or sentences in the location of the four cardinal directions (west, south, east and north).

I named these thematic circles Contemplation Circles. Each Contemplation Circle was focused around a spiritual theme that would help point me to *a Transcendent Reality* and to an expanded vision of living my life with inner freedom. I perceived these circles as spirtual maps of consciousness - or theme targets - or wheels of distinction that empowered and supported my spiritual journey and the restoration of my health. Through these ongoing contemplations, I have received beneficial insights that have served the wellbeing of my body, heart, and mind, and have helped me to expand the way I love and accept myself.

Over many years of working with these Contemplation Circles on a daily basis, I began to see applications for them in various aspects of my spiritual practice. They started to organically have a life of their own. I was inwardly guided regarding how to use them in contemplation practices, affirmative prayer, foundational transformative practices, and to gain ever-larger perspective of my life, including my physical challenges.

In 2007, I experienced a transformational workshop called the Big Mind Process facilitated by Genpo Roshi, a Buddhist teacher and author. I was deeply moved by the ability of this process to bring a person to a direct experience of profound states of transcendence so quickly and effectively. The next morning, I began to create my own Contemplation Circles around my experience of the Big Mind Process. It felt natural to use a set of specific circles in a sequential form in my daily meditations. The result was very powerful. The depth of my meditations took on a new level of sublime communion, and I began to notice a much greater experience of self-love and acceptance of my life.

I used this system of meditation for a year, continuing to receive fulfilling results - and was then guided to put this meditation process into a form that could be shared with others. The first book I wrote is called, **Master of Freedom**. This book was written as a universal creation story that portrays "The Great Story" of the creation of the Universe, the 13.8 billion year process of infinitely intelligent evolution. **Master of Freedom** is the archetypal story of life awakening throughout the Universe - in relation to our current human journey of transformation, the spirituality of humanity. It offers a poetic glimpse of our sacred destiny, which is to live an awakened life of inner freedom - and to learn to love all of life unconditionally.

Then in November of 2008, I was given the inner guidance to take 365 of my 400-plus Contemplation Circles and organize them in such a way as to write a thematic narrative for every day of the year. I started writing these narratives on December 21, 2008, the Winter Solstice. That year, I wrote a 350-word narrative for 365 consecutive days. This daily set of contemplative narratives, accompanied by its adjacent Contemplation Circle, I called **Journey of *The Great Circle***.

I do not call myself a spiritual teacher, nor am I some kind of healer, psychological counselor, or expert of esoteric spiritual studies. I am simply a conscious person who is passionate about living life fully and discovering what really matters, but also a person, like many, who has suffered a great deal during my life adventure. Yet by some form of *grace*, I have embraced the conscious awareness to take responsibility for my healing, and through inner transformative work have gained a greater experience of inner freedom.

Initially, I did not begin this time of deep contemplation in Nature with a pre-conceived idea to write a book. The creative process of these contemplations grew over time on its own, and I feel this book was written through me rather than by me. I was benefiting tremendously from these contemplations and insights, living with greater peace, happiness, joy, and harmony, and my guidance informed me to put them into a book for the benefit of others.

The Daily Practice of Being *an Artist of Life*

JOURNEY OF *THE GREAT CIRCLE* is a daily transformative program to assist people interested in developing larger perspectives of what life is truly about in order to cultivate an ongoing experience of inner freedom and an awareness of loving oneself and others unconditionally. It uses *the evolutionary perspective* to help create an understanding of the "Bigger Picture" of our human reality.

This system of contemplative practices focuses on the daily practice of being an *artist of life* in which a person lives in a state of inner freedom, maintains an ongoing alignment with *Life*, and learns to effectively contribute his or her creative gifts and talents in service to others - and to all of life. In this series of narratives, living in inner freedom is described as an awakened individual (referred to as a **Master of Freedom**) who has discovered how to live life masterfully and who has learned to respond to every experience with gratitude, surrender, and complete acceptance of what is.

The insights from **Journey of *The Great Circle*** assist in understanding that this universal awakening is a part of the intrinsic evolution that's taking place everywhere in the Cosmos. Thus it's taking place on our little blue planet - and is also taking place within you and me. Every person has the potential to be a conscious self-reflective human being becoming aware of the natural unfolding of evolutionary principles within the Universe and throughout the Earth. When we become aware of, and deeply study, *the evolutionary perspective* (the unfolding perspective of the Universe that has been naturally evolving for 13.8 billion years) and we perceive how we are all an integral part of this constant and ever-expanding evolution, we then begin to understand that this *journey of spiritual awakening* is one of the most natural processes unfolding within every human being. It is just one step in the never-ending unfolding journey within a vast Universe of Infinite Awakenings.

The Intention for Journey of *The Great Circle*

This book is designed to assist individuals to respond to life's challenges with harmony and grace, as well as to understand the blessing and obligation it is to contribute one's unique gifts and talents to the creation of a more glorious world. In other words, these narratives are designed to inspire people to cultivate inner freedom and to joyously offer their creative gifts to others as an *artist of life*.

My intention in sharing this book
is that it be helpful
in discovering the magnificence
of who you really are.

My hope
is that the contemplative practices in this work
may aid you
to more easily navigate your life
to a place of peace and inner freedom.

✶ INTRODUCTION – POLISHING THE DIAMOND ✶

Bringing Light to *the Art of Life*

IMAGINE WALKING THROUGH AN ART MUSEUM that displays many exquisite masterpieces of paintings and sculpture. Now visualize that it's late at night when all of the lights are turned off - and every room is completely dark. In this moment you would not be able to see anything in the museum. All of the magnificent works of art would be right in front of you, but without any light to illuminate them, you couldn't enjoy them.

Now imagine that you light a match. The sudden light from the match would allow you to get a glimpse of some of the artistic majesty around you. Yet if you turned on a strong flashlight, it would provide even more illumination for you to enjoy a bigger spectrum of the art collection. And, of course, if the main lights in the museum were suddenly turned on, you would be able to appreciate the total experience of beauty and grace from all the masterpieces around you.

Certainly before the overhead lights were turned on, the art and sculpture were right there close to you the entire time, but were veiled and hidden in the dark. But with the aid of the light, you were able to observe what was always present.

Similar to the lit match, the flashlight, or the main lights in the museum, ever-greater spiritual awareness (ever-larger perspectives of what our life is truly about and what really matters) is like a powerful light that comes into "the mansion of our heart and mind" to illuminate the reality we perceive. More expansive perspectives of reality transform "the darkness of our mind", so we can easily see the truth, goodness, and beauty that is always there. What is always present within us, and what *the Essence of Life* yearns for us to fully experience, is the radiant magnificence of who we really are. We are constantly being invited by *Life* to rediscover our ever-present magnificence - by turning on the light of our conscious awareness.

There is a constant stream of *Transcendent Energy*, a *Field of Unlimited Creativity*, which surrounds us and permeates within us in every moment. This *Boundless and Transcendent Creativity* is who we really are. Yet sometimes "the darkness" of our habitual belief in separation, fear, and other loveless thoughts can inhibit us from seeing our own beauty, our own "magnificent work of art". Every one of us is a living masterpiece that is ever-evolving, a creative work in progress. Our life is the outer creative expression of our inner development. We are continually learning to unveil the exquisite beauty and majesty of who we truly are. Each day we fashion the blank canvas of our life to create the next version of our masterpiece. Every day we're embarked on a journey of learning to artfully live our lives in a way that expresses the natural states of peace, happiness, joy, and harmony. These are the natural states of our *True Eternal Nature*.

Greater spiritual awareness is what naturally nurtures the creative artist within us - or what we can call *the artist of life*. There are many time-tested ways to cultivate *the artist* within us - and to turn on "the light of our spiritual awareness", including meditation, self-inquiry, deep contemplation, and devotional prayer - to name a few. Yet another important way is to fully recognize that in the present moment, our life is always unfolding perfectly just as it is - for life simply is the way it is. This sublime recognition is a radical acceptance of our life.

The Daily Practice of *the Art of Life*

Like being helplessly and powerfully drawn toward some mysterious invisible magnet, we seem to be constantly pulled by unseen forces that attempt to compel us to seek for something other than what we already are. Our modern society, as well as the unconscious people around us, sometimes tell us that we are not OK the way we are, that we are somehow flawed and need to be fixed, that something within us is not right, and that what is wrong in us must be changed into what others believe is right.

The unconscious result of our society's dysfunctional conditioning is that it keeps pulling us away from the creative power of the present moment. This kind of social conditioning persists in attempting to catapult us to some future reality where, at some illusory time, our lives will hopefully be fixed, changed, holy, or enlightened. It falsely promises that we will finally be transformed into what we've been taught by others to believe life should actually look like.

If we habitually succumb to "the mysterious pull of this magnet", this collective illusion propagated within our society, then we typically begin our personal quest to be fixed, or to rid ourselves of our flaws, by first trying to eliminate our suffering. And sometimes from a religious point of view, this illusory quest compels us to attempt the pursuit of spiritual enlightenment - or some kind of spiritual transformation, so we may someday be like the elevated saints and gurus we have learned to venerate.

Of course there is nothing wrong with gaining inspiration from the wealth of great spiritual wayshowers that have come before us, especially if they're pointing us to our own innate power and invincible *True Nature*. Yet seeking to be fixed, as if we were broken, can become the kind of illusory spiritual quest in which we join millions of other people across the globe in seeking something to magically transform our lives, but which in actuality, we already have and already are. *We already are, and have always been, the perfect expression of truth, goodness, and beauty that the Infinite Intelligence of the Universe perfectly unfolds within us through a natural process of universal and personal evolution.* We are all living in a boundless *Field of Unlimited Creativity* which is always present to further our inner development and spiritual evolution.

As we intentionally open our heart so we may explore an even deeper and more meaningful spiritual quest, we begin to feel the inner attraction of an authentic "spiritual magnet", our true *journey of awakening.* This *journey of discovery* is primarily about the full realization of who we really are. This "attraction" is the natural tug of *the Transcendent Impulse* within us. It is the natural impulse to learn that, in the present moment, our life is unfolding perfectly just as it is.

Over time we begin to recognize the perfection unfolding within the creative expressions in every form of life. We are part of that perfection which includes each living creature on our planet and every phenomenal structure within the Universe. This awareness allows us to be truly grateful for everything, to humbly surrender our attachments and resistance, to fully accept ourselves just as we are, and to celebrate the essential Oneness of which we are a part.

This is *Life's* universal invitation to love and accept ourselves completely and unconditionally with all of our individual flaws and personality traits. It's a heightened recognition that the challenging parts of our life are not problems, but rather sacred gifts we can use to "polish the diamond" within us. We use these gifts so we may transform into a more radiant expression of our highest self. We attain this awareness - not by being habitually attached to getting rid of our suffering or our challenges - but by embracing each challenge as "a gift in disguise" offered for our personal and collective transformation. These are life's exquisite opportunities to let our pain or suffering point us to what our life is truly about - and what really matters.

As we arrive at this level of spiritual awareness, we become immune to the societal influences and programming of "the magnet of dysfunctional conditioning". We then experience a transformative shift from living under the unconscious urge of constantly seeking for what we do not have - to celebrating the magnificence of who we already are and joyously living *the art of life.*

Being and *Becoming*

Living our lives in the present moment is where true creativity exists, as well as the genuine experience of unconditional love. Authentically living in present moment awareness, or Presence, allows us to be consciously aware of two fundamental and paradoxical streams of life that are constantly expressing within us: **Being** and **Becoming**.

Being is the absolute reality where everything in our life is unfolding perfectly just as it is. A life that is unfolding perfectly is one that lives in the sacred sanctuary of present moment awareness. With this awareness there's a knowing that because of the perfection in our life, there is nothing to do and nowhere to go, and that nothing needs to be changed, altered or fixed. **Being** is also an awareness of the Oneness within all of life, and in that Perfect Oneness rests the experience of true happiness and peace of mind.

At the same time, living in Presence allows us to experience the paradoxical and complimentary stream of life called **Becoming**. The journey of **Becoming** is the constant natural yearning within us to develop our highest potential, to strive for ever-higher levels of awareness, to expand into new horizons and uncharted territory of unlimited possibilities, and to poetically "reach for the stars". This ongoing personal growth and inner development comes from an intrinsic longing to contribute to the creation of a more glorious world within an awareness of joy and creativity, rather than from an awareness of needing to fix something that is wrong with us - or the unconscious attachment to relieve our suffering.

Cultivating Inner Freedom

There are many beautifully written self-help books, which certainly play an important role in elevating a person's conscious awareness and alleviating suffering. As it has been already stated, **Journey of *The Great Circle*** is not about helping you change the outer circumstances of your lives, fix your emotional or psychological flaws, or get rid of your problems. These writings aim to inspire you to live a life of devoted practice so as to cultivate inner freedom, self-love, and an unconditional love for all of life. Yet with this wealth of self-cultivation, the areas of one's life are constructively affected. This book is also designed to point you to the conscious awareness of your *True Eternal Nature*, the supreme holiness and magnificence of who you really are.

It's pretty obvious that everyone has their own set of difficult opportunities to deal with, and there doesn't appear to be any way to bypass life's many challenges. Some challenges can be very hard to cope with, yet challenge is one of the most natural parts of evolving life. For without the dynamic challenges, chaos, and turbulence within the Universe there would be no galaxies, nor stars, nor planets. Thus there would be no intelligent life on Earth, and there would be no conscious awakening within you and me.

Therefore, with intention, we can choose to use our challenges as sacred gifts in order to become ever more free. We can make use of these opportunities to consciously develop a more awakened awareness, for true healing is learning to maintain a perfect balance within us that supports the evolution of all of life. No matter how much money we have, how great our health may be, how wonderful our marriage or significant relationship is, or how successful our career may be unfolding, we will always be presented with challenging situations that will invite us to expand our ability to experience true inner freedom.

Inner freedom does not come from changing the external conditions of our lives, but is fostered from how we're able to respond to the events and challenges of our life from inside the chamber of our heart. The heart is the integral part of us we must keep open and aligned with *the Source of Life*, so the sublime energy of *Limitless Love* can continuously flow through us unimpeded.

Embodying Inner Freedom

Inner freedom is the unconditional love and acceptance of ourselves and others in which we fully realize that our life is unfolding perfectly just as it is. Since the nature of life is to move through continuous cycles of order and chaos, balance and imbalance, challenges will always be an intrinsic and important part of our ever-evolving life. A masterful ability to love and accept life just the way it is, simply witnessing these experiences without judgment, allows for inner freedom to be embodied within the everyday unfolding of life's constant stream of challenges and treasures.

Just as turning on the main lights in a darkened museum allows us to see all the artistic masterpieces present, as we illuminate the light of our own awareness to the supreme majesty and magnificence of who we are, we re-establish our ability to live in self-mastery. In these writings, a person who realizes and lives with this elevated awareness is referred to as a **Master of Freedom**.

Transformative Practice

This innate yearning to embody inner freedom and joyously express our unique creativity is enhanced by developing a system of personal practice that helps us consciously live our visionary intentions. Through the use of daily transformative practices, we "polish the diamond of our inner being" and use the personal expressions of our creativity to help manifest a more peaceful and compassionate world. Transformative practice is what establishes new belief systems, new world views, new perspectives of life, and new behavior. Practice is what also slowly eliminates destructive habits and dysfunctional patterns in our life.

As we develop a more expanded awareness, "life becomes practice" and "practice becomes life". And both our life and our practice are informed and guided by consciously living in a state of Presence, a state of present moment awareness. From this state, we practice *the art of life*, like a musician practices his or her instrument, or a painter practices his or her craft, to co-create with life in sculpting a more beautiful world. Whether we practice the piano or tennis, compose a symphony, develop a life-enhancing personality trait, or help to relieve hunger on our planet, transformative practice is all about living in the joy of being an *artist of life*. It's about jumping into the natural stream of evolving life that inwardly directs us towards truth, goodness, and beauty - and towards expressions of unconditional love and service to others.

The essence of this book is intended to inspire and provide the mechanisms for the power of daily practice. Each day presents a unique awareness perspective to contemplate regarding the nature of your life. Each day provides an opportunity to expand your awareness of what your life is truly about - and what really matters. It is of great benefit to bring these contemplations out into the glory of Nature - to sit next to a creek - or lie upon the earth at the top of a hill - or lean against a tall tree. As you exercise the "muscles" of your *body, heart, mind, and Spirit* each day with steady determination and commitment, you are assisting *Life* in creatively sculpting its next expression of awakening within you.

Remember that you already are, and have always been, a supremely gifted *artist of life*. There is no one else who can create the exquisite masterpieces which only you can create. So while you enjoy your daily practice as you read and contemplate each day's theme within this book of narratives, you are practicing *the art of life*. And remember that your daily practice is not only for your personal benefit. We are all intimately connected as one global family as we ascend the infinite ladder of awareness. Our daily practice benefits all the men, women, children, and myriad creatures of the world. Practice well.

You Are A Diamond

You are a perfect diamond
    Longing to become more perfect
        A luminescent jewel
            Shimmering upon the necklace of this ephemeral world   ·
           Forged from the supreme fire
               Within the heart of the Universe

You are a multifaceted gem of sublime majesty and grace
    Through which *Life* focuses its celestial starlight
    So it may glisten endlessly within you

You are a beloved *artist of life*
    Fashioning unparalleled hues upon the blank canvas of each new day
    To create the next rendering of your magnificent masterpiece

You are an invincible prism of the *Soul*
    Chiseled into form so *the Fullness* of the Cosmos can savor
    More of the luminous spectrum of its sensual wonders and hallowed glories

You are an ascending aeronaut spiraling heavenwards
    Climbing the infinite ladder of possibility
        Navigating tumultuous storms and immaculate skies
           Terrestrial chaos and galactic order
               The sacred gifts you use to share the omniscient nature of your truest self

You are a sovereign sculptor of untethered intentions
    Each one polishing the ever-effulgent diamond of your life
        So you may launch new portals of pristine freedom
           For the invisible lines of destiny to dance through you

Your mission - to dance with the *Light*
    Your purpose - to polish the perfection
        Your meaning of it all - to give for the good of all

It's just what diamonds
    Who spend their life *Being*
        In the course of *Becoming*
           Do

Today in our contemporary time, the perspective of *evolutionary spirituality*
has shifted our focus from our self-oriented and personal desires
to become enlightened, spiritually awake, or enter heaven just for ourselves
to an understanding that authentic enlightenment
is about living an awakened life of inner freedom
in which we love all of life unconditionally
and use our creative gifts and talents
to serve the wellbeing of others.

✳ HOW TO BENEFIT FROM THIS BOOK ✳

The Daily Narratives and Contemplation Circles

JOURNEY OF *THE GREAT CIRCLE* has been designed to provide a set of contemplative narratives of various spiritual themes to be used as a daily transformative practice for cultivating peace of mind and inner freedom. Engaging daily in this form of inner development, especially for an entire year, you will be inwardly pointed to the most natural ways to experience greater peace, happiness, joy, and harmony.

Each of the 365 contemplative themes has a narrative displayed on the left page and a corresponding Contemplation Circle on the right. The Contemplation Circle illustrates a short summary of the daily narrative in four concise statements or words. Each Contemplation Circle can be used to quickly reconnect and summarize the primary ideas that have been described in the narrative.

The Contemplation Circles are typically read in the clockwise direction starting with the north node (top quadrant) yet there are often variations of how the Circles can be read. Many have arrows pointing in a specific direction for further contemplation. Generally, the counter-clockwise direction of the Circles represents the evolution of consciousness, and the clockwise direction represents the evolution of creation.

The Four Seasonal Volumes

The complete set of 365 contemplative narratives has been divided into four seasonal volumes. Each has a specific theme for its series of daily practices. The Winter Volume is oriented toward practices for the **cultivation of spiritual wellbeing**; the Spring Volume for **wellbeing of the mind**; the Summer Volume for **wellbeing of the heart**; and the Autumn Volume for **wellbeing of the body**.

Each of the four volumes contains sixteen primary Contemplation Circles that are repeated in all four volumes. The specific Contemplation Circle is the same within each volume, but the narrative is different, allowing you to explore and gain a deeper understanding of the main theme.

How to Use the First Two Seasonal Narratives – March 19th and 20th

The first two narratives of this volume, March 19th and March 20th, explore the spiritual meaning and transcendent qualities of the spring season. Both of these narratives have two dates printed at the top of the page. This is because the spring equinox, the first day of spring, will usually occur on one of those two dates depending on the relationship of the Earth's orbit with the Sun for any given year. The title of the first narrative is written as "Gifts of Spring – March 19th or 20th" and the second is written as "Qualities Within the Seasons of Life – March 19th or 20th".

When the spring equinox takes place on March 19th, read the first two narratives as they are sequentially laid out. When the spring equinox occurs on March 20th, read the narrative entitled "Qualities Within the Seasons of Life" first on March 19th, and then read "Gifts of Spring" on March 20th, the actual day of the spring equinox for that year.

Transformative Practices

A primary intention of this book is to encourage the use of daily transformative practice as a means to discover effective ways to embody and anchor the ideas and concepts into the heart as a direct experience. Consistent self-cultivation is the center of spiritual development. Throughout each of the four volumes there are a series of transformative practices that may be incorporated into one's daily life. The prominent focus is based upon four foundational transformative practices. These are:

1) meditation, 2) contemplation, 3) appreciation, and 4) prayer.

It is suggested for the spiritual development of the reader that some form of each of these four practices be experienced frequently. Change usually happens slowly and incrementally through constant repetition on a daily basis. In order to master a sport, an art, a science, or a business, one must practice ardently. It takes this same effort to develop our spiritual nature.

You may be interested in exploring the suggested meditative practices in the narrative from January 14th called "Meditation Practices" in the Winter Volume or explore various meditation practices that you discover elsewhere. You can also explore a specific form of the practice of contemplation in the narrative from April 5th called "A Contemplation Practice" in the Spring Volume. Daily appreciation is seemingly straightforward, yet you may get additional inspiration from the July 6th narrative called "Spheres of Appreciation" in the Summer Volume. And you may deepen your exploration of the power of prayer in the October 8th narrative called "The Practice of Prayer" in the Autumn Volume.

Daily Affirmation Statements

At the top of each contemplative narrative is a short affirmation printed in italics. This affirmation expresses one of the key themes within the daily narrative. For best results, the affirmation can be repeated at various times throughout the day. In the back of the book, all affirmation statements are printed for each day within a given volume. They are designed to be copied onto a piece of 8.5" x 11" paper. You can cut along the dotted lines and then take the individual affirmation with you as a reminder of the theme you are embracing for that specific day.

Visionary Archetypes as Transformative Practice

A visionary archetype is similar to the image of a distant horizon, for it represents qualities and virtues of ever-higher levels of human consciousness that we can envision on our personal horizon, yet desire to embody right now in our life. It is a poetic image of our greater potential or possibility, which we have yet to realize, until we have bravely traveled past boundaries of our current beliefs about who we think we are.

Visionary archetypes are symbolic templates that point us to higher stages of inner development and to the qualities and realms of creative expression we strive to achieve. They can be thought of as pictorial representations of superior moral qualities which can empower and motivate us to reach for something greater in ourselves, a promise of a more positive future for our life.

We can use these archetypes as a spiritual tool and blueprint of potential to assist us in imagining a more perfect expression of ourselves, and to hold within us an expansive vision of what is possible. It is suggested that each person seek their own inner guidance regarding how to use these visionary archetypes as a means to envision and embody the highest possibilities of who they really are.

Throughout each volume there are four sets of visionary archetypes that can be used as a transformative practice to envision and embody one's creative potential and spiritual sovereignty. The four sets are: 1) The Archetypes of Spiritual Awakening, 2) The Archetypes of Life Mastery, 3) The Archetypes of Higher Knowledge, and 4) The Archetypes of Conscious Contribution.

The Archetypes of Life Mastery, the Archetypes of Higher Knowledge, and the Archetypes of Conscious Contribution are all visionary archetypes. The Archetypes of Spiritual Awakening are four archetypes that represent our *spiritual journey*, or *journey of awakening*. The ultimate culmination of our *journey of awakening* is consciously living a life of inner freedom represented by the archetype of the **Master of Freedom**. All of the other visionary archetypes are facets of our unlimited potential, pointing to our sacred destiny as a **Master of Freedom**.

A Tool of Inner Guidance

There are additional ways to benefit from this book other than consecutively reading the daily narratives. You can also utilize this book to find guidance and inspiration by opening any volume to any place within the seasonal narratives, reading that specific narrative, and discovering how the narrative applies to your life at that moment. In this way, **Journey of *The Great Circle*** becomes "a tool of inner guidance" and can be used when you need a form of spiritual guidance or when you are seeking a moment of inspiration for your day.

The Great Circle as "a Spiritual Map of an Awakening Life"

The Great Circle is a map of consciousness and creation. It is a way to clearly understand the dynamics at play in our world and in our life. **The Great Circle** illustrates how our inner development determines and gives creative shape to how our external reality is expressed in our life. It portrays the universal dynamics relating to our inward expansion of awareness mirrored as our outward creative expression.

The primary function of **The Great Circle** as a transformative tool is to simply portray a useful collection of thoughts and ideas for the purpose of deeply comprehending the nature of existence. With this awareness we develop a greater understanding of what our life is truly about and thus cultivate an unconditional love for each expression of life.

There are many examples of traditional iconic images that represent **The Great Circle**, such as the Yin Yang symbol, the Star of David, the Medicine Wheel, and the Sacred Cross. In this book, the following symbolic image, *"The Great Circle* Portal - a Window Into *Being* and *Becoming"*, is also used to visually illustrate **The Great Circle** as "A Spiritual Map of an Awakening Life".

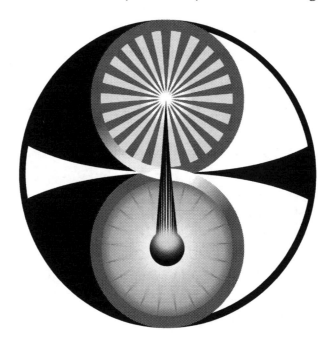

This image has been placed at each chapter of the contemplative practices to subconsciously assist you in deepening your understanding of the universal dynamics that are at play in the world and in your life. It can also be used to cultivate a comprehension of your purpose in life, your life mission, the meaning of life, and an awareness of your *True Nature*. Here is the significance of the Circle:

First, there is both a vertical line and a horizontal line within the larger circle of the image. The vertical line represents *Being* - or *Infinite Intelligence* - or God *(the Divine Transcendent* aspect of life). The horizontal line represents *Becoming*, our *journey of inner development*, our *spiritual journey.*

Over the vertical line within the large circle there is a Vertical Infinity Sign (a figure eight) that perpetually descends to the bottom of the circle and then ascends to the top repeating continuously. This Vertical Infinity Sign represents the constant yearning of our current physical lifetime (bottom circle) to merge with *the Transcendent, the Source of Life* (top circle) and *the Transcendent* (top circle) that constantly yearns to manifest ever-new expressions of creativity in our current physical lifetime (bottom circle). This natural and constant yearning (which is both the longing for spiritual awakening and spiritual embodiment) exists within us and within all forms of life. It is called *the Transcendent Impulse.*

The Vertical Infinity Sign represents *the Transcendent Impulse* as the top circle merging with the bottom circle - Consciousness merging with Creation - God merging with the Universe - *Divinity* merging with humanity - *Spirit* merging with the body - *Infinite Intelligence* merging with the myriad forms of Nature - *The One* merging with the Many.

The top circle within the Vertical Infinity Sign is a cosmic tunnel, like an inter-dimensional portal or quantum vortex, constantly moving towards the center. The center of this circle represents God, *the Source of All That Is, Universal Consciousness*.

The bottom circle has a Black Centerpoint or Singularity which represents material form, the physical body, or a focused point of creative manifestation.

The thick black line from the center of the top circle to the center of the bottom circle represents the perpetual alignment and Oneness of our current physical incarnation with *the Divine Transcendent (God, Infinite Intelligence, the Source of Life).*

Master of Freedom Logo

This image represents our *Fully Awakened Self*, one's *True Eternal Nature* completely experienced and lived within one's physical body. It is the embodied realization of a person who lives a life of inner freedom, loves all of life unconditionally, and serves the good of all with their creative gifts and talents. It is every person's sacred destiny to embody the *Awakened Self* and fully experience life as a **Master of Freedom.**

Infinite Awakenings Logo

This image represents the perpetual evolution - or the constant "awakenings" - that naturally take place in every aspect of Nature symbolized by the diamond, the flower, the bird, and the human being.

At one time, millions of years ago, there was only a plethora of green vegetation on the planet. The beautiful manifestation of flowers had not yet arrived on the evolutionary scene. But over time and with gradual development, evolving life eventually found a way to empower a brand new emergent form to arise; the very first flower.

For the first flower to take shape on Earth, a radical shift in consciousness was required within the plant kingdom. This new expression of vegetative form could poetically be thought of as an "enlightenment" or "awakening" of the plant kingdom. A similar kind of radical shift in consciousness also occurred in the mineral kingdom with the first diamond - and millions of years later, in the animal kingdom with the first flight of a bird.

The same expansive evolutionary impulses in consciousness are happening right now throughout the world as they continuously have from the beginning of the Universe. Each person on the planet is now, consciously or unconsciously, evolving and developing into his or her destiny as an awakened human.

The Story of Awakening Within the First Narratives

In the conceptual design of **Journey of The Great Circle**, there is a poetic interweaving of themes within the first four contemplative narratives of each volume. Together these four narratives reveal "a hidden archetypal story" regarding every person's *spiritual journey of discovery*.

The first four narratives in the Spring Volume are:

1) Gifts of Spring
2) Qualities Within the Seasons of Life
3) The Great Story of Awakening
4) *Journey of Awakening*

The daily practice of contemplative narratives can easily be accomplished without the understanding of this conceptual design. Yet for those who are interested, the concept of how these four narratives are woven together is described at the end of the book in the section called "The Story of Awakening Within the First Narratives".

Life as Practice

One of the foundational themes within the contemplative narratives of **Journey of *The Great Circle*** is to experience the spiritual power of daily transformative practice. In order to embody something that we desire in our life, it usually requires dedicated practice and committed perseverance.

When we intend to align our awareness with *the Source of Life*, it also takes practice to embody this alignment as an ongoing experience in every moment. When we intend to be grateful for all that we're learning from every experience of our life, it takes practice. When we intend to live a life of inner freedom, it takes practice. When we intend to love all of life unconditionally, it takes practice.

If a person is committed to the practice of learning to play the piano, in the beginning it requires a lot of focused attention on every detail of how to move the fingers across the keyboard. Yet over time as one implements daily exercises and perseverance, eventually playing the piano becomes natural and effortless. It is as if some invisible *Field of Energy* is playing through the person - as the piano becomes a natural creative extension of his or her body.

The same thing occurs with spiritual practice. For with the daily dedication of placing our attention on the spiritual desires of our heart, we naturally and effortlessly learn how to respond to life's glories and challenges with ease, grace, and conscious responsibility. This is what these 365 daily contemplative narratives are designed to help you manifest in your life. There comes a sacred moment on our journey of discovery when we deeply recognize the authentic joy of practicing each day to be the best version of ourselves. And in that sublime moment, daily transformative practice becomes one of the most fulfilling and meaningful facets of our life.

Therefore practice with all the vibrant joy in your heart so you may walk through this life, gracefully and naturally, as a **Master of Freedom.**

Our journey of awakening is about learning what is true, developing potential, expanding awareness, and then creatively expressing our inner development. The Universe uses – and even requires – challenge, chaos, and crisis as evolutionary catalysts to generate more elevated awareness and greater expressions of our creativity.

DAILY
CONTEMPLATION
PRACTICES
FOR
SPRING

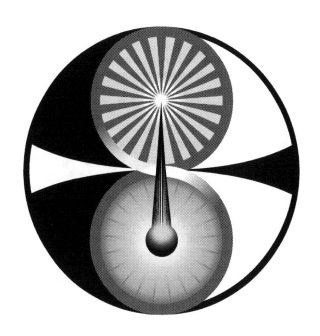

1

THE DANCE
OF THE INFINITE
SEASONS

GIFTS OF SPRING

I have a personal mission to use my unique creative talents to help co-create a better world.

For some people the experience of a barren and frigid wintertime can feel exceedingly long,
Yet the colder weather of winter has offered many of us a time for self-reflection
In which our hearts are made ready for the next season of our life.

At last, **the beginning of spring** has come carrying its warmth to the natural world
And it seems, for most of Nature's creatures, there's "a new music in the air",
For migrating birds are now returning - singing their mating songs,
People are buzzing like bees with renewed energy from the milder weather,
And everything appears to have a refreshing hum to it.

Today is the northern hemisphere's celebration of *the vernal equinox*, the first day of spring,
An ancient, as well as contemporary, rite of passage moving us from winter into spring.

The word "equinox" (which is derived from Latin) means "equal night",
And describes the two specific times of the year, both the start of spring and autumn,
When the light of day and the dark of night are of equal duration.

The spring equinox heralds a celestial moment in the perpetual flow of time
When life is ready "to spring forth once again", to manifest brand new possibilities,
And is eager "to plant into the fertile soil of our creative garden"
The visions we received during winter that our heart longs to bring forth.

It's a time to contribute to the grand vision of a planet in greater harmony and balance,
A world that lives in the balance between our masculine and feminine energies,
Between the expansion of our consciousness and expression of our creativity,
Between our basic human need for internal stillness and external activity,
Between sublime silence and the music that yearns to burst forth.

From this place of balance within us, we can empower our **unlimited creativity**
And nurture the seeds of our inspired ideas that have emerged from within our hearts
During moments of self-reflection.

From this state of equilibrium - and our alignment with *the Source of Life*
Spring is a time of **outward expression** or mission regarding our vision for the future
Based on all we've received from our inner guidance and winter's contemplation.

Spring reminds us we are all artists of life *(the creative artists of our daily offerings)*
Painting our revelations and new possibilities on the blank canvas of each new day.

In a manner of speaking, we're all sculptors of our potential, conceiving with our imagination
And shaping our vision of the world into what our heart has envisioned is possible.

And we are all composers of *a unique visionary music* that's being heard for the first time
As we humbly share our novel love songs birthed from our own *journey of discovery*,
Songs that we radiate out into the world so we may help co-create
Brand new renderings of the Universe - and superior versions of our lives.

Circle of the Gifts of Spring
(Transcendent Qualities Within the Seasons of Life)

OUTWARD EXPRESSION
A TIME OF OUTWARD EXPRESSION OR MISSION REGARDING MY VISION FOR THE FUTURE BASED ON MY INNER GUIDANCE AND WINTER'S CONTEMPLATION

CONTRIBUTION TO FAMILY
A TIME OF CULTIVATION FOR GENERATING GREATER SAFETY, LOVE, EMPOWERMENT, AND CONNECTION WITH "MY EXTENDED FAMILY"

ACCEPTANCE
A TIME OF DEEPENING THE FULL ACCEPTANCE THAT MY LIFE IS UNFOLDING PERFECTLY AND OF COURAGEOUSLY EMBRACING MY LIFE JUST AS IT IS

ENDLESS CREATIVITY
A TIME OF CREATIVITY IN WHICH I PLANT THE SEEDS OF INSPIRED IDEAS THAT HAVE EMERGED IN MY HEART DURING MOMENTS OF SELF-REFLECTION

QUALITIES WITHIN THE SEASONS OF LIFE

The creative impulse within me is the same Infinitely Creative Intelligence that spins the Cosmos.

Whenever we embark on a journey to travel somewhere
    We usually require the aid of some kind of wheel,
        Such as the rubber tires of a bicycle or car, the metal wheels of a train,
            Or the spinning turbines of a jet plane.

The annual journey of the Earth's cyclic flow of time, that is - **the turning of the seasons**,
    Is also typically illustrated in the form of a clockwise wheel or circle
        With four cardinal points portraying the four distinct seasons of the year.

This symbolic circle represents an inherent movement perpetually occurring in Nature
    That constantly advances from the renewal of winter
        To the new beginning of spring,
            From spring to the growth phase of summer,
                And from summer to the harvest of autumn.

Wherever there is progressive movement or change in the world,
    There must be a complimentary force that initiates and animates this movement,
        And the animating force of the Earth's seasonal cycle
            Is *the Natural Intelligence of Universal Creativity.*

It is the same *Song of Creativity* that all creatures on our planet instinctively "dance" to,
    For birds know when to build their nests,
        The blossoms of flowers know when to burst from their buds,
            Bears and lizards know when to awaken from hibernation,
                And butterflies know when to emerge from their cocoons.

This *Infinitely Creative Intelligence* is "the invisible hand that spins the Cosmos"
    Initiating the next turn of the wheel,
        Climbing up the spiral of infinite cycles,
            Exploring all the seasons of existence,
                And thus unfolding this unique moment of **spring's new birth**.

It is the same *Universal Impulse of Creativity* within the human species that discovered fire,
    That inspired the first rock art in caves,
        And composed the musical splendors of classical symphonies.

It is the creative longing that built bridges to new worlds, majestic schooners to foreign shores,
    And will build future spaceships to distant stars.

It is the natural creativity within you and me guiding us to continually develop and grow
    So we might discover "the fires of loving compassion", foster a deep reverence for life,
        And learn to be of service in helping to fashion a more awakened world.

And at this time, we're all being invited by *Life* to "dance to the next verse of Creation's Song",
    To do the transformational work that will awaken us from the sleep of our ignorance,
        And to emerge from our cocoons of limitation so we may soar with true freedom.

Circle of Qualities Within the Seasons of Life

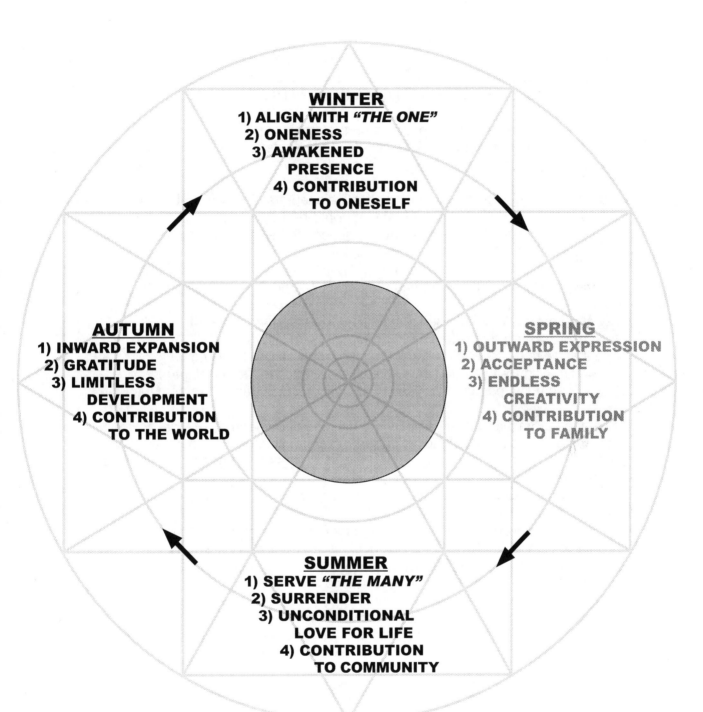

WINTER
1) ALIGN WITH *"THE ONE"*
2) ONENESS
3) AWAKENED
   PRESENCE
4) CONTRIBUTION
   TO ONESELF

SPRING
1) OUTWARD EXPRESSION
2) ACCEPTANCE
3) ENDLESS
   CREATIVITY
4) CONTRIBUTION
   TO FAMILY

AUTUMN
1) INWARD EXPANSION
2) GRATITUDE
3) LIMITLESS
   DEVELOPMENT
4) CONTRIBUTION
   TO THE WORLD

SUMMER
1) SERVE *"THE MANY"*
2) SURRENDER
3) UNCONDITIONAL
   LOVE FOR LIFE
4) CONTRIBUTION
   TO COMMUNITY

THE GREAT STORY OF AWAKENING

My spiritual journey is the same as my Soul's longing to learn to love all of life unconditionally.

If you look closely at the four characteristic qualities which are represented within each season,
    You will notice that a specific arrangement of these key seasonal qualities
        Forms an unfolding "pathway of destiny" which all people shall eventually travel
            As every human being advances along the natural evolutionary journey
                Towards their destiny of living an awakened life.

We can use and arrange the various qualities on the previous page as building blocks
    To form "four distinct life stages", "four well-defined chapters" of a story of discovery
        That portrays themes regarding our *spiritual journey* - our *journey of awakening*.

Take a moment to imagine that these four distinctive chapters of **a Great Story of Awakening**
    Are all visually symbolized by a group of four horse-drawn chariots
        In which each "charioteer" represents an aspect of the forward impulse of our life,
            Each "chariot" represents a particular stage, or chapter, of our story,
                And "the four horses pulling each chariot"
                    Represent the four primary qualities of that specific chapter.

These four chapters can then be used to help us understand more clearly
    That each of us is living our life as an epic *journey of discovery*,
        And that we're all on a sacred quest to learn what our life is truly about
            And to ultimately realize who we really are *(our True Eternal Nature)*
                Through a personal process of expansive growth and development.

The first "charioteer" in the north signifies the beginning of our *journey of awakening*
    Guiding the "chariot" representing **The Great Circle** (a spiritual map of an awakening life)
        With the "horses": <u>inward expansion</u>, <u>outward expression</u>, <u>alignment</u>, and <u>service</u>,
            Where we learn of the universal dynamics that are at play within our life
                And expand our awareness of what is true - and what really matters.

Our "hero's journey" continues in the second chapter with the "charioteer" in the east
    Directing the next "chariot" which is a symbol for the **Pillars of Awakening**,
        Drawn by the "four horses" of <u>gratitude</u>, <u>surrender</u>, <u>acceptance</u>, and <u>Oneness</u>,
            Which depict qualities that help us transform our suffering into freedom.

The "charioteer" in the south guides the third "chariot" that represents the **Master of Freedom**
    Who masters life with <u>limitless development</u>, <u>unconditional love</u>, <u>awakened presence</u>,
        And <u>endless creativity</u> - embodying an awakened life of inner freedom.

The final chapter of this story *(our journey of awakening)* is led by the "charioteer" in the west
    Guiding the fourth "chariot" that portrays the **Spheres of Contribution**, in other words,
        Taking action by responding to the natural impulse within us to contribute to others.

The Great Story of Awakening is a transformative archetypal longing within each of us
    That points us to our *spiritual awakening,* which is our internal journey from fear to *Love*,
        A journey that travels through expanded awareness - in order to be transformed -
            So we may learn to master our life - and ultimately, serve the good of all.

Circle of The Great Story of Awakening
(My *Spiritual Journey* In Relation to the Infinite Seasons of Life)

THE GREAT CIRCLE
MY *JOURNEY OF AWAKENING*
IS TO MINDFULLY EXPAND MY
AWARENESS OF WHAT IS TRUE
AND SERVE THE GOOD OF ALL
+ + +
WIN - ALIGN WITH *"THE ONE"*
SPR - OUTWARD EXPRESSION
SUM - SERVE *"THE MANY"*
AUT - INWARD EXPANSION

SPHERES
OF CONTRIBUTION
I RESPONSIBLY SUSTAIN
BALANCE REGARDING
MY CONTRIBUTIONS TO:
+ + +
WIN - MYSELF
SPR - FAMILY
SUM - COMMUNITY
AUT - THE WORLD

PILLARS
OF AWAKENING
WITH DAILY PRACTICE I
TRANSFORM SUFFERING
INTO INNER FREEDOM
+ + +
WIN - ONENESS
SPR - ACCEPTANCE
SUM - SURRENDER
AUT - GRATITUDE

MASTER
OF FREEDOM
ULTIMATELY I DISCOVER
HOW TO MASTER THE KEYS
TO LIVING AN AWAKENED LIFE
+ + +
WIN - AWAKENED PRESENCE
SPR - ENDLESS CREATIVITY
SUM - UNCONDITIONAL LOVE
AUT - INNER DEVELOPMENT

9

JOURNEY OF AWAKENING

Today I expand my awareness of what my life is truly about - and what really matters.

Every person's psychological development can be thought of as "the story of a hero's journey",
    The continuous inner growth of humanity that has been maturing over generations
        As each individual within our human community develops greater awareness,
            Which is then expressed as a more conscious and compassionate life.

As science helps us understand *the evolutionary story* that everyone is an integral part of,
    There are more and more people who have gained the heart wisdom and compassion
        To proactively engage in a more conscious role within our unfolding human story.

It's as if, for thousands of years, humans have been partially asleep to "life's Bigger Picture" -
    Yet with the support of science, many are waking to their key part to play in this "story".

The first chapter, or stage, within our **journey of awakening** is focused on our **development**
    As we expand our awareness of what our life is truly about - and develop our potential.

During this process of discovery, we become like an empty cup which has a destiny to be filled
    So that more inclusive perspectives and a greater understanding of what really matters
        Can pour into us - and supply us with effective ways to live a more fulfilling life.

Then we must look within to examine whether our life is heading in the direction we intend,
    Or whether we're traveling on "a dead-end road" that cannot take us to our desired goal.

If the latter is so, we can find means to **transform** our dysfunctional habits and unloving beliefs
    Into more compassionate, caring, and love-centered beliefs - and ways to live our life
        In which we cultivate various attributes such as gratitude, surrender, and acceptance.

The third stage is about fostering conscious responsibility as we embody our new awareness
    Through the personal discipline of transformative practice.

By aligning with, and surrendering all of our choices and actions to, *a Transcendent Power*,
    We cultivate the kind of **mastery** that becomes an embodied experience of freedom.

Through our alignment with *the Source of Life*, our investigation of what our life is truly about,
    And our commitment to our daily transformative practices
        We ultimately realize the gift of an awakened life of inner freedom.

At this vital point of our *journey*, after traveling the internal path of expanding our awareness,
    Transforming our beliefs, and embodying the mastery of inner freedom in our daily life,
        The next stage of our *journey of awakening* is to take creative action.

Therefore from our awakened awareness, it becomes natural and obvious
    That we are to **contribute our creative gifts and talents to the good of all**.

This amazing life journey can be thought of as an epic archetypal story - yet in every moment,
    We can either choose to listen to an old handed-down story about our imagined limitations
        Or choose to be a co-creator with *Life* of an expansive story that yearns to be created.

Circle of the *Journey of Awakening*
(Key Stages of the Transformative Quest For Inner Freedom)

DEVELOPMENT
FIRST STAGE:
I EXPAND MY AWARENESS
OF WHAT MY LIFE
IS TRULY ABOUT AND
WHAT REALLY MATTERS,
FOSTER MORE INCLUSION
OF OTHERS, AND DEVELOP
MY UNLIMITED POTENTIAL

CONTRIBUTION
FOURTH STAGE:
AS I LIVE A LIFE OF INNER
FREEDOM, I CONTRIBUTE
MY CREATIVE GIFTS
AND TALENTS
TO THE GOOD OF ALL
- AND HELP CO-CREATE
A BETTER WORLD

TRANSFORMATION
SECOND STAGE:
I ENGAGE IN PRACTICES
THAT HELP ME TRANS-
FORM MY BELIEFS WHICH
NO LONGER SERVE *LIFE*
INTO MORE CARING,
COMPASSIONATE, AND
LOVE-CENTERED BELIEFS

MASTERY
THIRD STAGE:
I EMBODY THE MASTERY
OF LIVING A LIFE OF INNER
FREEDOM THROUGH MY
DAILY ALIGNMENT WITH
THE SOURCE OF LIFE AND
COMMITMENT TO TRANS-
FORMATIVE PRACTICE

TRANSFORMATION

I transform myself as I replace fear-based beliefs with love-centered beliefs that empower me.

During this vibrant time of spring's new birth, the hibernating creatures of the Earth
    Are awakening from their long season of winter's slumber.

Many forms of reptiles are emerging from their earthen burrows
    And the warming air is an instinctual signal for snakes to shed their worn-out skins.

For each of us as well, spring represents a time to shed our unloving ways,
    To let go of any fear-based beliefs that we, for unconscious reasons, have clung to,
        And to relinquish our dysfunctional habits and patterns
            That, over time, we've acquired during our life.

These habitual patterns and beliefs do not make us wrong or bad for having them,
    Nor do they make us inferior humans for being caught in their grip -
        For we can only live our life and express who we are at our current level of awareness.

Yet they do demonstrate that we have been unaware, asleep, or unconscious
    Of a more free and unrestricted way to intentionally travel the winding road of life.

If we've spent time during winter in self-reflection, we've most likely been offered new insights
    And have been presented with new possibilities of how we may transform our life.

Now with the rebirth of spring at hand once again,
    It's time to plant the seeds of insight we've been given in the silent womb of winter
        With our commitment to using **daily transformative practices**
            To cultivate new empowering ways to live our life.

This season represents a time to unlearn the old ways that do not serve us any more
    And, thereby, heighten our awareness of *an Infinitely Creative Intelligence*
        That's perpetually pointing us toward living a life of inner freedom
            And contributing our creative gifts and talents to the wellbeing of others.

Furthermore, spring symbolizes an inherent call for **transformation**
    By inviting us to courageously let go of our attachments to how we want life to be,
        Accepting what is, and fully embracing the constant changes in our life.

We transform by consciously replacing harmful fear-based **habits or beliefs**
    With love-centered beliefs that empower us.

Transformation also comes from integrating **more inclusive perspectives of life**
    And learning what really matters, for we can always make more constructive life choices
        When we understand the larger vantage and dynamics of what has true value.

Then - when we have boldly "shed our old worn-out skins"
    And have learned to embody into our life these transformative modes of possibility,
        We can more easily "glide across the sands of time"
            And travel the winding road of life with grace and peace of mind.

Circle of Transformation

CHANGE BELIEFS
I TRANSFORM MYSELF
BY REPLACING
HARMFUL
FEAR-BASED HABITS
OR BELIEFS WITH
LOVE-CENTERED BELIEFS
THAT EMPOWER ME

PRACTICES
I TRANSFORM MYSELF
THRU MY COMMITMENT
TO USING DAILY TRANS-
FORMATIVE PRACTICES
TO CULTIVATE NEW
EMPOWERING WAYS
TO LIVE MY LIFE

ACCEPTANCE
I TRANSFORM MYSELF
BY LETTING GO
OF MY ATTACHMENTS,
ACCEPTING MY LIFE
JUST AS IT IS, AND
FULLY EMBRACING THE
CHANGES IN MY LIFE

PERSPECTIVE
I TRANSFORM MYSELF
BY INTEGRATING MORE
INCLUSIVE PERSPECTIVES
OF LIFE INTO
MY CURRENT AWARENESS
- AND LEARNING
WHAT REALLY MATTERS

TRANSFORMATIVE PRACTICE

Today I use daily transformative practice as a powerful way to learn to love unconditionally.

All radios and televisions are built with a number of fundamental electronic components,
　　And one essential component that enables them to receive proper signals is the *tuner*.

In the early days of the radio when it was first being introduced,
　　Radios had to be hand-tuned to a frequency using a rudimentary sliding mechanism
　　　　That required patience and precise calibration to receive a station.

Of course, the more precise these sliding tuners could be aligned to a radio frequency,
　　The clearer the reception - and the better one could hear the music or broadcast.

Similarly, our body, heart, and mind are also *vibrational receivers of Life Force energy*
　　That must be tuned daily to the frequencies of *a Universal Creative Intelligence*
　　　　If we desire to experience an optimal alignment with the limitless energy of life.

Just as it takes practice to make the necessary adjustments on a sliding tuner of an old radio,
　　The basics of learning to align our "human receivers" with *the Source of Life* is simple,
　　　　Yet sustaining this is not always easy but can be cultivated with daily **practice**.

When we were newborn infants, the only "practice" in our life was to survive in this new world,
　　But as we grew older, our "forms of practice" naturally changed to learning how to fit in,
　　　　Acquiring a good education, developing relationships, starting a career,
　　　　　　And, sometimes, spending time in our life pursuing our creative talents.

Most people learn "to practice" a business craft or trade so as to fiscally support themselves,
　　And some spend their lives "practicing" their natural gifts - which express a creative art.

Everything we focus our attention on is "practice" - and as we mature from our life experiences,
　　A longing begins that calls us "to consciously practice" cultivating our inner spiritual life.

Transformative practice is taking action in ways in which we devote ourselves
　　To consciously expanding our awareness in relation to what really matters,
　　　　The disciplined actions and exercises we engage in
　　　　　　To help us become kinder, more loving, and more compassionate.

This form of practice is essentially about maintaining an attunement with *the Source of Life*
　　And, thus, **committing ourselves to the cultivation of our spiritual development**.

It's the focused act of, each day, **aligning our awareness with *the Infinite Presence of Love***
　　Which then aligns us with a natural yearning to love all of life unconditionally.

As we gain higher levels of conscious development, the role of practice changes once again,
　　For in the fullness of time, we begin to notice how "life is practice" - and "practice is life",
　　　　And that our ongoing personal evolution - is actually the same as the journey of life.

Life is always inviting us to be precisely attuned to this *Universal Creative Intelligence*
　　So we may continuously hear - and respond - and dance - to *"the Song of the Infinite"*.

Circle of Transformative Practice

DISCIPLINE
TRANS. PRACTICE –
**THE DISCIPLINED
ACTIONS AND EXERCISES
I ENGAGE IN TO HELP ME
BECOME KINDER,
MORE LOVING, AND
MORE COMPASSIONATE**

DEVOTION
TRANS. PRACTICE –
**TAKING ACTION IN WAYS
IN WHICH I DEVOTE
MYSELF TO CONSCIOUSLY
EXPANDING MY AWARE-
NESS IN RELATION TO
WHAT REALLY MATTERS**

COMMITMENT
TRANS. PRACTICE –
**THE ACTIONS I TAKE
OF COMMITTING MYSELF
TO THE CULTIVATION
OF MY INNER
DEVELOPMENT
AND SPIRITUAL GROWTH**

ALIGNMENT
TRANS. PRACTICE –
**THE ACTIONS OF ALIGNING
MY AWARENESS WITH
*THE INFINITE PRESENCE
OF LOVE* - AND LEARNING'
TO LOVE ALL OF LIFE
UNCONDITIONALLY**

FAITH

I have unwavering faith in the Transcendent Power that's pointing me to my greater potential.

In the United States of America during the late 1800's and all through the 1900's,
    A number of industrial companies built huge steamships
        With engines that were powered by the burning of coal or wood
            Generating tremendous steam pressure in turbines
                Which turned large paddle wheels or massive propellers.

The fuel was burned in the "hidden" furnace of the vessel located below the main decks,
    And, from the view of most passengers, it seemed to magically thrust the ship forward.

For the last one hundred years, the engines within our cars and trucks have been fueled
    By an "unseen" supply of gasoline or diesel that was "hidden" in the fuel tanks.

Without these "hidden or unseen" sources of power, our vehicles would not be able to move
    And we would not, as conveniently as we do, travel to where we want to go.

The spiritual development or expanded awareness which is potential within each of us
    Can be likened to a vehicle or ship that's propelled forward with the proper fuel,
        And, of course, spiritual growth requires a very different form of "unseen power".

One form of "inner fuel" (i.e. human virtue) that's essential to propel our awareness forward
    To the sacred place within us where we realize who we really are - is the virtue of **faith**.

Faith is a spiritual knowing, for it's **the unwavering belief** that *a Transcendent Power*,
    The Infinite Intelligence of the Universe, is always pointing us to our greater potential.

Faith can be thought of as **complete trust** that something benevolent will occur in our life
    Without our understanding exactly how or when.

Faith (like the coal or wood of an old steamship) is "an unseen fuel" that dwells within us
    Igniting a desire "to touch a distant star", "to reach a farther shoreline",
        "To climb a higher mountain" which we have not yet ascended.

It's an aspect of the inward expansive principle that sparks a vision of possibility from within
    So that the outward expressive principle can bring it into manifestation in our life.

A strong faith is **the visionary acceptance**
    That some form of good will eventually be manifested in a particular situation,
        The doubtless knowing that all facets of our life
        Are constantly unfolding in a beneficent manner.

Without "the inner fuel" of *faith*, "the amazing vehicle we refer to as our life"
    Has a more challenging time "climbing the steep mountain path"
        Which gradually takes us ever upward to a clearer vantage of the summit
            Where we can gaze out onto a whole new vista of possibility,
                A place that only unwavering belief and trust in something greater
                    Will lead us to.

Circle of Faith

UNWAVERING BELIEF
FAITH –
THE UNWAVERING BELIEF
THAT *A GREATER POWER,*
THE INFINITE INTELLIGENCE
OF THE UNIVERSE,
IS ALWAYS LEADING ME
TO MY GREATER POTENTIAL

VISIONARY ACCEPTANCE
FAITH –
THE ACCEPTANCE
THAT SOME FORM
OF GOOD
IS EVENTUALLY
BEING MANIFESTED IN A
PARTICULAR SITUATION

DOUBTLESS KNOWING
FAITH –
THE INNER KNOWING
WITHOUT DOUBT THAT
ALL FACETS OF MY LIFE
ARE CONSTANTLY
UNFOLDING IN
A BENEFICENT MANNER

COMPLETE TRUST
FAITH –
THE COMPLETE TRUST THAT
SOMETHING BENEVOLENT
IS ALWAYS TAKING PLACE
IN MY LIFE WITHOUT
MY UNDERSTANDING
EXACTLY HOW OR WHEN

MARCH 26
INNOCENCE

Today I willingly surrender everything in my life to the Infinite Presence of Love.

The feature film "Forrest Gump" was a blockbuster hit in 1994
And is an inspiring movie that portrays many of the powerful qualities of **innocence**.

In the film, Forrest, a man who by society's view is a developmentally challenged individual,
Learns to compensate for his "so-called limitations"
By fostering other strong, virtuous, and self-defining characteristics.

Through his intention to overcome his personal trials - and through the blessings of *grace*,
He develops a presence of life that allows him to experience a sense of appreciation
For whatever reality puts in front of him,
He feels a vulnerability that puts him in touch with what is truly important,
He joyously includes everyone around him as his potential friend,
And he innocently aligns himself with the natural flow of life.

Forrest Gump represents a person who is real, authentic, and innocent,
And who, in the movie, expresses his uniqueness in his own triumphant way.

Of course, it is not our function to attempt to be like Forrest Gump (or like anyone else)
Because it's our responsibility to learn to express the fullness of our own uniqueness,
Yet we can certainly benefit by cultivating some of his empowering qualities.

Innocence is the quality of *radical presence (of being totally alive and present to life)*
In which we feel profound gratitude for everything in our life,
Thus, it can be thought of as our willingness and openness
To being grateful for the learning we receive from every life experience.

Innocence is the quality of *radical vulnerability* in which we're able to fully surrender
Everything in our life to the *Infinite Presence of Love*.

It's so much easier to let go in the direction of the river's natural flow
Than to fight the current by trying to swim upstream,
In other words - than to be out-of-touch with the guiding presence within our heart.

Innocence is the quality of *radical inclusion* of everyone and everything
In which we accept that, in this moment, our life is unfolding perfectly just as it is.

If we are blatantly honest with ourselves, then we must see that life *is* the way it is
Including all of its glorious moments, as well as all of its challenging opportunities,
For when we choose to resist life as it is, we experience suffering.

Innocence is also the quality of *radical alignment* with *the Source of Life*
In which we're aware of the part of us that is eternal and can never be wounded.

One of life's great spiritual teachers stated, *"If you want to enter the Kingdom of Heaven,*
You must, once again, learn to be as innocent as a child",
Which means, with innocence, we can learn to live in Heaven here on Earth.

Circle of Innocence
(In Relation to the Pillars of Awakening)

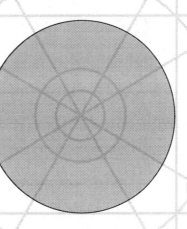

ONENESS
INNOCENCE –
THE QUALITY OF *RADICAL*
ALIGNMENT WITH *LIFE*
IN WHICH I'M AWARE
OF THE PART OF ME
THAT IS ETERNAL AND
CAN NEVER BE WOUNDED

GRATITUDE
INNOCENCE –
THE QUALITY OF
RADICAL PRESENCE
IN WHICH I FEEL
PROFOUND GRATITUDE
FOR EVERYTHING
IN MY LIFE

ACCEPTANCE
INNOCENCE –
THE QUALITY OF
RADICAL INCLUSION
OF EVERYONE, IN WHICH
I ACCEPT THAT MY LIFE
IS UNFOLDING
PERFECTLY JUST AS IT IS

SURRENDER
INNOCENCE –
THE QUALITY OF
RADICAL VULNERABILITY
IN WHICH I SURRENDER
EVERYTHING IN MY LIFE
TO *THE INFINITE*
PRESENCE OF LOVE

POLARITIES OF EXISTENCE

Universal Consciousness and my Eternal Self are one - thus the Universe and I are one.

Most people are familiar with the biblical story of Noah and the Great Flood
   In which Noah was a man who was told by God to build a very large wooden boat
      And to fill it with one male and one female from every animal species on Earth.

The physical world we live in is full of numerous dualities that consist of opposite polarities
   Such as masculine and feminine, light and dark, internal and external, hot and cold, etc.

If we ponder the nature of reality, we discover another *set of polarities* beyond earthly dualities
   Which offers us the existential paradox that both *the transcendent realm* of the formless
      And *the material realm* of the phenomenal world of form
         Somehow both exist simultaneously, and in the same space,
            And we will now explore four fundamental **polarities of existence**.

Concerning **The Great Circle**, which is a spiritual map of the key dynamics at play in our lives,
   There is the expansion of our inward evolving consciousness which is unbounded and formless
      As well as our evolving creativity which manifests as our outward expressions of form.

In relation to **the universal perspective of reality** (in other words, "the Big Picture of life"),
   There is <u>God</u> *(Infinite Intelligence)* that exists in the formless invisible realm of *Being*,
      And <u>the Universe</u> as the expression of form in the visible realm of *Becoming*.

From **a personal perspective of life** (how we personally experience the world we live in),
   We are an embodiment of our *Eternal Self* that is formless and present everywhere,
      Yet our physical <u>body</u> has the appearance of a solid form in the material realm.

Regarding the destiny of our **spiritual awakening**, the wisdom of our heart constantly reveals to us
   That we are one with *Limitless Love* - which is without form,
      And that this *Love* is outwardly mirrored in the world as our creative <u>contributions</u> to others.

And when we look deeply at each one of these various descriptions of *the transcendent realm*,
   Consciousness, *God*, *Eternal Self*, *Limitless Love*, we experience the same *Sublime Essence*
      For they are all distinctive words for the one *Transcendent Power of existence*.

<u>Universal Consciousness</u> is the same as *God*, <u>God</u> is actually another word for *Eternal Self*,
   Eternal Self is another way of describing *Limitless Love*,
      And <u>Limitless Love</u> is identical to the *Universal Consciousness* in all of existence.

Yet if all of the various exalted descriptions of *the transcendent realm* are one and the same,
   Then it points us to the awareness that *the many material forms* are the same as well,
      Which means our body is, unfathomably, one and the same as the Universe,
         And from a quantum perspective, we are truly one with all of creation.

The polarities of existence show the paradox that both *the transcendent and material realms*
   Exist at the same time as complimentary realms of *Being* and *Becoming*,
      And this awareness helps us realize that we, in the **form** of our individual body,
         Are actually merged completely with the **formless** realm of *"The One"*.

Circle of the Polarities of Existence
(In Relation to the Transcendent and Material Realms of My Life)

THE GREAT CIRCLE
PERSPECTIVE
+
TRANSCENDENT:
CONSCIOUSNESS
+ MERGED WITH +
MATERIAL:
CREATION

**PERSONAL
PERSPECTIVE**
+
TRANSCENDENT:
ETERNAL SELF
+ MERGED WITH +
MATERIAL:
BODY

**UNIVERSAL
PERSPECTIVE**
+
TRANSCENDENT:
GOD
+ MERGED WITH +
MATERIAL:
UNIVERSE

**AWAKENED
PERSPECTIVE**
+
TRANSCENDENT:
LIMITLESS LOVE
+ MERGED WITH +
MATERIAL:
CONTRIBUTION

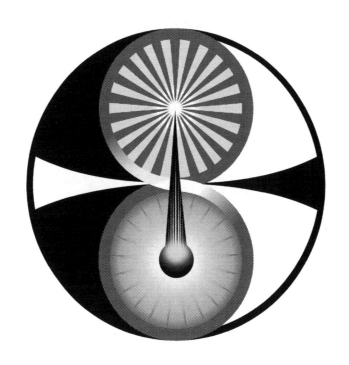

II

THE POETRY
OF
THE GREAT CIRCLE

THE GREAT CIRCLE

My inner development gives creative shape to how my external reality is experienced in my life.

As we keep learning about the nature of reality regarding the Universe, the Earth, and all of life
We sooner or later come to realize that the world we live in contains many paradoxes.

A paradox is defined as two statements that express ideas which are contradictory
Where both statements appear to be true at the same time,
Even though this arguably battles against one's common rational thinking.

Some of the elegant discoveries of quantum physics since the early 1900s
Have pointed humanity to examples of scientific paradoxes.

One fundamental paradox relating to quantum physics was revealed
When scientists learned how to observe extremely small sub-atomic particles
And noticed that these particles had the uncanny ability
"To wink in and out of existence",
In other words - to exist in one moment - and then not exist in the next.

These tiny particles would mysteriously emerge from a dimensionless *Virtual Realm,*
An invisible *Void*, which the scientific community has named *The Unified Field.*

Scientists noticed that sub-atomic particles would seem to appear for a very short time
(In the phenomenal reality we experience as the physical realm)
And then disappear back into the imperceptible void of *The Unified Field.*

The transition zone from the internal invisible *Virtual Realm* to the external *physical realm*
(As well as its opposite direction, which is the transition zone from the visible *physical world*
To the *Virtual Realm)* is referred to as *the quantum realm.*

It's difficult for the human mind to truly comprehend
How something that exists in our physical world can emerge from essentially nothing.

Throughout human history, philosophers have developed various *maps of existence*
To help us understand the underlying dynamics of life - as well as life's paradoxes.

The Great Circle is "a spiritual map of an awakening life" that portrays the universal dynamics
Of one's inward expansion of awareness mirrored as one's outward creative expressions,
Illustrating that our awareness expands based on **our evolving consciousness**
Which is mirrored in the world as expressions of **our evolving creativity**.

Within **The Great Circle**, these two evolutionary impulses can be depicted in scientific terms
As two interrelated aspects - the interior and exterior impulses of the quantum realm.

It also links *The Unified Field* (i.e. **"The One" Source of All That Is - Unity without form**),
With physical reality (i.e. **"The Many" forms of Nature that are unfolding perfectly**).

We are being invited to embrace this paradox - and learn that the transformation of our body
Outwardly mirrors the developmental growth and inward changes of our consciousness.

The Great Circle
(A Spiritual Map of an Awakening Life)

"THE ONE"
PERFECT ONENESS,
UNITY WITHOUT FORM,
THE ONE TRANSCENDENT
SOURCE OF ALL THAT IS,
INFINITE INTELLIGENCE,
LIMITLESS LOVE,
MY TRUE NATURE
WHICH IS ETERNAL
(BEING)

INNER DEVELOPMENT
INWARD EXPANSION
OF MY AWARENESS
+
INTERIOR EVOLVING
CONSCIOUSNESS
+
MY SPIRITUAL
AWAKENING
(BECOMING)

OUTER TRANSFORMATION
OUTWARD EXPRESSION
OF MY HEALING
+
EXTERIOR EVOLVING
CREATIVITY
+
MY CONSCIOUS
CONTRIBUTION
(BECOMING)

"THE MANY"
THE PERFECTION WITHIN
EACH FORM OF LIFE,
THE MANY UNIQUE
FORMS WITHIN NATURE,
INCLUDING MY BODY,
ALL UNFOLDING
PERFECTLY
IN THE PRESENT MOMENT
(BEING)

THE GREAT CIRCLE OF HEART WISDOM AND COMPASSION

Learning what my life is truly about and what really matters transforms into greater compassion.

If you watch the evening news on television or the Internet
    You might view a story about the irresponsible and destructive impact
        That segments of humanity, at times, inflict on itself, on the global environment,
            Or on large numbers of species throughout our planet.

And if you were also to look at this human impact from a metaphorical perspective,
    You might sense that the evolutionary growth of humanity can be seen as analogous
        To a person who progresses from a young infant to a mature adult,
            And that, right now, humanity seems to be in its "young adolescent stage".

If a supposedly adult person hasn't yet developed compassion and heart wisdom,
    Then like an immature child or adolescent, that person is more likely to act irresponsibly.

Yet if we can learn to see the evolutionary role of our humanity from "a Big Picture vantage",
    We may begin to see that the emergence of intelligent self-reflective human life on Earth
        Has the possibility - and obligation - to shift from its current destructive influence
            To an influence that can catapult evolution forward in magnificent ways.

The seemingly unlimited capacity of our human mind to consciously co-create future realities
    Through the power of our focused intentions (joined with our elevated emotions)
        Has the potential to be a beneficial gift for the unfolding of evolution on our planet
            If we can learn to align our awareness with *the Natural Intelligence of Life.*

Just like most children go to school to learn how to grow up as educated informed adults,
    Every person will benefit if they can "go to school" so as to discover what really matters
        And expand their understanding regarding what life is truly about.

As we all learn the gift of more inclusive perspectives of reality from our experiences of life
    (Which include human developmental perspectives and evolutionary perspectives),
        Our consciousness can more easily expand and develop in constructive ways.

Through our diverse **life experiences** and conscious participation with our ongoing education
    (I.e. from spiritual study, mindfulness, contemplation, and the practice of inner silence)
        We are offered opportunities to learn to embrace the perfection of each moment.

As our awareness expands about what really matters, knowledge expands into **heart wisdom**,
    While, simultaneously, *the Source of Life* mirrors outwardly our heightened awareness
        Which manifests as the creative gifts, talents, and expressions of our new beliefs
            And, in this case, as our **greater compassion** and contributions to others.

From a universal perspective, these four seemingly distinct aspects of our being,
    "The One", our life experience, heart wisdom, and our greater compassion are all one unity,
        One constantly evolving **Great Circle** that's unfolding as our everyday reality.

The more we each become passionately dedicated to expanding our awareness in this way,
    The more the stories we watch on the evening news will reflect an ever-awakening world.

The Great Circle of Heart Wisdom and Compassion
(In Relation to Expansive and Expressive Impulses of Life)

"THE ONE"
THE LIMITLESS SOURCE
OF ALL THAT IS
(INFINITE INTELLIGENCE)
OUTWARDLY MIRRORS
MY INNER DEVELOPMENT
AND EXPANDING
AWARENESS INTO MY
BODY, HEART, AND MIND

HEART WISDOM
GREATER KNOWLEDGE,
LIFE EXPERIENCE,
AND MY EXPANDING
AWARENESS OF WHAT
MY LIFE IS TRULY ABOUT
TRANSFORM INTO
THE CULTIVATION
OF HEART WISDOM

**GREATER
COMPASSION**
MY GROWING HEART
WISDOM AND INNER
DEVELOPMENT IS
EXPRESSED IN MY LIFE
AS MY NEW BELIEFS,
GREATER COMPASSION,
AND CONTRIBUTIONS

LIFE EXPERIENCE
MY NEW BELIEFS
AND NEW ILLUMINATING
LIFE EXPERIENCES
OFFER ME ADDITIONAL
OPPORTUNITIES
TO LEARN TO EMBRACE
THE PERFECTION
OF EACH MOMENT

27

THE GREAT CIRCLE OF THE STAR OF DAVID

I see the world with eyes of Love, and thus all I perceive points me to my journey of self-mastery.

It would be hard for a day to go by without seeing various visual symbols portrayed in places
 Like TV commercials, magazine ads, Internet sites, and the daily mail we receive.

These kinds of graphic symbols are simple pictorial images
 That point to, and represent, a specific concept or idea.

Illustrative symbols were the initial basis for the birth of humanity's written languages,
 And these "pictures" or "hieroglyphs" morphed into the letters of the world's alphabets.

Numerous spiritual traditions from around the world developed certain religious symbols
 Which visually represented their beliefs and concepts about God - and about life,
  As well as expressed particular aspects of their tradition's spiritual principles.

Over many generations of using a particular religious symbol,
 The symbol's meaning would evolve and take on different degrees of spiritual depth
  Depending on the level of awareness associated with the people who used it.

As cultures changed, the same religious symbol could embrace multiple layers of meaning,
 Much like there are many layers of rainbow colors in the spectrum from one ray of light.

A popular meaning (or "lower spectrum of meaning") arose for the common people,
 And a more nuanced (or "middle spectrum of meaning") emerged for the religious elite.

Yet for the mystics, those spiritual pioneers who were passionately driven
 To explore the inward caverns of the mind and deeply investigate the nature of reality,
  "An even higher spectrum of mystical or esoteric meaning"
   Radiated through these religious symbols
    Which only a specific group of people were able to understand.

In the Jewish tradition, the image of **the Star of David** is one of these multi-layered symbols
 That holds diverse degrees of meaning based on the level of one's consciousness.

At the mystical level, the Star of David points us to the same place (the same understanding)
 Which "the spiritual map of an awakened life" called **The Great Circle** points us to
  Merging the spiritual (transcendent) and physical (bodily) impulses of our life.

The ascending triangle visually represents the expansion of our **evolving consciousness**
 And the descending triangle shows our **evolving creativity** as the expressive impulse.

The point at the top of the Star symbolizes **"The One"**, the essence within us which is eternal,
 And the bottom point represents **"The Many"**, depicting each life as it unfolds perfectly.

As we keep a watchful eye and observe the rich variety of religious symbols
 Which are used throughout the cultures of the world,
  Begin to notice how these unique symbols can point us
   To a greater understanding of our own *spiritual journey*.

The Great Circle of the Star of David

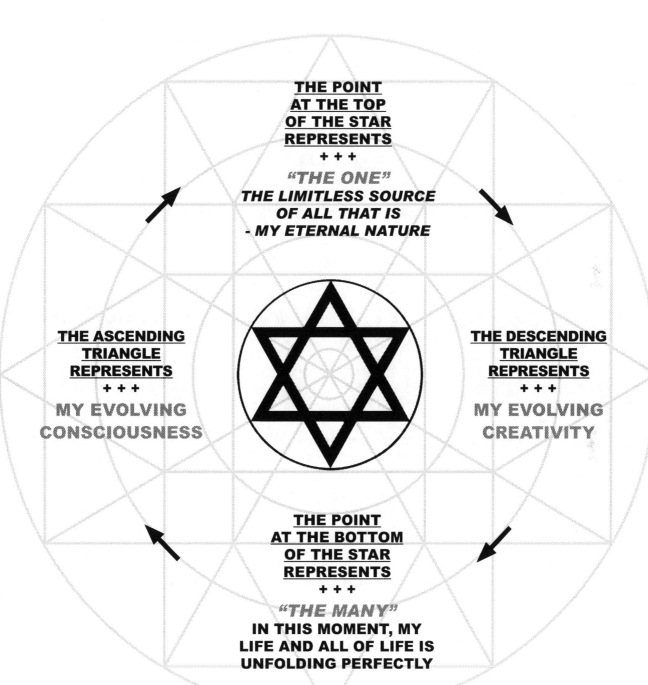

THE POINT
AT THE TOP
OF THE STAR
REPRESENTS
+ + +

"THE ONE"
THE LIMITLESS SOURCE
OF ALL THAT IS
- MY ETERNAL NATURE

THE ASCENDING
TRIANGLE
REPRESENTS
+ + +

MY EVOLVING
CONSCIOUSNESS

THE DESCENDING
TRIANGLE
REPRESENTS
+ + +

MY EVOLVING
CREATIVITY

THE POINT
AT THE BOTTOM
OF THE STAR
REPRESENTS
+ + +

"THE MANY"
IN THIS MOMENT, MY
LIFE AND ALL OF LIFE IS
UNFOLDING PERFECTLY

THE PERPETUAL UNFOLDING OF *INFINITE CREATIVITY*

The Creative Intelligence of the Universe is constantly inviting me to realize my Eternal Nature.

The world's religious traditions have been proclaiming to humanity for thousands of years -
There is a divine presence called God that exists everywhere and created everything.

Yet in today's world, the contemporary teachers of leading-edge spirituality
Are telling us a very similar declaration, but using different phrases to express the same idea,
Such as - *"There is a Universal Consciousness of infinitely intelligent creativity*
That has animated the entire Universe for 13.8 billion years
Which is always present within the core of everything,
And is the Creative Intelligence which directs
The future unfolding of the Cosmos".

If we try to search for this essential intelligence by examining the tiniest fragments of matter
With the most powerful electron microscope in the world, we will not see it.

This **Universal Consciousness of Infinite Creativity** is invisible and formless,
Limitless and unbounded - and yet it exists everywhere and always.

Searching for it would be similar to a fish swimming in the sea through vast stretches of water
And then trying to look in every direction to find the ocean.

The natural movement of this *Creative Impulse* is everywhere, for it's *the Dance of Life* itself,
And it has been perpetually unfolding into ever higher stages of expression
As the Universe has evolved throughout its *spiral of time.*

It was the infinitely intelligent **Evolutionary Impulse**
Exploring existence at the very beginning of the Cosmos
That arranged the colossal formations of galaxies,
Produced the nuclear furnaces and explosions of massive stars,
Shaped innumerable solar systems and planets,
And sculpted the great diversity of biological life on Earth.

It's the same *Universal Consciousness* that pulses through the instincts of every animal,
Innately knowing how to further the **survival and progression of its species**.

It is the same *Creative Intelligence* that invites you and me
To recognize that our heartfelt intentions, in the form of **conscious creative choices**,
Have focusing power to shape our future reality.

This *Intelligence* is inviting us to expand our awareness - and learn what our life is truly about
So we may fully realize that this spark of **Infinite Creativity** is always flowing in us
As *the transcendent Creative Power* within the Universe -
And as *the Eternal and Unchanging Nature* of who we really are.

Each of us is constantly immersed in a vast sea of unlimited possibilities
And no matter which direction "we swim", we are always being shown *The Way*
By the sublime whispers within this boundless "Ocean of Creativity".

Circle of the Perpetual Unfolding of *Infinite Creativity*
(From a Macro to a Micro Perspective)

**UNIVERSAL
CONSCIOUSNESS**
THE INFINITE CREATIVITY
OF THE UNIVERSE
IS THE LIMITLESS
CREATIVITY ANIMATING
ALL OF EXISTENCE,
THE SOURCE
OF ALL CREATIVE POWER

*THE EVOLUTIONARY
IMPULSE*
WITHIN THE UNIVERSE,
THIS CREATIVITY IS *THE
INTELLIGENT IMPULSE*
THAT DIRECTS THE
EVOLUTION OF EVERY
LIFE FORM INTO HIGHER
STAGES OF EXPRESSION

**CONSCIOUS
CREATIVITY**
WITHIN THE HUMAN MIND,
THIS CREATIVITY IS
EXPRESSED AS FOCUSED
INTENTION, IN THE FORM
OF CONSCIOUS CHOICES,
WITH CREATIVE POWER
TO SHAPE THE FUTURE

PROCREATION
ON PLANET EARTH,
THIS CREATIVITY IS
THE ESSENTIAL FORCE
THAT DIRECTS THE
BASIC INSTINCTS OF ALL
EVOLVING ORGANISMS
WHICH FURTHERS THEIR
SPECIES' SURVIVAL

THE LIMITLESS FIELD OF INFINITE CREATIVITY

The Infinite Creativity of the Universe is the same limitless creativity that flows through me.

Powerful rays of light are continually being hurled from the Sun
 And stream toward the Earth at a speed of 186,000 miles per second
  Illuminating our planet with the gifts and wonders of ever-evolving life.

Physicists tell us that *light* exhibits properties of both a *particle* and a *wave*
 Depending on where one places their attention in the moment of observation.

Light contains the intriguing paradox of possessing both characteristics at the same time,
 Being a *wave* as an invisible expression of possibility, *a field of potential*,
  As well as a *particle* producing a visible expression of *energy in manifest form*
   Constantly winking in and out of physical reality.

Thus, *physical light* is the merging of *a Limitless Field of Infinite Creativity* with physical matter,
 A vital blending together of *invisible pure potentiality* with visible forms of energy,
  While *Transcendent Light* is the fundamental core of everything in the Universe
   And, therefore, *the Unbounded Essence* within every person.

The particle property of physical light is brought into expression by **Infinite Creativity**,
 The vast intelligent power of **Life Force energy** that streams through all manifested forms
  And fashions all structures of Nature into higher stages of complexity.

For thousands of years **the Infinite Intelligence of Life** has been called God by many,
 For it is the *Universal Consciousness* that directs every creature on Earth
  Into higher stages of order, diversity, and cooperation.

It is this *Infinite Creativity* that forms galaxies, stars, mountains, amoebas, and dandelions,
 And brings the laughter of children into the world.

Infinite Creativity can also be depicted from a science vantage as **the Evolutionary Impulse**
 That vibrates at the core of all phenomenal structures inwardly directing their unfolding,
  An impulse that constantly explores how to bring ever-new possibilities into form.

From a religious perspective it is called *"the Love of God"*, or **the Field of Love**,
 The Divine Universal Intelligence that shapes every stone, flower, and animal,
  As well as each artistic expression of human ingenuity.

It is this **Limitless Field of Infinite Creativity** that has fashioned civilized societies,
 Just governance, the wondrous works of art, sculpture, and music,
  And is the creative power to send spaceships to distant planets.

Infinite Creativity is the *Universal Life Force* that's constantly flowing through each of us,
 Just as light constantly streams into us from rays beaming from the surface of the Sun,
  And from the cosmic rays that radiate from the center of our Milky Way Galaxy,
   And from the luminous hub of massive galactic clusters,
    And from the dazzling marrow of the Universe,
     As well as from "the very Heart of God".

Circle of *the Limitless Field of Infinite Creativity*
(Various Names for *the Transcendent Power* of the Universe)

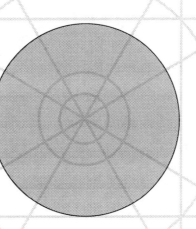

THE EVOLUTIONARY IMPULSE
INFINITE CREATIVITY –
THE IMPULSE OF EVOLUTION
THAT VIBRATES
AT THE CORE OF ALL
PHENOMENAL STRUCTURES
INWARDLY DIRECTING
THEIR UNFOLDING

LIFE FORCE ENERGY
INFINITE CREATIVITY –
THE LIFE FORCE ENERGY
THAT STREAMS THROUGH
ALL MANIFESTED FORMS
- AND FASHIONS ALL
STRUCTURES OF NATURE
INTO HIGHER STAGES
OF COMPLEXITY

INFINITE INTELLIGENCE
INFINITE CREATIVITY –
THE UNIVERSAL INTELLI-
GENCE THAT DIRECTS
EVERYTHING IN THE
COSMOS INTO HIGHER
ORDER, DIVERSITY,
AND COOPERATION

THE FIELD OF LOVE
INFINITE CREATIVITY –
THE INTELLIGENT *FIELD*
OF LOVE THAT SHAPES
EVERY STONE, FLOWER,
CREATURE, AND EACH
ARTISTIC EXPRESSION
OF HUMAN INGENUITY

33

GOD AS "THE CREATION"

I am in awe of the vast Intelligence that animates the countless elegant expressions of Nature.

As humanity continues its quest to expand its understanding of the nature of reality,
    More and more distinctions will continue to emerge in every area of human endeavor.

As further scientific information is discovered, additional fields of scientific study arise
    And, thus, brand new categories of technical specialists are needed.

As biologists constantly gain knowledge about the intricate workings of the human body,
    Additional supplementary medical and biological spheres of study result.

Throughout history, as humanity has implemented more civilized ways to govern
    And has created further distinctions and refinements in state and national laws,
        A larger spectrum of professional judicial expertise has been required.

And from our creative investigations, as we discover new unique styles of music,
    More musical genres are being explored and available to expand our sonic horizons.

In today's world, creating ever-finer distinctions in every sector of life
    Is a natural part of the modern human experience.

And further distinctions are also occurring in the area of spirituality,
    Especially in the sphere of humanity's evolving relationship with God.

In past times when people used the word "God", it referred to one basic definition of the divine,
    Yet at this current period in human evolution, many of the world's spiritual traditions
        Are now expressing at least three different and unique distinctions of God.

For example, God can be experienced as **"The Transcendent"**,
    The non-personal eternal and unbounded *Field of Limitless Consciousness,*
        God can also be experienced as **"The Beloved"**,
            A Supreme Presence in which one can have a personal relationship with,
                And God can be experienced as **"The Creation"**,
                    The vast *Intelligence* abiding within the elegant expressions
                    Of the natural world and the Universe.

God as "The Creation" can be thought of as *the Universal Field of Infinite Intelligence*
    That creatively animates all phenomenal forms of life,
        ***The Divine Spark of Energy* that's embodied in all manifestations of Nature,**
        ***The Evolutionary Impulse* that directs the unfolding of the Cosmos.**

Some of the cultural traditions that have expressed this particular distinction of God
    Are the Native Americans of the North American continent, the Taoists of China,
        The Celtic sects of Europe, and the shamans of South America.

As we continue along our *journey of awakening*, we're each being inwardly invited by *Life*
    To not only experience God as one of these individual distinctions,
        But to boldly embrace the mystery and paradox that God is all three at once.

Circle of God as "The Creation"
(Third Person Perspective of the Divine)

FIELD OF INFINITE INTELLIGENCE
GOD EXPERIENCED AS *THE UNBOUNDED FIELD OF INFINITE INTELLIGENCE* FROM WHICH ALL THE MYRIAD FORMS OF CREATION ARISE

THE INTELLIGENCE WITHIN NATURE
GOD EXPERIENCED AS *THE VAST INTELLIGENCE* THAT ABIDES WITHIN THE COUNTLESS ELEGANT EXPRESSIONS OF THE NATURAL WORLD

UNIVERSAL CREATIVE ENERGY
GOD EXPERIENCED AS *THE UNIVERSAL CREATIVE ENERGY* THAT ANIMATES ALL PHENOMENAL FORMS OF LIFE

THE EVOLUTIONARY IMPULSE
GOD EXPERIENCED AS *THE IMPULSE OF EVOLUTION* THAT CREATIVELY DIRECTS THE CONSTANT UNFOLDING OF THE UNIVERSE

III

MIND
AWARENESS
PRACTICES

FOUNDATIONAL TRANSFORMATIVE PRACTICES

Consistent self-cultivation is the center of my spiritual development.

In order to determine which team will first receive the ball at the beginning of a football game,
    An umpire will decide it with the toss of a coin.

Just like there are two sides to every coin (the so-called "heads side" and the "tails side"),
    There are also two fundamental sides, or facets, which are advantageous for us to develop
        As we become aware that life is fundamentally about our *journey of awakening*.

There is the facet of our journey involved in attaining a clear vision of what really matters
    (Which is also the side of cultivating greater awareness of what our life is truly about),
        And there is the facet of integrating this growing awareness into our life
            Through the discipline and engagement of daily transformative practice.

By following our heart, we can take beneficial steps to support our *awakening journey*
    As we move toward a balance of awareness (clear vision) - and practice (integration).

When we aspire to tone the muscles of our body,
    We can choose to practice a certain system of physical exercises
        That are designed to achieve the intended goals we have established.

And if we want "to tone our spiritual muscles", such as deepening our gratitude or compassion,
    Or cultivating kindness, then it aids us to engage in the transformative practices
        That can help facilitate the attainment of our goals.

Numerous religious traditions around the world have developed thousands of spiritual practices
    To assist in furthering a person along their *spiritual journey*.

And even though this plethora of practices comes from diverse cultures and takes many forms,
    They generally fall into four specific categories
        And typically consist of a few **foundational transformative practices**.

Most spiritual traditions practice some form of inner silence,
    Whether it's **meditation**, mindfulness, or some other method of quieting the thoughts,
        In order to align with *the Source of Life* - and awaken to our *Eternal Nature*.

Contemplation is a foundational practice that can help a spiritual seeker
    Expand his or her ever-changing perspectives and awareness
        By reflecting on "the Big Questions" regarding what life is truly about.

Two other foundational practices are **appreciation** for the gifts we receive each day,
    And **prayer**, in the form of asking *Life* how we are to serve the wellbeing of others.

When we "toss the coin of our *quest for what is true* into the air of higher awareness",
    We must be willing to engage both the heads side and the tails side at the same time,
        Both "the awareness" and "the practice",
            Both the clear vision of who we really are
                And the effective means to integrate our awareness into mastery.

Circle of Foundational Transformative Practices
(Primary Ways to Cultivate and Maintain Inner Freedom)

MEDITATION
THE PRACTICE
OF EXPERIENCING INNER
SILENCE SO AS TO STILL
MY MIND, ALIGN MY AWARE-
NESS WITH *THE SOURCE
OF LIFE*, AND AWAKEN
TO MY *ETERNAL NATURE*

PRAYER
THE PRACTICE
OF ASKING *LIFE*
HOW I AM TO SERVE,
AND CONTRIBUTE TO,
THE WELLBEING OF
OTHERS - AND ACTING
ON WHAT I RECEIVE

CONTEMPLATION
THE PRACTICE OF
CONSCIOUSLY EXPAND-
ING MY AWARENESS
BY REFLECTING ON
"THE BIG QUESTIONS"
REGARDING WHAT MY
LIFE IS TRULY ABOUT

APPRECIATION
THE PRACTICE OF BEING
THANKFUL FOR THE GIFTS
I RECEIVE EACH DAY,
BEING GRATEFUL MY LIFE
IS UNFOLDING PERFECTLY,
AND FULLY APPRECIATING
MYSELF FOR WHO I AM

39

CONTEMPLATION

I consistently cultivate an awareness of what really matters - and what my life is truly about.

When a professional highway architect designs a new road,
    He or she envisions a complete picture of where the road is going
        With knowledge of the road's starting point, as well as its final destination.

Similarly, if you want to design "a new positive pathway for your life"
    (A future road or favorable direction you would like your heart to travel),
        It serves to hold a clear vision of who you want to be - and where you want to go.

The practice of **contemplation** (expanding our awareness by reflecting on "the Big Questions"
    Regarding what our life is truly about) is one of the transformative tools we can use
        To cultivate more inclusive perspectives and insights about what really matters.

We can think of contemplation as being analogous to sitting near a beautiful alpine lake
    And watching the movement of the surface water begin to get calmer and tranquil
        The more we observe it, and the more we keep the focus of our attention on it.

If we continue this analogy, then at one point within our observation, the water becomes so still
    That the lake's surface appears to turn into a serene reflective mirror.

Next, imagine that the wind blows a tiny feather over the lake, gently landing on the water
    And as it does, the feather creates a very soft ripple on the lake's quiet surface.

This soft ripple of water begins to travel across the lake first as a small subtle wave,
    But then begins to grow in size - and expands as larger and larger circles
        Which symbolizes the receiving of larger glimpses into The Great Story of Life.

If you were to look closely at the primary dynamics of contemplation as a spiritual practice,
    You would observe the following four basic components.

First, you relax into an **alignment** with "a sphere of vast knowledge and universal wisdom"
    That transcends and exists beyond your personal mind,
        Which is analogous to the water of a lake getting calmer over a period of time.

Then, you **surrender** the activity of your mind (let go of your thoughts, feelings, and desires),
    Discovering a silent state of mind within you, which is like the still mirrored waters
        Of a serene alpine lake reflecting the surrounding images.

Next, you softy drop in **an existential question or inquiry** into *this subtle field of awareness*,
    Which is symbolized by a tiny feather gently landing on the tranquil water of the lake.

Finally, you simply wait, and watch, and patiently listen to what comes to you
    Allowing the moment to **reveal** insights, intuitions, and expanded awareness
        Represented by "the ripples of the lake poetically unfolding its visionary story".

We are "the architects of our dreams" each day co-creating with *the Limitless Source of Life*,
    Constantly designing the creative pathways of the next leg of our *journey of awakening*.

Circle of Contemplation
(A Transformative Practice)

ALIGNMENT
CONTEMPLATION –
AN INNER ALIGNMENT
WITH "A SPHERE
OF VAST KNOWLEDGE
AND UNIVERSAL WISDOM"
THAT TRANSCENDS
MY INDIVIDUAL SELF

REVELATION
CONTEMPLATION –
CONSCIOUSLY
LISTENING TO AN
INWARD CLARITY THAT
REVEALS INSIGHTS,
INTUITIONS, AND
EXPANDED AWARENESS

SURRENDER
CONTEMPLATION –
MY ABILITY
TO SURRENDER MY
MIND SO AS TO ACCESS
"A FIELD OF LIMITLESS
INFORMATION" THAT
EXISTS BEYOND MY MIND

INQUIRY
CONTEMPLATION –
THE PROCESS
OF GENTLY PLACING
INTO MY MIND
AN EXISTENTIAL
QUESTION ABOUT
WHAT REALLY MATTERS

A CONTEMPLATION PRACTICE

I frequently quiet my mind so as to receive heart wisdom and insights from my Eternal Self.

Just like with the development of any desired life skill
    Such as learning to be an accomplished cook,
        Skiing capably down a snowy mountainside,
            Or playing a musical instrument proficiently,
                The art of contemplation is also a skill that must be practiced
                In order to enjoy the full harvest of its fruits.

In our Western culture, engaging in **contemplation as a spiritual practice**
    Is not a concept that is common to most people in our everyday world.

At present, it's not typically encouraged in our youth, fostered as part of our adult lives,
    Taught or venerated in our societies, and is sometimes thought of as something
        Only reclusive monks, philosophers, or theoretical physicists would do.

The world we live in might be very different today
    If "a course in contemplation" had been taught to all children in early school years.

Imagine going to your first class of elementary school
    And taking an introductory course in Contemplation 101.

Then attending your next year of school with the more advanced version of Contemplation 201,
    Contemplation 301 in your third year, and so forth with each additional school year.

A teacher in this class might have taught you a practice called ***Alignment with the Field***,
    Which is a basic contemplation practice that uses the following steps.

First find a quiet place, unfocus your eyes as you gaze at some chosen object,
    Such as a flower, the leaves of a tree, the flowing water of a stream, a passing cloud,
        Or the flickering of a candle, and **align** with *the Natural Intelligence of Life*.

As you do this, empty your mind of all thoughts or desires of accomplishing anything
    As you **surrender** to an inward spaciousness of silence
        Until you sense a deep connection with *a Field of Higher Awareness*.

As this occurs, gently place into this *Field* a question you would like to investigate,
    Either an **inquiry** concerning your personal life,
        Or a pursuit of some greater perspective of what your life is truly about,
            Or simply, an existential question like "Why am I here?" or "Who am I?"

Then from the quiet state of your serene mind,
    Be willing to patiently listen - and receive from the depths of your inner being
        New **revelations**, heart wisdom, and insights from your *Eternal Self*
            That you write down so you may review them at a later time.

It's never too late to further our education, for we are all "children of the Universe"
    Perpetually developing, expanding, and learning within "the Universe-ity of Life".

Circle of a Contemplation Practice
(A Transformative Exercise - *Alignment With The Field*)

ALIGNMENT
1) UNFOCUS YOUR EYES
AS YOU GAZE
AT A CHOSEN OBJECT,
SUCH AS A FLOWER,
THE LEAVES OF A TREE,
A CLOUD, OR A CANDLE,
WHILE ALIGNING WITH
THE INTELLIGENCE OF LIFE

SURRENDER
2) LET GO OF ALL
THOUGHTS OR DESIRES
AS YOU SURRENDER
TO AN INWARD
SPACIOUSNESS OF
SILENCE AND CONNECT
WITH *A FIELD
OF HIGHER AWARENESS*

INQUIRY
3) FROM A CONSCIOUS
PLACE OF DETACHMENT
ABOUT ANY NEED
FOR AN ANSWER, ASK
A QUESTION SUCH AS:
*WHO AM I? - WHY AM
I HERE? - WHAT IS THE
MEANING OF MY LIFE?*

REVELATION
4) FROM THE QUIET
STATE OF A SERENE
MIND, BE WILLING TO
PATIENTLY LISTEN AND
RECEIVE FROM WITHIN
YOU - REVELATIONS,
HEART WISDOM,
AND INSIGHTS

43

IV

THE SONG
OF EMBODIED
LOVE

THE NATURAL STATES THAT EMERGE FROM *BEING*

I nurture a quiet mind allowing the natural states of peace, happiness, joy and harmony to arise.

When the clear still water of a small pond is stirred up as the result of a raging storm
 The pond is invaded by floating particles of mud and sand from the turbulence
  Which are then dispersed throughout the pool,
   And for a time, there remains little visibility in the water.

In order for the pond to revert back to its pristine clarity and return to its natural state,
 The water requires a calm period of stillness to allow everything to settle.

Similarly, when we are feeling "out of balance"
 From the everyday storms and emotional events of our lives
  Or from the turbulence of our self-created stress,
   Our inner being can become cloudy and confused
    And our natural clarity can be temporarily blurred.

Like the image of a murky pond restoring itself after an agitating storm,
 We also can regain peace of mind by engaging in a period of stillness
  So as to return our inner being to its *natural state*.

When we enter the silence within our heart, align with *Life*, and experience a time of renewal,
 Then "our inner pond" is given the opportunity to become calm
  And its "disturbed waters" can begin to return to clarity once again.

It's from this place of quiet connection and attunement with *the Infinite Presence of Love*,
 It's from this sanctuary of communion with *the Source of All That Is*,
  That our most **natural states that emerge from *Being*** are revealed.

When we take the time to flow into stillness,
 Our body can naturally experience a sacred **harmony**.

When we choose to become serene and quiet,
 Our heart can unveil an authentic **joy**.

When we live our life in a manner in which we are fully present,
 Our mind can relax into a true **happiness**.

And when our mind is silent,
 We can experience a sublime **peace** that's always available to us.

As we align our awareness with *"the Song of Perfect Oneness"*, *"the Mystery of Eternity"*,
 "The Ocean of Limitless Love" - the states that emerge from *Being* naturally arise.

Could it be that *the Source of Life* is constantly inviting us
 To bring "our turbulent pond" to the haven of silence
  So we can respond to any situation from an awareness of inner freedom
   And merge with this vast *Ocean*, with the natural states of *Embodied Love,*
    In order that we may dive, once again, into its pristine clarity?

Circle of the Natural States That Emerge From *Being*

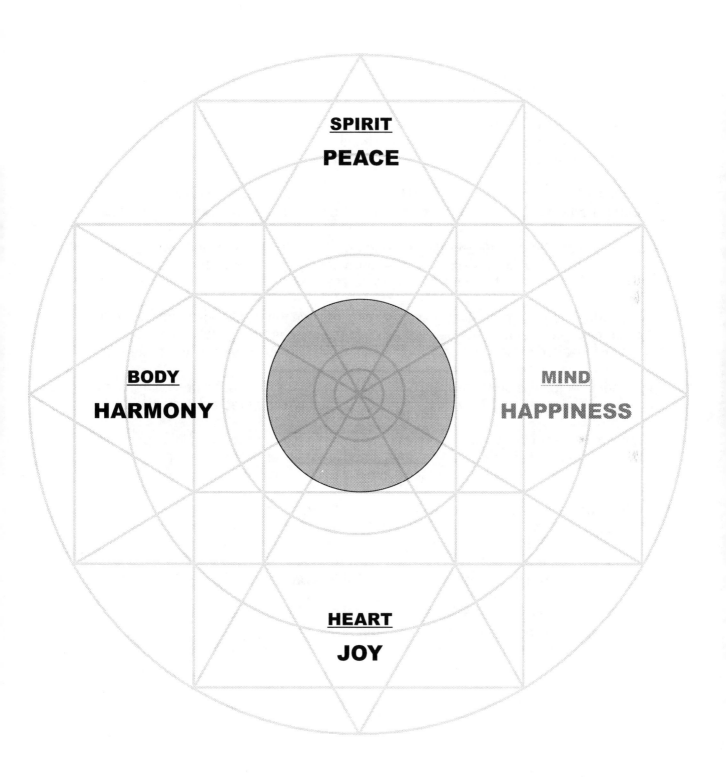

SPIRIT
PEACE

BODY
HARMONY

MIND
HAPPINESS

HEART
JOY

THE NATURAL STATE OF HAPPINESS

Today I choose to be happy for the blessed gift of simply being alive.

There is something magical about being around a happy glowing infant who is full of laughter
Which has an infectious way of reminding us that every person on our planet
(Whether rich or poor, from the east or west, north or south)
Also has a deep inborn desire to be happy.

The Infinitely Intelligent Creative Power that animates and sustains all creatures on Earth
Is constantly surging through our heart and mind,
And is always arousing within us, a natural yearning to experience happiness.

But a sustained experience of happiness does not come easy for many people who struggle,
Which is partly due to the adverse programing they've received from facets of society.

Yet despite societal programing, we can learn to maintain happiness by embodying a key skill,
A fundamental capacity in which we consciously recognize we each have the ability
To simply choose to live our life in this natural state.

By using certain transformative practices to help us remove the blockages to the flow of *Love*,
We can discover how to surrender to the constant changes taking place in our life
And, thus, to choose to be grateful for what we're learning from every experience.

With greater mindfulness and self-observation, we can learn to live in the present moment
Where we choose to direct our mind on thoughts that are centered in loving awareness.

As we realize how to accept, within the present moment, that our life is unfolding perfectly,
We can embrace life just as it is and, thus, choose to live with more altruistic qualities
Such as kindness, service to others, generosity, and integrity.

True happiness is actually a *choice*, a sense of fulfillment from the heart of the Universe
For choosing to live our life in **gratitude** for the blessed gift of simply being alive.

It's the inherent reward we receive
For choosing to feel and express a greater depth of **compassion** and love for others.

Happiness can be thought of as the fulfillment we experience when we choose to live our life
Intentionally directing our mind on the **highest possible thoughts**,
Thoughts that help us co-creatively build with others, a more enlightened world.

This expansive facet of happiness comes to us as a sacred offering from *Life*
For traveling the developmental road of consciously cultivating our mind and heart,
And arriving at (in a way of speaking) "the place where we have always been".

This "sacred place" is our natural and instinctive home, the sanctuary of the present moment,
Where we choose to live in **alignment** with *the Source of Life*.

At this awakened stage of awareness, happiness is a **natural state that emerges from *Being***,
And is to be found all along the journey of our life - not just at the final destination.

Circle of the Natural State of Happiness

ALIGNMENT
HAPPINESS –
**A SUBLIME AND
NATURAL STATE THAT
I EXPERIENCE WHEN MY
CONSCIOUS AWARENESS
IS ALIGNED WITH**
THE SOURCE OF LIFE

GRATITUDE
HAPPINESS –
**A SENSE
OF FULFILLMENT WHICH
COMES FROM <u>CHOOSING</u>
TO BE GRATEFUL
FOR THE BLESSED GIFT
OF SIMPLY BEING ALIVE**

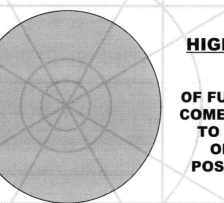

HIGHER THOUGHTS
HAPPINESS –
**A SENSE
OF FULFILLMENT WHICH
COMES FROM <u>CHOOSING</u>
TO DIRECT MY MIND
ON THE HIGHEST
POSSIBLE THOUGHTS**

COMPASSION
HAPPINESS –
**A SENSE OF
FULFILLMENT WHICH
COMES FROM <u>CHOOSING</u>
TO EXPRESS A GREATER
DEPTH OF COMPASSION
AND LOVE FOR OTHERS**

PILLARS OF AWAKENING

I accept that my life is unfolding perfectly just as it is.

As a visualization exercise, let's go on a metaphorical journey of imagining a cliff diver
Who courageously leaps off a high overhang as he descends into the ocean below,
Which symbolizes "our personal dive into freedom" - the opportunity life gives us
To awaken every day to a more glorious expression of our vast potential.

Each of the four sections of his dive - being present, the leap, the free-fall, and the merging -
Poetically represents one of the four **Pillars of Awakening** displayed here as:
1) <u>**Gratitude**</u> for what we're learning from every experience of our life,
2) <u>**Surrender**</u> everything to *a Greater Power* and let go of our attachments,
3) <u>**Acceptance**</u> that our life is unfolding perfectly just as it is,
And **4) an awareness of our <u>Oneness</u>** with all of life.

Now - imagine a fearless diver with a sun-bronzed sculpted body
Walking confidently to the rim of a high rock precipice
That overlooks the rippling waters of the azure sea below.

Picture the following scene in which the diver stops for a moment at the edge of the cliff
To gaze out in all directions at the beautiful panorama around him,
And then with a radiant smile on his face, becomes very present and centered,
Feeling **gratitude** for the wondrous gift of every breath he breathes
And for the energy of aliveness pulsing through him.

Envision that he's now ready to proceed, with his feet firmly planted on the rim of the rocky cliff,
Looking down at the churning water below,
Adrenaline surging through the fibers of every muscle,
And then with an explosive leap, he catapults himself forward,
Surrendering to a graceful dive,
While letting go of the solid ground of *the known*.

At this point the diver descends, the gravity of the Earth pulling on him,
As he fully embraces his free-fall, **accepting** the inevitable trajectory of his body,
And sensing that invisible wings assist him in his downward flight.

Finally, his body plunges into the ocean depths
As he enters through the portal on the water's surface, merges with the blue vastness,
And experiences sublime **Oneness** with the sea.

If we truly desire to "dive into inner freedom" - and learn to love all of life unconditionally
(I.e. live a conscious life in which we experience an awakened awareness
And a compassionate life of service to others),
We ultimately must respond to this ongoing invitation
To embody these qualities in our life as our natural way of being.

For as we learn "to dive into life" by courageously living these **Pillars of Awakening** each day,
They will lead us to authentic spiritual freedom "as our eyes gaze out in all directions"
Eager to offer our creative gifts and talents to an ever-awakening world.

Circle of the Pillars of Awakening
(Attributes For Cultivating Inner Freedom and a Life of Mastery)

ONENESS
I AM AWARE
OF MY ONENESS
WITH ALL
OF LIFE

GRATITUDE
I AM GRATEFUL
FOR WHAT I'M LEARNING
FROM EVERY
EXPERIENCE OF MY LIFE

ACCEPTANCE
I ACCEPT
THAT MY LIFE IS
UNFOLDING PERFECTLY
JUST AS IT IS

SURRENDER
I LET GO
OF MY ATTACHMENTS
AND SURRENDER MY LIFE
TO *A GREATER POWER*

ACCEPTANCE

I realize that my life is unfolding perfectly just as it is - and thus, I fully accept "what is".

Majestic schooners that carry multiple tall masts billowing with full sails
  Are catapulted forward along their ocean journey by the powerful force of the wind.

Experienced sailors know that in order for their vessels to go where they want them to go,
  They must, sometimes, navigate their ships in the direction of the wind.

In our daily journey, **acceptance** is the ability to flow with our life experiences just as they are
  By facing them directly into "the winds of the present moment"
    So we may fearlessly advance forward to where *the Source of Life* is leading us.

Acceptance is the mature capacity "to sail our ships" through both "the joys of clear skies",
  As well as "the storms of our life", unattached to the changing seasons of life's events.

Acceptance can also be thought of as boldly **embracing "what is"**,
  Which is fully accepting every situation that arises in our life each day.

It's letting go of the polarizing labels and definitions we tend to place on everything,
  Such as "good or bad", "right or wrong", "holy or evil",
    And allowing life to be just as it is.

Acceptance can be likened to climbing to the summit of a high mountain
  And, thereby, gaining the awareness of a much more expansive perspective,
    So eventually we can look out at **the perfect unfolding within our life**.

From the higher vantage of living our life in present moment awareness,
  We discover "a Bigger Picture", a wider view, of what really matters
    And how each event in our life is intimately connected to a greater wholeness.

Acceptance can also be seen as the recognition and **trust**
  That we have opportunities to learn valuable lessons from every experience of our life.

Whether a situation we undergo appears positive or negative when it's happening,
  We can, aligned with *the Source of Life*, use any situation
    As a means to free ourselves from limitation, develop our potential,
      And discover what our life is truly about.

Acceptance is an attribute that calls us to live with an open mind and heart,
  And which offers authentic **forgiveness** for ourselves and others
    Concerning the various challenges that may arise.

It's like standing at the bow of a majestic schooner
  With our arms wide open and fully extended,
    Directly facing the warm Sun and the force of the wind,
      And then for a brief moment,
        Receiving a glimpse of a *sublime inner knowing*
          That our life is always unfolding perfectly.

Circle of Acceptance

EMBRACING LIFE
ACCEPTANCE –
MY ABILITY
TO BOLDLY EMBRACE
"WHAT IS", WHICH IS
FULLY ACCEPTING EVERY
SITUATION THAT ARISES
IN MY LIFE EACH DAY

TRUST
ACCEPTANCE –
THE RECOGNITION
AND TRUST THAT
I HAVE OPPORTUNITIES
TO LEARN VALUABLE
LESSONS FROM EVERY
EXPERIENCE OF MY LIFE

PRESENCE
ACCEPTANCE –
THE UNDERSTANDING
THAT AS I LIVE MY LIFE
IN PRESENT MOMENT
AWARENESS - MY LIFE IS
UNFOLDING PERFECTLY
JUST AS IT IS

FORGIVENESS
ACCEPTANCE –
LIVING WITH
AN OPEN MIND
AND HEART THAT
OFFERS AUTHENTIC
FORGIVENESS FOR
MYSELF AND OTHERS

53

PATIENCE

I align myself with Life - and thus, I am intuitively guided to take right action at the proper time.

In the spring when we plant new seeds in the fertile soil of our gardens, we must be patient
Knowing that, in time, the seedlings will emerge effortlessly from the moist ground
Into the nurturing light of the Sun.

Nature's growth cycle has its own timing we must honor
And, therefore, we cannot dig into the soil to see how the seed is coming along
Because it will disturb its intrinsic unfolding process.

Thus, we must wait, be unwavering in our trust of its natural development, and be patient
Understanding the seedling will appear out of the ground at the proper time.

From a spiritual perspective, we can define *patience* as the virtue we embody
When we unwaveringly **trust** in the perfect unfolding of our life, relinquish our control,
And let go of any attachments to our desires.

A blue heron is a large bird with long thin legs
That can stand at the side of a river completely still for an extended period of time
And wait for the perfect moment to strike its prey,
Which will, sooner or later, come swimming by in the water in front of it.

Another important aspect of *patience* is - being aligned with *the Source of Life*
In order to be intuitively guided to **take right action at the proper time**.

Some hawks and eagles instinctively build their large nests
At the very top of tall pine trees.

Their nests must be constructed in such a way that they can withstand high winds,
Battering rain, and all manner of storms.

True patience is also being able to consciously **accept and embrace**
Whatever "storm" may arise in our life without resistance, knowing it will pass.

There is *an Infinitely Intelligent Creative Power* that's constantly inviting us
To discover how to live our life from the exquisite richness of *the present moment*,
To take a courageous leap into the vital experience of **presence**
Where we most easily develop our greater potential and possibilities.

Patience, from this perspective, is the awakened awareness we cultivate through practice
And through living our life in the present moment.

As we continue to plant, in "the springtime of our hearts and minds",
The seeds of possibility that envision a more peaceful world for others and ourselves,
With *patience*, these seeds will naturally blossom within us - and within the world.

Awakened awareness is developed from the discipline of daily practice,
And, like the passage from the chrysalis to the butterfly, daily practice requires *patience*.

Circle of Patience
(From a Spiritual Perspective)

TRUST
PATIENCE –
TRUSTING IN THE PERFECT UNFOLDING OF MY LIFE, RELINQUISHING CONTROL, AND LETTING GO OF MY ATTACHMENTS TO MY DESIRES

PRESENCE
PATIENCE –
THE AWAKENED AWARENESS I CULTIVATE THROUGH PRACTICE AND THROUGH LIVING MY LIFE IN THE PRESENT MOMENT

ACCEPTANCE
PATIENCE –
BEING ABLE TO CONSCIOUSLY ACCEPT AND EMBRACE WHATEVER ARISES IN MY LIFE WITHOUT RESISTANCE

RIGHT TIMING
PATIENCE –
BEING ALIGNED WITH *THE SOURCE OF LIFE* IN ORDER TO BE INTUITIVELY GUIDED TO TAKE RIGHT ACTION AT THE PROPER TIME

55

PAIN VERSUS SUFFERING

I consciously respond to each experience of pain in my life and accept it as part of "what is".

The experience of pain, as well as its opposite, the experience of pleasure,
    Are natural and essential aspects of a dualistic world, and are foundational to life
        In ways that are similar to all other fundamental polarities,
            Such as light and darkness, expansion and contraction,
            Attraction and repulsion, male and female, etc.

Pain is an unpleasant experience that we're all familiar with
    And everyone on the planet, most of the time begrudgingly, has no choice
        But to, on occasion, be subjected to this aspect of reality.

A majority of people also undergo *suffering* as an ordinary, recurrent experience of their lives,
    Yet this isn't true for everyone, especially those leading-edge pioneers of consciousness
        Who have gained an expansive spiritual perspective of what their lives are truly about
        And who have *awakened* to a higher, more enlightened awareness.

There is a distinct difference between *pain* and *suffering*
    That must be clarified as we attempt to make sense of this world,
        And as we continue to cultivate our *journey of awakening*.

Suffering comes from our **attachment** of wanting some painful aspect of our life
    To be different than it is,
        Whereas *pain* is the **acceptance** of an experience of discomfort as "what is".

Suffering comes from **resisting** our experiences of *pain* that arise in our life
    And fighting against the obvious fact that reality "is as it is",
        Rather than **embracing** our life which has encounters of discomfort and anguish.

Suffering can also come from our thoughts of self-imposed fears,
    From clinging to the regrets and resentments of the past,
        Or the apprehensive expectations and anxieties of the future.

It comes from defending false ideas about ourselves (e.g. we're unworthy or not good enough)
    Which creates **"an illusion within our mind"**, instead of seeing **reality** the way it is.

Experiencing *an epiphany of awareness*, or a glimpse of our *True Nature*,
    Helps make us more conscious of the constant magnetic pull of our *spiritual journey*,
        And can remind us that, ultimately, *suffering* comes from the confusion
            Of not knowing who we really are (not knowing our *Eternal Self)*.

When *pain* appears in our life, *suffering* is like an attempt to swim upstream
    And struggle **against** the natural direction of the river's **flow** (what is actually occurring)
        In order to fulfill our personal desires and habitual needs
            To have life be the way we think it should be.

Acceptance that our life is unfolding perfectly just as it is, including when *pain* arises,
    Is like effortlessly flowing downstream with the natural current of "the River of Life".

Circle of Pain Versus Suffering

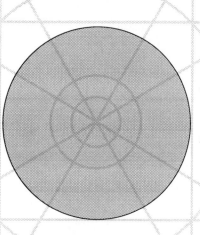

WITH THE FLOW VS. AGAINST

PAIN – IS LIKE FLOWING DOWNSTREAM WITH THE CURRENT OF A RIVER AS DISCOMFORT ARISES

SUFFERING – IS LIKE SWIMMING UPSTREAM AGAINST THE CURRENT WHENEVER PAIN ARISES

EMBRACING LIFE VS. RESISTANCE

PAIN – IS EMBRACING AN EXPERIENCE OF DISCOMFORT AS "WHAT IS"

SUFFERING – IS WHAT WE SELF-CREATE WHEN WE RESIST PAIN "JUST AS IT IS"

ACCEPTANCE VS. ATTACHMENT

PAIN – IS THE ACCEPTANCE OF AN EXPERIENCE OF DISCOMFORT OR CHANGE

SUFFERING – COMES FROM THE ATTACHMENT OF WANTING SOME PAINFUL ASPECT OF LIFE TO BE DIFFERENT THAN IT IS

REALITY VS. ILLUSION

PAIN – LIKE PLEASURE, IS PART OF THE WORLD OF DUALITY: LIGHT AND DARKNESS, EXPANSION AND CONTRACTION, ETC

SUFFERING – IS AN EXPER- IENCE CREATED AS "AN ILLUSION OF THE MIND"

PATHWAYS OF SELF-INQUIRY

Asking questions about the purpose and meaning of my life helps me cultivate peace of mind.

If you want to build something like a house, a chair, or a fence,
It's beneficial to have the appropriate tools handy
So you can more easily and proficiently accomplish your task.

For many of us who have a strong yearning to explore the spiritual facets of our nature,
The deep existential questions of life are "effective tools" our minds can use
To help us cultivate inner freedom and expanded levels of awareness.

Asking ourselves questions about purpose, meaning, and mission is an awareness practice
That can help us on our path of cultivating peace of mind.

Powerful life-defining questions can be like the seeds of tomorrow's harvest
And when these questions are "planted in the fertile soil of an open mind and heart",
In time, their insightful fruits burst forth from *the Unlimited Ground of Being*.

The Infinite Intelligence of the Universe is always seeking new creative pathways
For the next expression of its ever-unfolding potential,
And for many of us, *self-inquiry* is a valuable pathway to explore our limitless potential.

There are numerous **pathways of self-inquiry** that are possible for us to experience,
Many self-examining explorations that lead us to sacred places of investigation
Where we question who we really are, why we are here,
And what our life is truly about.

For many people, **suffering** seems to be the most common path that initiates self-inquiry,
Since a time of suffering can shake one to the core - and stir a feeling of intense unrest,
An unrest that awakens a hunger to seek answers to "the Big Questions of life".

Yet suffering stems from a lack of higher awareness, an ignorance of the truth of what is,
And, over time as awareness begins to grow, other *paths of inquiry* start to appear.

Self-inquiry can arise in us from developing greater **compassion and empathy**,
Through noticing the pain and suffering of others,
And then being compelled to find ways to serve them by relieving their pain.

The awe of **inspiration** also leads to *self-inquiry* from being uplifted by Nature, beauty, and art,
Or by the encouragement of other people who inspire us to ask the important questions.

With the *grace* that comes from **aligning our awareness with *the Source of Life***
And with a fuller understanding and perspective of what really matters,
We can shift from using suffering as the primary generator of our *inquiry*
To the joy of developing ourselves and expanding our consciousness.

When we're able to take conscious responsibility for the choices we make and actions we take,
Compassion, inspiration, and alignment can become the fertile gardens
From which the seeds of our deepest questions begin to sprout forth.

Circle of Pathways of Self-Inquiry

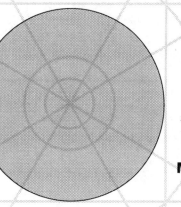

ALIGNMENT
SELF-INQUIRY
ARISES OUT
OF MY ALIGNMENT
WITH *THE SOURCE OF LIFE*
WHERE I CONNECT WITH
MY INNATE YEARNING TO
EXPAND MY AWARENESS

SUFFERING
SELF-INQUIRY
ARISES OUT OF MY
PERSONAL SUFFERING,
BORN FROM A CRISIS
THAT MOTIVATES
AN INNER SEARCH INTO
"THE BIG QUESTIONS"

INSPIRATION
SELF-INQUIRY
ARISES FROM
THE UPLIFTMENT OR
AWE OF NATURE, FORMS
OF BEAUTY, OR ART,
INSPIRING ME TO ASK
MEANINGFUL QUESTIONS

COMPASSION
SELF-INQUIRY
ARISES FROM
COMPASSIONATELY
NOTICING THE
SUFFERING OF OTHERS,
AND THEN FINDING WAYS
TO RELIEVE THEIR PAIN

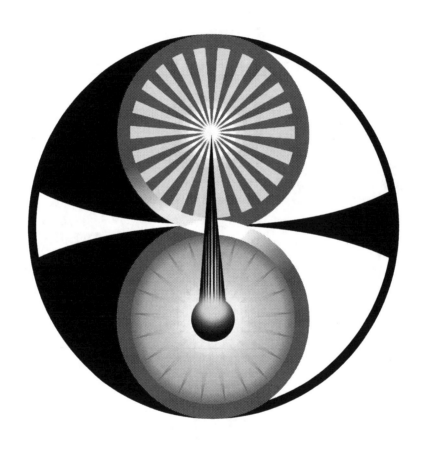

V

MIND
AWARENESS
PRACTICES

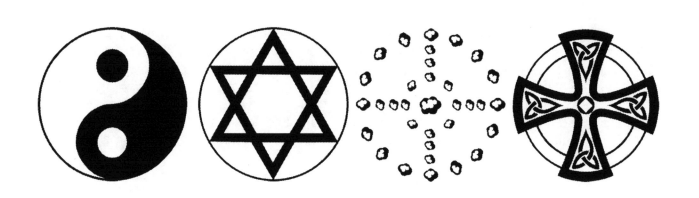

SELF-INQUIRY

I frequently ask myself "the Big Questions of life" as a way of discovering who I really am.

Many young children seem to be born into this world as curious as a cat
    Relentlessly asking questions such as "What is this?" and "How does that work?"
        And typically their favorite question - "Why?"

When you and I were children, we most likely tried to enhance our knowledge of life
    By asking the people around us numerous questions
        So we could learn more about the nature of everything
            That existed in our small and personal world.

As we grew older, a natural desire developed to find out about our inner nature as well,
    A longing to answer the existential life-defining questions which began to arise in us,
        Such as the burning questions about the purpose of life
            And is there **meaning** to our life.

Other areas of inquiry that seemed to surface were focused on questions about **death** and **life**,
    Such as "What happens after I die?" or "How do I live the best life I can live?"

These "Big Questions" eventually included **the transcendent ones**,
    Like "Is there *a Greater Power?*", "What is God?", and "Who am I?"

There is a mysterious potency in these questions, for these questions have an intrinsic ability
    To take us beyond the well-worn tracks and habitual pathways of our mind
        Enabling us to experience other roads of awareness we've never traveled before
            And explore brand new realms of the possible.

The more profound a question is,
    The more power it potentially has to transform our reality.

The puzzling thing about the deep **self-inquiry** of transcendent questions like "Who am I?"
    Is that these questions have no solid answers to hold onto, no exact solutions to grasp,
        For they only point us to a direct personal experience of unfathomable *Being*
            And a life-long journey of inner development and never-ending *Becoming*.

As we ask these questions, they inwardly lead us to an unfolding spiral of *infinite awakenings*
    Which reveals an unlimited creative realm of spiritual adventures where *Life* yearns to take us.

The power here is not necessarily in the answers, but in our courage to ask the questions
    And in allowing the process to open up "brand new pathways to our spiritual horizons".

An unseen universal force is thereby unleashed from these kinds of questions
    That "shapes our tomorrows" into our creative potential and our endless possibilities.

So when we ask these powerful questions often, they hold the promise to transform and heal
    Creating an opportunity for us to experience radical transformation,
        And perhaps, one day, emerge into a higher realm of human consciousness,
            As if we are being metamorphosized from a caterpillar into a butterfly.

Circle of Self-Inquiry
(A Transformative Practice)

TRANSCENDENCE
WHAT
IS
GOD?
+ + +
WHO
AM
I?

LIFE
WHAT IS
TRUE, GOOD,
AND BEAUTIFUL?
+ + +
HOW DO I LIVE
THE BEST LIFE
I CAN LIVE?

MEANING
WHAT IS
THE MEANING
OF MY LIFE?
+ + +
IS THERE
A PURPOSE
TO LIFE?

DEATH
WHAT
HAPPENS
AFTER I DIE?
+ + +
DO I HAVE
AN *ETERNAL
NATURE?*

63

CULTIVATING HAPPINESS

Today I choose to be happy which serves me to effectively respond to each situation in my life.

When some people look at a tall modern building
    They typically don't see one of the important and key components of the construction -
        The foundation on which it's built.

In order to support the entire structure and deal with the immense stresses it will undergo,
    Architects design the foundation of a lofty building so it anchors deep into the earth.

Without this kind of strong foundation in place to properly secure it,
    The building will not be constructed in a safe manner.

As we continue to build on our *journey of life* by consciously cultivating our inner awareness,
    One of the things we discover is that **the happiness we desire**
        Must be supported by a strong foundation of right thinking and action.

For example, **a well-rested body** that receives adequate sleep and daily periods of silence
    Helps to create a strong footing for the myriad experiences we encounter each day.

A non-restful body can make it harder to feel happy by being in a constant mode of stress,
    Thus always seeking a state of equilibrium in an attempt to be rejuvenated and restored.

Another valuable foundational support that contributes to our happiness
    Is proper **nutrition**, sufficient water intake, and balanced body chemistry.

A vibrant healthy body maintained through appropriate exercise, ample hydration,
    And nourished with natural foods, is the bedrock for everything we do,
        And is the physical foundation that enhances the attainment of our desires.

For some people, additional vitamin and mineral supplementation is, at times, required
    To allow full development of the body and healthy neural pathways within the brain.

Of course, it's natural for daily life to provide many normal stresses
    Like the various challenges of our careers, family life, time concerns, finances,
        And the surprises and crises that occasionally occur.

Yet we can promote a greater level of peace by **being mindful**
    Not to add self-imposed stress from any self-created fears and concerns
        Which may be unconsciously generated from old dysfunctional habits and beliefs.

And one of the strongest ways to support our happiness
    Is to, each day, deliberately choose the **intention** to be happy,
        For there is much power in our innate ability to choose the way we want to feel.

Could it be that with a strong conscious foundation, we can build our life - choice by choice -
    Thought by thought - feeling by feeling - growing higher and higher in awareness
        And thereby perceiving our world from a greater vantage of what really matters
            Where "the light of happiness" naturally radiates as who we truly are?

Circle of Cultivating Happiness
(Transformative Practices)

REST
I MAKE IT A PRIORITY
TO RECEIVE
ADEQUATE SLEEP
AND DAILY PERIODS
OF SILENCE

NUTRITION
I MAINTAIN
PROPER NUTRITION,
AMPLE HYDRATION,
AND BALANCED
BODY CHEMISTRY

INTENTION
I CONSCIOUSLY
CHOOSE TO BE HAPPY
AS I RESPOND TO
EACH SITUATION THAT
ARISES IN MY LIFE

MINDFULNESS
I AM MINDFUL
TO LIVE MY LIFE
WITHOUT CREATING
SELF-IMPOSED
STRESS

NATURAL INTERESTS

Active engagement in the interests I'm passionate about awakens a greater purpose for my life.

Because of their intrinsic connection to their innate instincts
Most animals respond to life by carrying out daily functions that are *natural* to them.

In the wild of Nature, birds *naturally* know how to build nests for their young,
Bees *naturally* know how to acquire honey in support of the collective hive,
And monarch butterflies *naturally* know how to embark on the annual trek
Of their long migration to the north - and back again.

These are a few examples of how certain species express an "inborn" or "instinctual" form
Of *natural interest* in relation to their basic survival needs.

Mammals, like all other species of animals, are strongly driven by *the impulse to survive*,
Which directs all creatures to seek safety, secure nourishment, and procreate.

When mammals feel extended periods of safety, they are drawn to experiences of enjoyment,
And from their times of play, they begin to develop more evolved forms of "interests",
Which seem to naturally arise from an innate *impulse to pursue pleasure*.

And some mammals have even responded to a more evolved impulse, *the impulse to create*,
By discovering and using simple tools; e.g. sticks that improve ways of finding food.

But it appears only we humans have evolved the complex emotions and rational thinking
Which inwardly activate us, not only by *the impulse to survive*, *the impulse of pleasure*,
And *the impulse to create*, but also by a natural *impulse to spiritually awaken*.

For us humans, **natural interest** has developed into the kinds of *interest* we are **attracted to**
That cultivate a feeling in us of wakefulness, aliveness, and enthusiasm for life.

Furthermore, it can be thought of as the *interests* that **naturally inspire us**
To investigate the deeper philosophical questions of life,
The profound questions which enliven a sense of purpose for our lives.

Natural interests can also point us to what **creatively challenges and motivates us**
To expand beyond our personal limits, fears, and boundaries.

Today, many people live in a world where they have created lifestyles of constriction
In which they do a number of things they don't want to do, yet feel they should do,
Engage in careers they hate to be in,
And are involved in various other "activities of mental imprisonment".

When we release ourselves from these self-imposed prisons of "shoulds" and "supposed to's"
And instead, practice each day to be ever more aware of, and consciously involved in,
Our *natural interests (those facets of our life that we're **passionate about**)*,
Then *Life* will direct us (like it has directed all creatures for billions of years)
To discover the most natural ways to fulfill our own unique mission
And awaken our true purpose for being alive.

Circle of Natural Interests

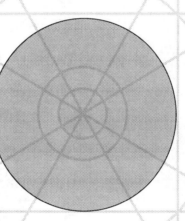

ALIVENESS
NATURAL INTERESTS –
THE INTERESTS
I AM GENUINELY
ATTRACTED TO THAT
CREATE IN ME A FEELING
OF ALIVENESS AND
ENTHUSIASM FOR LIFE

PASSIONS
NATURAL INTERESTS –
THE INTERESTS
THAT SPRING FORTH
FROM MY JOYS
AND PASSIONS WHICH
GENERATE A SENSE
OF TIMELESSNESS

INSPIRATION
NATURAL INTERESTS –
THE INTERESTS
THAT INSPIRE ME
TO INVESTIGATE
THE DEEPER QUESTIONS
OF LIFE WHICH ENLIVEN
A SENSE OF PURPOSE

MOTIVATION
NATURAL INTERESTS –
THE INTERESTS THAT
CREATIVELY CHALLENGE
AND MOTIVATE ME
TO EXPAND BEYOND
MY PERSONAL LIMITS,
FEARS, AND BOUNDARIES

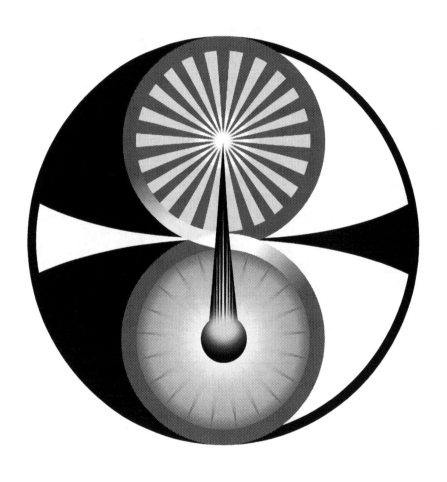

VI

ARCHETYPES
OF CONSCIOUS
CONTRIBUTION

EVOLUTION OF PRIMARY HUMAN IMPULSES

I realize that everything I experience is in my life to help me spiritually awaken to who I really am.

Whenever we climb a staircase to get to a higher floor of a building
    It's obvious we must first place our feet on the lower steps
        And then go up each ascending step before we can reach the top of the stairs.

Similarly in the long evolutionary progression of life,
    There are foundational levels or steps that must first be established
        Before the next higher step can then be taken.

Within all sentient beings on Earth, there is an innate and basic will to survive,
    A primary impulse that's built into every creature to ensure the furtherance of its existence
        So life within its species will carry on.

In the beginning of humanity's evolutionary journey, **the impulse to survive** was foremost,
    Especially when the harsh and hostile environment of the primitive world
        Contained many life-threatening dangers.

Over time with greater adaptation and better skills, some of these challenges were diminished,
    Which allowed more energy and time available to explore new experiences.

With these evolutionary developments, the intrinsic impulse to seek pleasure and avoid pain
    Activated many to delve into such things as enjoying food beyond its survival function,
        Investigating the frolicsome experiences of play and fun,
            And cherishing the rich sensations of the physical body.

Therefore, *the impulse to survive* can be seen as a necessary and foundational step
    That brought humanity to its next level, **the exploration of pleasure**.

Then with further human progress that occurred over thousands of years,
    More time became available to bring into material form
        The wondrous and imaginative ideas of the creative mind,
            For the joyful urges of individual creativity and inner development
                Began to flourish as an essential impulse of the heart.

The instinctual impulse to survive and *the impulse of pleasure* were both important steps
    That naturally led humanity to **the exploration of conscious creativity**.

Today in our modern world, as we continue to expand our awareness and compassion,
    A new and novel impulse has begun to arise within a great number of people,
        A natural longing to deeply question the very nature of existence,
            An inquiry about what life is truly about - and what really matters,
                A primary impulse to spiritually awaken to our Eternal Nature.

Could it be that everything we experience in life is an integral part of our spiritual awakening,
    And that every action we engage in, every choice we make, every step we take
        Is *a yearning of awakening* that helps us learn how to ascend a bit further
            Up "the stairway of awareness" so we may ultimately discover who we really are?

Circle of the Evolution of Primary Human Impulses

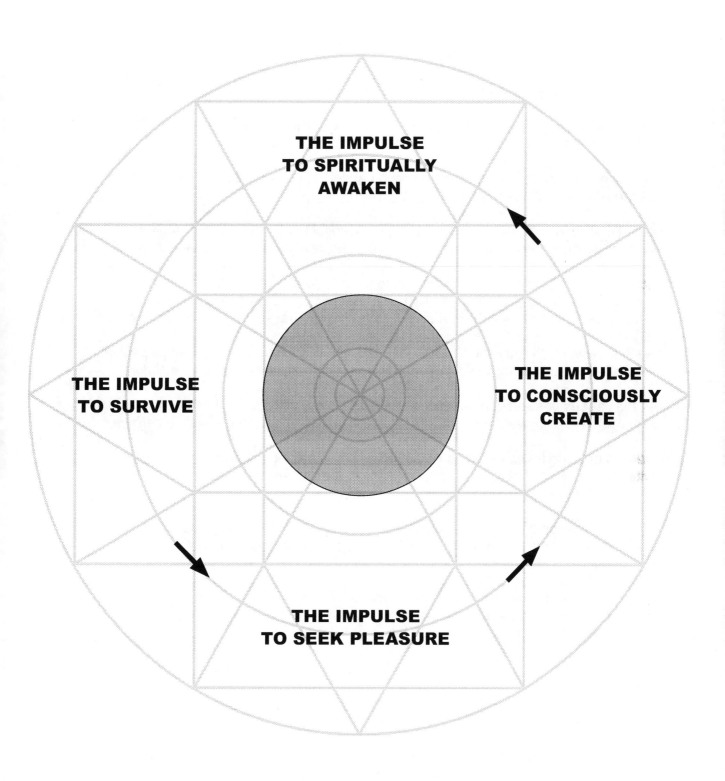

PRIMARY EMOTIONAL NEEDS

My longing to feel safe, loved, empowered, and connected leads me to realizing who I really am.

If you visit an airport, or walk through a shopping mall, or go where there are lots of people,
You can easily observe that all individuals have their own distinctive facial features,
Their different personality traits, their characteristic skin tone,
And a body type which makes them unique.

Yet simultaneously, all human beings, at the very core of their essential nature,
Are basically the same - and each person generally feels similar inherent longings.

This amazing diversity of people can be likened to endless clouds floating against a blue sky
As the billowy contours form an array of unique shapes and limitless patterns in the air.

Yet just like all clouds are similar - because the essential nature of each individual cloud
Is made of *the same water vapor*, so do all people have *the same Essential Nature*.

Within the heart of every unique person on the planet, there is a collective natural yearning,
A fundamental longing to be nourished by **the same primary emotional needs**:
The need **to feel safe**, **to feel loved**, **to feel empowered**, and **to feel connected**.

These four basic needs develop from our natural impulses to survive and to seek pleasure,
To create and, ultimately, to spiritually awaken to the realization of our *True Nature*.

When the various perceived threats and challenges to our physical and emotional survival
Are, over time, removed from our awareness, a feeling of **safety** naturally emerges.

The feeling of being **loved** can emerge out of the pleasure and intimacy
Of bonding with, trusting, and enjoying the blessings of, another person,
As well as deeply trusting in *Life*.

When we experience the encouraging support of others, or acknowledge our personal success
Which comes from the accomplishments of our own courageous acts of creativity,
A feeling of **empowerment** ensues.

Our experiences of feeling safe, loved, and empowered form a strong foundation within us
In which we feel **connected** with the beauty and goodness within all of life,
With what really matters, and with *the Source of All That Is*.

It is our sustained alignment with *the Source of Life*, moment by moment,
That guides us to the realization of our next higher stage of awareness,
A stage where we feel an absolute <u>safety</u>, a transcendent <u>love</u> of self,
A universal feeling of <u>empowerment</u>, and a <u>connection</u> with everything.

The desire to experience these emotional longings naturally springs forth in the human heart
For they are **the primary emotional needs** that all people strive for.

They form "four pillars of an inner bridge" that lead us to an awareness of who we really are,
A promise of what we can become, and a sacred destiny of living in authentic freedom.

Circle of Primary Emotional Needs

CONNECTION
**THE FEELING OF BEING
CONNECTED COMES FROM
ALIGNING MY AWARENESS
WITH *THE SOURCE OF LIFE*,
KNOWING MY *TRUE NATURE*,
AND CULTIVATING
*SPIRITUAL AWAKENING***

SAFETY
**THE FEELING OF
SAFETY COMES FROM
OVERCOMING ANY
PERCEIVED THREAT
OR CHALLENGE
TO MY *SURVIVAL* BOTH
PHYSICAL & EMOTIONAL**

EMPOWERMENT
**THE FEELING OF BEING
EMPOWERED COMES
FROM THE ENCOURAGING
SUPPORT OF OTHERS
AND FROM THE SUCCESS
OF MY COURGEOUS
ACTS OF *CREATIVITY***

LOVE
**THE FEELING OF BEING
LOVED COMES FROM
THE *PLEASURE*
AND INTIMACY OF BONDING
WITH, AND TRUSTING,
ANOTHER PERSON, AS
WELL AS TRUSTING IN *LIFE***

SPHERES OF CONTRIBUTION

I feel a natural yearning in me constantly inviting me to contribute my creative gifts and talents.

Within the intricate world of Nature, life has evolved a tapestry of interconnected ecosystems
Weaving together diverse living creatures and unique environments
Which are dependent on one another for their individual survival.

Through eons of Nature's evolutionary exploration, life has discovered that in order to prosper,
It's more effective for certain species to work together than to oppose one another.

For example, bees fly from flower to flower performing their daily dance of existence
Receiving nectar from each flower while, at the same time, bees pollinate the flowers.

In a similar manner, birds eat the seeds from many plants and trees,
And then help spread their seeds to "the four corners of the globe".

There is a common phrase we hear occasionally, *"the birds and the bees"*,
That symbolically represents human procreation, and can refer to human love as well.

It also relates to *the Infinite Creativity of Life, the Ocean of Love* that animates all of creation,
Which most animals on our planet are instinctively attuned to.

Yet somewhere along the long evolutionary road of life, humans became disconnected from
And, over time, unconscious of this instinctive attunement with the natural world.

Many great thinkers and philosophers have postulated ideas and theories why this occurred,
But no one seems to know for sure how this severing of the connection happened.

At present, **the impulse to survive** life's daily challenges is still felt by everyone on the planet,
But a majority of people are largely dealing with emotional, rather than physical survival.

Over many millennia, humans have deeply explored the utter extremes of **seeking pleasure**,
Yet much of the civilized world has now attained a healthy balance of this key impulse.

In the last few thousand years, **the impulse to consciously create** has been a natural force
That has urged humans to manifest vast creative innovations to further benefit the world.

Today, humanity is also strongly affected by an innate **impulse to spiritually awaken**,
A natural yearning that invites all people to consciously align with *the Source of Life*.

An alignment with *the Essence of Life* inwardly invites each of us to collectively work together,
To be intimately connected with the Earth's ecosystems, to foster cooperation
By **contributing our creative gifts and talents to the wellbeing of others**.

In order for us to effectively contribute our creative gifts toward manifesting a better **world**,
We can develop greater integrity and cooperation within our **communities**.

In order to help cultivate cooperative communities, we can nourish strong healthy **families**,
Because healthy families are the fundamental units in "the living body of humanity".

Circle of the Spheres of Contribution

CONTRIBUTION TO ONESELF
I CONTRIBUTE TO THE CARE OF MY PERSONAL WELLBEING AND HAPPINESS SO I'M TRULY ABLE TO SERVE OTHERS

CONTRIBUTION TO FAMILY
I CONTRIBUTE TO MY FAMILY AND "LOVED ONES" BY HELPING THEM FEEL SAFE, LOVED, EMPOWERED, AND CONNECTED TO *LIFE*

CONTRIBUTION TO THE WORLD
I CONTRIBUTE MY CREATIVE GIFTS AND TALENTS TO THE WELLBEING OF OTHERS SO I MAY HELP BUILD A BETTER WORLD

CONTRIBUTION TO COMMUNITY
I CONTRIBUTE TO MY LOCAL COMMUNITY BY CULTIVATING INTEGROUS RELATIONSHIPS, EQUAL OPPORTUNITIES, AND COOPERATION

APRIL 19

CONTRIBUTION TO FAMILY

I support my "loved ones" by helping each person feel safe, loved, empowered, and connected.

The human body consists of over thirty trillion cells of various types,
    Which must all function in harmony in order to work as one integrated healthy organism.

These individual cells are what make up the varied organs and biological systems of our body,
    And they must be kept in a healthy state for our body to thrive and maintain balance.

Individual people can be thought of as similar to individual cells within "the body of humanity",
    Whereas families can be likened to the biological systems of "the body of our society",
        And in order for our community or society to function effectively,
            Our fundamental family units must be strong and healthy.

Of course, it's important for children to be raised in families that are nurturing and supportive
    So they can grow up feeling safe, loved, empowered, and connected to what matters.

Family is the core vessel where all members first look to fulfill these *primary emotional needs*
    And where each person yearns to feel the nurturing gifts of *the family nest*.

Each family unit remains strong when **every family member is aware to serve one another**
    With the following four foundational gifts:

1) To do one's best to provide protection for one's "family" (and this extends to all "loved ones")
    By keeping each person **safe**, healthy, and away from harm.

We all want to live in the kind of home
    Where we feel the security of a safe and protected environment.

2) To, frequently and vulnerably, share and express one's **love** and affection
    With the members of one's "family".

It is scientifically proven that we each grow healthier and have stronger immune systems
    When we experience love and emotional nurturance from another,
        And without it, "the flower of our inner being" may begin to wither.

3) To regularly **empower** the members of one's "family" to be the best they can be
    And consciously support them in developing their unique creative potential.

Just like a seed grows stronger when it's given abundant sunshine and proper nutrients,
    People grow stronger when they are empowered and supported,
        And given the encouragement that assists them to creatively blossom.

4) To maintain an intimate **connection** with "family" through ongoing open communication
    And by sharing time and meaningful activities with each person.

Just like healthy cells are the bedrock of a healthy body, when we cultivate healthy "families",
    We develop the important foundations for strong communities,
        Which, in turn, contribute to the building of a harmonious and peaceful world.

Circle of Contribution to Family

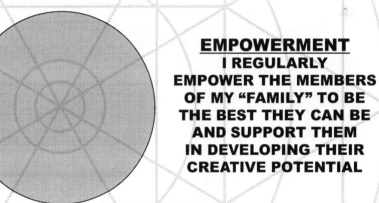

CONNECTION
I MAINTAIN AN INTIMATE
CONNECTION WITH
MY "FAMILY" THROUGH
ONGOING OPEN
COMMUNICATION AND
BY SHARING TIME AND
ACTIVITIES WITH THEM

SAFETY
I CONSCIOUSLY
PROVIDE PROTECTION
FOR MY "FAMILY"
BY DOING WHAT I CAN
TO KEEP EACH PERSON
SAFE, HEALTHY,
AND AWAY FROM HARM

EMPOWERMENT
I REGULARLY
EMPOWER THE MEMBERS
OF MY "FAMILY" TO BE
THE BEST THEY CAN BE
AND SUPPORT THEM
IN DEVELOPING THEIR
CREATIVE POTENTIAL

LOVE
I, FREQUENTLY
AND VULNERABLY,
SHARE AND EXPRESS
MY LOVE
AND AFFECTION
WITH THE MEMBERS
OF MY "FAMILY"

FAMILY ARCHETYPES

Today I use the power of my imagination to envision myself expressing my creative potential.

Archetypes (the way we're using them here) are visionary images or symbolic personas
Which represent beneficial virtues and qualities that we desire to embody in our life,
And can be thought of as "blueprints of possibility", "portraits of our potential".

Since the family unit is a fundamental and important component of our communities
And a vital influential factor in the further development of our societies,
We can use a set of specific symbolic images called **the family archetypes**
To envision in us the essential qualities that support healthy communities,
And, by invoking their qualities, support our own inner development.

The four iconic symbols of **the family archetypes** portrayed here -
The child, the mother, the father, and **the ancestors** -
Represent various aspects of our *journey of discovery*, our journey of self-mastery.

In relation to our emotional body, these four archetypes represent a natural impulse within us
That yearns to fulfill our **primary emotional needs**, (see April 17th)
Our fundamental human longing to feel <u>safe</u> and protected,
To feel <u>loved</u> and nurtured, to feel <u>empowered</u> and supported,
And to feel <u>connected</u> with the goodness and beauty of life.

They also symbolize **the Pillars of Awakening** we instinctively strive for, (see April 8th)
Four essential qualities which can powerfully transform our life
From one of suffering - to a life that embraces peace of mind and joy of heart.

The **Pillars of Awakening** are <u>gratitude</u> for what we're learning from each of our life experiences,
<u>Surrendering</u> everything in our life to *a Greater Power*,
<u>Accepting</u> that our life is unfolding perfectly just as it is,
And living with the expansive awareness that we are <u>one</u> with all of life.

Furthermore, these symbols correspond to **the four foundational transformative practices**,
<u>Meditation</u>, <u>contemplation</u>, <u>appreciation</u>, and <u>prayer</u>, (see April 3rd)
Which if we use them, can help us cultivate an awakened life of inner freedom.

These archetypes also represent **the individual facets of our unfolding journey of life**
That each of us inwardly travels along our spiritual arc of discovery. (see May 27th)

The child symbolizes the <u>transformation</u> of our egoic nature as the Young Awakening Self,
The mother portrays <u>compassion</u> - the Servant of Love, our Compassionate Heart,
And **the father** depicts <u>heart wisdom</u> - *the Source of Life, Infinite Presence.*

The archetype of **the ancestor** represents the transcendent guidance that leads us to <u>mastery</u>
And to the full integration of the various facets of self unfolding within us.

It is our Compassionate Heart - completely merged with *Infinite Presence,*
In other words, it is the Servant of Love - in loving service to *the Limitless Source of Life*
That, when consciously embodied in our life, is realized as a Master of Freedom.

Circle of Family Archetypes
(Symbolic Images Representing Beneficial Qualities to Embody)

ANCESTORS
(DIVINE GUIDANCE)
1) CONNECTION
2) ONENESS
3) MEDITATION
4) MASTERY

CHILD
(DIVINE INNOCENCE)
1) SAFETY
2) GRATITUDE
3) PRAYER
4) TRANSFORMATION

FATHER
(DIVINE MASCULINE)
1) EMPOWERMENT
2) ACCEPTANCE
3) CONTEMPLATION
4) HEART WISDOM

MOTHER
(DIVINE FEMININE)
1) LOVE
2) SURRENDER
3) APPRECIATION
4) COMPASSION

THE GREAT CIRCLE OF THE ARCHETYPES

I consciously use my creative imagination as a tool to help me envision all that I desire to be.

The symbolic image of **The Great Circle** is "a spiritual map of an awakening life"
And displays the universal dynamics at play within the world and within our life.

This circle represents the perpetual evolutionary nature of life
Which has been unfolding throughout the Cosmos for the last 13.8 billion years.

In a similar fashion, **The Great Circle** of the Archetypes (on the following page)
Is a visual representation that displays "the story of ever-unfolding development"
That each of us is experiencing at this present time as part of human evolution.

This constantly evolving story has also been referred to as our *journey of awakening*
And can be portrayed within this circle as four distinct sets of visionary archetypes.

The four quadrants of **The Great Circle** that portray the evolutionary nature of existence are:
1) **Limitless Love**, 2) **awakened life** - depicted as "the cultivation of inner freedom",
3) **evolving consciousness**, and 4) **evolving creativity**. (see March 28th)

Each of these primary dynamics listed above is represented by one of four archetypal groups,
And each set of images is symbolically aligned with one quadrant of the seasonal cycle.

Aligned with **summer** in the bottom quadrant, **the Archetypes of Life Mastery** (see May 1st)
Are mythological personas representing the key virtues, values, and qualities
Which help us cultivate a life of inner freedom
And embody our destiny of living an **awakened life**.

The Archetypes of Higher Knowledge, in the left quadrant of **autumn**, (see May 19th)
Represent a natural longing to develop our talents and expand our awareness
So we may experience greater expressions of our unlimited potential,
And thus are associated with **the evolution of consciousness**.

In the upper quadrant of **winter, the Archetypes of Spiritual Awakening** (see May 27th)
Represent our *spiritual journey* leading to the archetype of the Master of Freedom,
Which is the embodiment of loving all of life unconditionally
And living a life in service to others that's guided by **Limitless Love**.

The Archetypes of Conscious Contribution, in the right quadrant of **spring**, (see April 22nd)
Represent a longing to contribute our gifts - and express our ever **evolving creativity**.

The inherent rotational movement of this circle (like the constant turning of the seasonal cycle)
Symbolically portrays *the journey of awakening* that each of us is embarked on
As an integral part of the natural *awakening* taking place within all people.

We can use the symbolic personas of these visionary archetypes in our daily practice
As ways to consciously imagine ourselves becoming all that we can be,
To embody their expansive qualities,
And to further cultivate the pathways of our *journey of self-mastery*.

The Great Circle of the Archetypes

WINTER

ARCHETYPES OF SPIRITUAL AWAKENING
ALL FOUR REPRESENT MY *JOURNEY OF AWAKENING* LEADING TO MY DESTINY AS A "MASTER OF FREEDOM", A LIFE IN SERVICE GUIDED BY

LIMITLESS LOVE

AUTUMN

ARCHETYPES OF HIGHER KNOWLEDGE
EACH ONE REPRESENTS A NATURAL LONGING TO DEVELOP MY POTENTIAL AND HIGHER STAGES OF

EVOLVING CONSCIOUSNESS

SPRING

ARCHETYPES OF CONSCIOUS CONTRIBUTION
EACH ONE REPRESENTS A NATURAL LONGING TO CONTRIBUTE MY GIFTS AND EXPRESS MY EVER

EVOLVING CREATIVITY

SUMMER

ARCHETYPES OF LIFE MASTERY
EACH ONE REPRESENTS THE KEY VIRTUES, VALUES, AND QUALITIES THAT HELP ME CULTIVATE INNER FREEDOM AND EMBODY MY DESTINY OF LIVING AN

AWAKENED LIFE

ARCHETYPES OF CONSCIOUS CONTRIBUTION

Today I offer my unique gifts and talents in ways that help create a better world.

The word *"contribution"* is typically considered a human action, but from "the Bigger Picture"
We can see that the intrinsic process of *contribution* has always been a primary factor
For every individual facet of creation since the beginning of the known Universe.

Another way of thinking about *contribution* is to view it as a part of the biological cycle of life,
Since every life form is always contributing back to life based on its development.

Each form of life *contributes* or *provides* its unique gifts to the perpetual unfolding of evolution
Through a natural process of expanding consciousness - which then creatively manifests.

Even every galaxy, solar system, star, and planet *contributes*, in its own way, to existence
As an outward manifestation within the Universe of an inward evolving consciousness.

Over time, as evolving life developed the complex cognitive capacities of the human brain,
Individual humans, for the first time in evolutionary history (as far we currently know),
Became self-aware of the creative gift of choosing to *consciously contribute* to others.

In every moment, *Life* is inviting each of us to increase our awareness of "this creative gift",
The gift of *consciously contributing* to the beneficent progression of evolution on Earth.

The Archetypes of Conscious Contribution consist of four symbolic images or templates
That we can use to envision how to effectively fulfill the purpose and mission of our life,
And are shown on the next page as the Visionary Healer, Visionary Storyteller,
Visionary Teacher, and Visionary Leader.

A Visionary Healer can be thought of as one who contributes to the wellbeing of another
By helping them reconnect with the unlimited source of all healing power
And by helping attune their mind, heart, and body with their *Eternal Nature*.

The contribution of **a Visionary Storyteller** is to uplift others with empowering stories
That help them expand their awareness of what really matters.

Visionary Teachers and **Visionary Leaders** assist people to imagine their unlimited potential,
And inspire them to achieve ever-greater possibilities not yet attained.

Visionaries possess a level of development that enables them to view "the Bigger Picture",
And this development allows one to see and integrate all areas of previous knowledge
In order to benefit the evolutionary unfoldment for every facet of life.

At times during humanity's past, it was as if humans were looking at a vivid rainbow in the sky
Yet were only capable of observing a tiny portion of the many colors of its full spectrum
Based on their current, yet limited, level of developmental awareness.

But now as humanity has evolved farther along the never-ending arc of human development,
One who can "look at the rainbow of possibility" from a more inclusive perspective of life
Will be able to see so much more of "the full spectrum of their vast creative potential".

Circle of Archetypes of Conscious Contribution

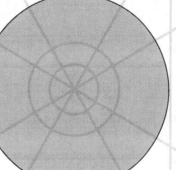

VISIONARY LEADER
IT IS THE PART OF ME THAT HELPS OTHERS EXPAND THEIR AWARENESS OF HOW TO BE A TRUE LEADER - AND TO EMBRACE LIFE AND ITS CHALLENGES FROM A MORE INCLUSIVE PERSPECTIVE AND VISION

VISIONARY HEALER
IT IS THE PART OF ME THAT HELPS OTHERS ATTUNE THEIR MIND, HEART, AND BODY WITH THEIR *ETERNAL NATURE* AND ALIGN WITH THE UNLIMITED SOURCE OF ALL HEALING POWER

VISIONARY TEACHER
IT IS THE PART OF ME THAT TEACHES OTHERS THROUGH EXAMPLE TO ALIGN WITH *THE SOURCE OF LIFE,* LEARN WHAT LIFE IS TRULY ABOUT, FOSTER BEAUTY, AND SERVE OTHERS

VISIONARY STORYTELLER
IT IS THE PART OF ME THAT SHARES WITH OTHERS EMPOWERING STORIES WHICH ARE INSPIRED FROM "A BIG PICTURE PERSPECTIVE" SO AS TO EXPAND AWARENESS OF WHAT REALLY MATTERS

VISIONARY TEACHER

I support the authentic goodness, inner beauty, and true creative potential within all people.

There always seems to be a few adventurous children that delight in the quest and challenge
    Of climbing the tall trees in their neighborhood.

A tall tree has many branches, some low, and some very high,
    And, of course, the vista of the surrounding area expands as one climbs up the tree
        For one can enjoy a more spacious panorama from the higher branches.

A Visionary Teacher is one who understands the world from "the higher branches of life",
    And imparts **knowledge to others from "a Big Picture view" of what life is truly about**,
        Being mindful to embrace and incorporate all the various levels of awareness.

It's a person who has experienced "the branches below" (i.e. the various levels of awareness)
    And can share with others a set of life skills and a maturity of judgment
        From his or her knowledge of those diverse levels of perspective.

We can envision **the Visionary Teacher** as someone with the quality of **supporting others**
    To express their own authentic goodness, inner beauty, and true creative potential.

When we empower, or give support to, another person by inspiring or encouraging them,
    We support the entire world at the same time - since we're all connected as one global family.

One of the best ways we can empower another person
    Is through **the everyday example of our own life**,
        Inspiring compassion, excellence, and integrity by our daily actions and choices.

Small children tend to emulate our actions and deeds
    Much more than they obey our words and requests.

In order to be truly effective at this,
    A Visionary Teacher first aligns his or her awareness with *the Source of Life*
        So as to take action, and share with others, from this *sacred connection*.

Each of us is constantly being invited by *Life* to contribute to the ever-unfolding progress of humanity
    And (in our own little or significant way) to be a catalyst for positive change.

We're also being invited to respond to the yearning within us to support the people we know
    By **empowering them to be all they can be**.

At the very core of our being, there is a teacher inside each of us known as *the wise advocate*
    Continuously directing us to discover ways to share our creative gifts and talents
        With a world that's eager and ready to receive them.

The archetype of **the Visionary Teacher** is a blueprint of possibility we can use in our daily practice
    To envision our life skillfully climbing "the Inner Tree of Consciousness",
        So we may courageously stand on "the higher branches"
            As we bestow our unique gifts and blessings to one another.

Circle of the Visionary Teacher
(An Archetype of Conscious Contribution)

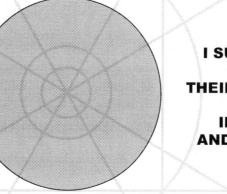

EMPOWERMENT
I DO WHAT I CAN
TO MOTIVATE OTHERS
SO THEY MAY ALIGN
THEIR AWARENESS WITH
THE SOURCE OF LIFE
- AND TO EMPOWER THEM
TO BE ALL THEY CAN BE

EXAMPLE
I, THROUGH
THE EVERYDAY EXAMPLE
OF MY OWN LIFE,
DO MY BEST TO
INSPIRE COMPASSION,
EXCELLENCE, AND
INTEGRITY IN OTHERS

SUPPORT
I SUPPORT OTHERS
TO EXPRESS
THEIR OWN AUTHENTIC
GOODNESS,
INNER BEAUTY,
AND TRUE CREATIVE
POTENTIAL

HIGHER KNOWLEDGE
I SHARE WITH OTHERS
THE EXPANSIVE
KNOWLEDGE
THAT EMERGES
FROM "A BIG PICTURE
PERSPECTIVE" OF WHAT
LIFE IS TRULY ABOUT

ALIGNMENT

Today I consciously align my awareness with the Source of Life, the Infinite Presence of Love.

When a professional opera singer loudly belts out a melody from a classical aria
    While standing next to an open unplayed grand piano,
        Many of the strings within the piano
            Will suddenly become alive with energy and begin to pulsate with sound.

This occurs because there are individual strings within a piano
    That interact to specific frequencies of the opera singer's voice,
        And as they respond to those frequencies, the strings will vibrate in resonance.

In other words, a piano string that vibrates to a particular frequency
    Will directly respond and vibrate to a singer's note of the same frequency.

In this example, there is an *alignment* of the piano strings with the voice of the opera singer
    Establishing a vibratory **entrainment** - or auditory **resonance**.

In our lives, we can use this image as a metaphor for our **alignment with *the Source of Life***
    In which the opera singer represents *the Voice of the Infinite*
        That is always singing "the Universal Music of Life",
        And the piano strings represent you and I.

In order for each of us "to play our true song" and contribute to the authentic mission of our life,
    "The strings of our heart" must be directly attuned to *the Music of the Eternal*,
        To *the Infinite Presence of Love*.

Alignment can be thought of as the process of **attuning** our personal consciousness
    With *Universal Consciousness (Infinite Intelligence)*.

It is establishing and maintaining a deep **communion** of our individual inner being
    That's integrated with *the Ocean of Being (the Source of Life)*.

This *alignment* is initiated through our conscious attention,
    And we can use certain transformative practices to help us sustain our alignment.

Through the joys and discipline of daily spiritual practice,
    Such as meditation, contemplation, appreciation, and prayer,
        We can discover how to maintain an ongoing attunement with *Life*.

Through our mindfulness of maintaining this *alignment*,
    We can also learn to be mindful of anything within our heart and mind
        That blocks us from experiencing the natural flow of *Love* in our daily life
            So everything that no longer serves us may be intentionally released.

As we renew our *alignment* moment to moment
    And, each day, stay attuned to *the Voice of the Infinite*,
        We eventually come to the simple realization
            That we are "the Singer" and, at the same time, we are *"the Song"*.

Circle of Alignment

ATTUNEMENT
ALIGNMENT –
THE EXPERIENCE OF
ATTUNING MY PERSONAL
CONSCIOUSNESS
WITH *UNIVERSAL
CONSCIOUSNESS*
(INFINITE INTELLIGENCE)

COMMUNION
ALIGNMENT –
ESTABLISHING
A DEEP COMMUNION
OF MY INDIVIDUAL
INNER BEING WITH
THE OCEAN OF BEING
(THE SOURCE OF LIFE)

RESONANCE
ALIGNMENT –
EXPERIENCING
A FULL RESONANCE
OF MY PERSONAL
VIBRATORY FIELD WITH
THE UNIFIED FIELD
(THE FIELD OF LOVE)

ENTRAINMENT
ALIGNMENT –
BRINGING MY OWN
AWARENESS INTO
SYNCHRONIZATION
WITH *INFINITE EVER-
PRESENT AWARENESS*
(INFINITE PRESENCE)

SUPPORT

Today I support the people in my life by honoring their intrinsic holiness and magnificence.

Take a moment to imagine what it would feel like if every leader from all countries of the world
Consciously supported their neighboring nations, and even their so-called enemies,
In ways that helped these countries manifest their highest potential.

Now also imagine that these world leaders were not focused on their own selfish agendas
But governed from a spiritual awareness that served the collective needs of the planet,
Seeing their nation as an integral part of creating a more harmonious world.

This all sounds very idealistic - and of course it is, yet just play along for another few moments
And let yourself enjoy the amazing power of your creative imagination.

Now imagine your favorite celebrities and film stars
Participating in movies, concerts, recordings, theatre, and even performing comedy,
Which all point their audiences to the profound discovery of their *True Nature*.

Conjure up a mental image of creative artists by the millions from every corner of the globe
Crafting sacred inspired art that arises from a deep spiritually awakened perspective.

At this point in our visualization, begin to envision that the people you work with every day
See you, and others around them, as *spiritual beings* consciously co-creating together.

And then imagine that everyone you meet during the day - the supermarket clerk, the waitress,
People at the post office and the gas station -
Are all individuals dedicated to demonstrating *conscious awakened living*.

Obviously, with everyone exhibiting this higher awareness, **support**, and empowerment,
Our world would be a very different place - it would be a much more awakened world.

If we want to support and build such a world, we cannot demand that everyone else change,
But we can certainly change how *we respond to reality* based on the choices we make.

For example, we can choose to support others through our own **example** of conscious living,
In other words - by living each day with greater conscious awareness in all that we do.

For when we live our life guided by *the Essence of Love*, we create an example for others
That has the potential to **empower** them to be the best they can be.

We can also decide to support another person by seeing him or her as their **True Eternal Self**
Honoring, in this moment, their intrinsic holiness and magnificence.

Furthermore, we can choose to take responsibility to live our life in a way that inspires others,
Supporting them to embody, and express, their **greater potential**.

As we cultivate an ongoing alignment with *the Source of Life (the Infinite Presence of Love),*
We will be guided each day how to manifest more of these aspects within our own life
And, thereby, discover how to be *a true leader within the world*.

<u>Circle of Support</u>
(From a Spiritual Perspective)

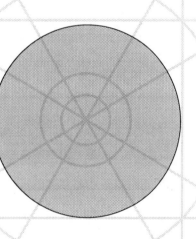

EMPOWERMENT
SUPPORT –
THE QUALITY
OF EMPOWERING
OTHERS TO BE
THE BEST THEY CAN BE
AND AWAKEN
TO WHO THEY REALLY ARE

PERSONAL EXAMPLE
SUPPORT –
THE QUALITY
OF BEING A PERSONAL
EXAMPLE OF,
AND DEMONSTRATING
IN MY LIFE, CONSCIOUS
AWAKENED LIVING

GREATER POTENTIAL
SUPPORT –
THE QUALITY
OF INSPIRING OTHERS
TO EMBODY,
AND EXPRESS, THEIR
GREATER POTENTIAL

TRUE ETERNAL SELF
SUPPORT –
THE QUALITY OF SEEING
OTHERS AS THEIR *TRUE
ETERNAL SELF* HONORING
THE HOLINESS
AND MAGNIFICENCE
OF WHO THEY REALLY ARE

EXEMPLAR

I choose to live the greatest life I can possibly live - and be the best person I can possibly be.

A professional dancer does not usually learn the choreography of a specific dance routine
    By reading about the movements in a book, or being told how to move with words alone.

Most dancers in a dance company learn a movement routine by watching the choreographer
    Give a visual example of the actual choreographed steps with his or her body,
        In other words - a live demonstration of the movements and design of the dance.

Similarly, teaching through the daily example of our own life
    Is one of the most powerful ways to inspire and influence the life of another person.

Most parents discover they cannot successfully teach their children
    By asking them to do one thing with their words
        While they then do the very opposite with their actions.

Parents must be consistent in their words and actions
    Because children imitate how their parents actually live their lives.

When you and I grew up and finally left the nest of our families
    To further our education through our unique life experiences,
        We continued to learn the lessons of life from the living example of many other people.

Yet just as other people are teachers for us by their living example,
    We also become teachers to those around us by *how we choose to live our life*.

We are constantly learning from the inspiring or destructive actions of others,
    And other people are also learning from the inspiring or destructive actions
        That *we teach them* through our own life example.

Most of us are naturally **motivated** and **empowered**
    By certain individuals around us who **demonstrate** how to live life more caringly
        Through the everyday example of their kindness and compassion.

We are powerfully supported in this way by those we will call **the Exemplars**,
    The spiritually developed people who are living near "the higher rungs of the ladder",
        And, metaphorically speaking, who abide near "the peaks of the mountains".

These are the ones who **inspire** us to express our greater possibilities and higher potential,
    Simply by being themselves, living authentic lives, and being truly aligned with *Life*.

We're all an integral part of a global human family
    That's constantly learning and growing in "the universal school of life".

Each of us is a perpetual student expanding and developing within this "school"
        And, at the same time, each of us is also a teacher
            Naturally sharing with one another what we've learned and what we know
                Through our everyday example of "the dance of life we choose to dance".

Circle of the Exemplar

EMPOWERMENT
AN EXEMPLAR –
ONE WHO EMPOWERS
OTHERS THROUGH
THE EVERYDAY
EXAMPLE OF THE WAY
THEY CONSCIOUSLY
LIVE THEIR LIFE

DEMONSTRATION
AN EXEMPLAR –
ONE WHO DEMONSTRATES
HOW TO LIVE MORE
AUTHENTICALLY
AND NATURALLY
THROUGH THE EXAMPLE
OF THEIR LIFE

INSPIRATION
AN EXEMPLAR –
ONE WHO INSPIRES
OTHERS TO DEVELOP
THEIR POTENTIAL,
JUST BY THE WAY
THEY CHOOSE
TO LIVE THEIR LIFE

MOTIVATION
AN EXEMPLAR –
ONE WHO MOTIVATES
OTHERS TO EXPAND
BEYOND THEIR
SELF-IMPOSED LIMITS,
SIMPLY BY BEING
WHO THEY ARE

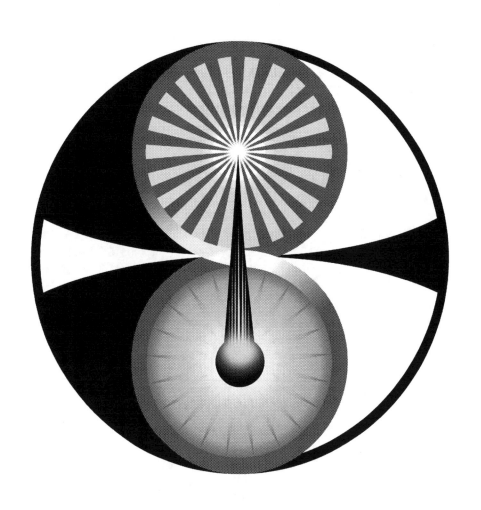

VII

MIND
AWARENESS
PRACTICES

WELLBEING OF THE MIND

Today I question what I believe is true - so I can be mindful to transform any loveless beliefs.

Even though biologists have been able to study and analyze in minute detail
    The numerous biological and genetic components of our physical bodies,
        And neuroscientists have mapped the various areas of the human brain,
            Still no one has been able to find the actual place that our minds occupy.

The tangible material whereabouts, or location in space, of the human mind
    Is a mysterious enigma - for the mind is so much vaster than the physical brain.

Some progressive-thinking scientists have postulated that our individual mind
    Is a part of, and connected to, *The Big Mind of the Universe* that exists everywhere,
        And, in some inexplicable way, we each individually experience
            Our own personal facet of the *One Universal Mind.*

Wherever our mind is, what we do know is our ability to choose and the quality of our choices
    Is what determines whether our mind stagnates and withers, or expands and develops.

So when we are speaking about **the wellbeing of our mind**,
    What we're exploring is our personal power of conscious choice
        To develop our mental capabilities - and transform any loveless beliefs.

For example, when we choose to **expand our awareness of what really matters**
    And learn more about the essential nature of reality,
        It helps us to embrace more inclusive perspectives of what our life is truly about
            Than we were previously aware of, or currently utilize,
                Which we may use to transform our beliefs and adjust our thinking.

The practice of **contemplating "the big existential questions of life"**
    Is another effective way to deepen our understanding of what we believe is true
        So we may widen our viewpoints - and realize our connectedness with all of life.

The mind without a clear sense of purpose
    Is like a small row boat without oars on a large ocean
        Being blown haphazardly in all directions by the ever-changing winds.

Whereas, the mind with **clarity of purpose and meaning**
    Is like a majestic ship with a strong rudder and tall sails,
        Which are central for navigating in the direction of one's choosing.

Our **imagination** is also a powerful means of focusing our mind toward realizing our potential
    Using it as a tool to envision expanded possibilities of what we can become
        So we may take appropriate action in co-creatively building a more peaceful world.

In our ongoing quest for wellbeing of our body, heart, and mind,
    Could it be that when our daily choices are consciously aligned with *the Source of Life,*
        We realize our "ship's course corrections" come directly from *"The Inner Captain"*
            Who always steers our vessel toward new shores of spiritual freedom?

Circle of Wellbeing of the Mind
(Transformative Practices)

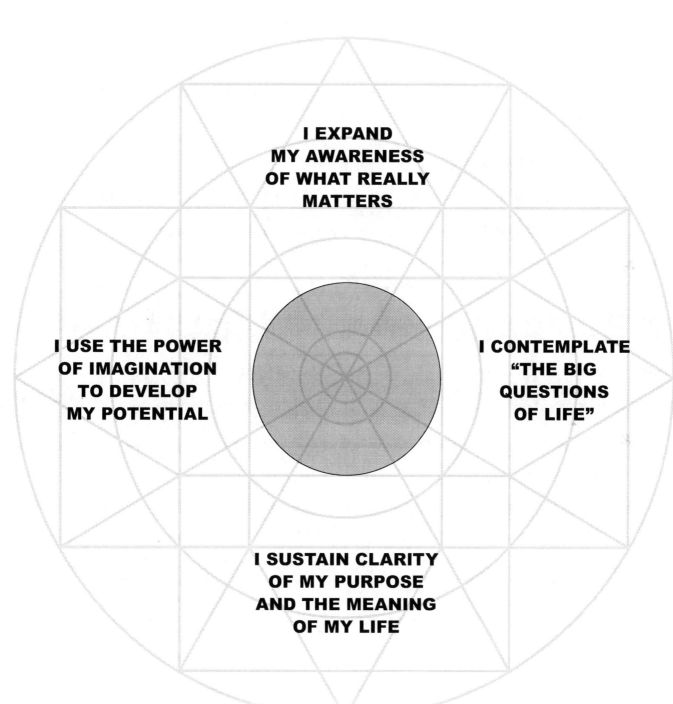

I EXPAND
MY AWARENESS
OF WHAT REALLY
MATTERS

I USE THE POWER
OF IMAGINATION
TO DEVELOP
MY POTENTIAL

I CONTEMPLATE
"THE BIG
QUESTIONS
OF LIFE"

I SUSTAIN CLARITY
OF MY PURPOSE
AND THE MEANING
OF MY LIFE

CULTIVATING THE GIFTS OF AN AWAKENED LIFE

Daily transformative practices help me cultivate peace of mind and a life of inner freedom.

Each time you turn on the external power button of a sound system to hear your favorite music,
    You activate an internal electronic device known as an amplifier
        Which magnifies the sound of the music, so you can adequately enjoy it.

An amplifier is a mechanism that takes a small signal and, through an electronic process,
    Expands or strengthens the intensity of that signal.

Without the signal amplifier to increase the sound coming out of the system's speakers,
    You would not be able to hear the music effectively.

The transformative practices we use each day can be thought of as our "personal amplifiers"
    Which help develop and amplify many beneficial gifts related to our life,
        Such as greater **health**, **happiness**, **heart wisdom**, and **inner freedom**.

Through the disciplined use of certain foundational practices,
    We can mindfully strengthen the embodiment of these awakened aspects within our life.

Almost everything we do in our life is made so much easier, and more enjoyable,
    When we live day-to-day within a physical body that radiates vibrant health.

We can actively choose to cultivate greater **health and wellbeing**
    By engaging in certain transformative practices
        That support our natural *Life Force*, or *Chi*, to flow through our body unimpeded.

A higher level of *Life Force energy* pulsing through us
    (Which can be facilitated by practices like Yoga, Tai Chi, Qigong, and breathwork)
        Also assists the beneficial development of our physical and emotional bodies.

Next we can expand our **happiness** every time we fully feel each emotion we encounter,
    Simply by completely experiencing it, whether it is anger, sadness, joy, confusion, etc.

If we should experience any repressed feelings, the practice of releasing bottled-up emotions
    Is a way of keeping our *Life Force* unblocked and flowing throughout our inner being.

The blossoming of our **heart wisdom** may be enhanced by practicing deep contemplation,
    Spiritual studies, as well as learning from my life experiences.

Of course every transformative practice is, in the end, about increasing our level of freedom
    By becoming present and awake, so we may learn to love all of life unconditionally.

Inner freedom can also be fostered through the practice of meditation,
    Or by some other means of attaining an internal stillness,
        And by aligning our awareness with *the Source of Life*.

If we truly desire to hear *the sublime Song of Life,* we can "access our personal amplifiers" each day
    To help us enjoy "dancing - ever more freely - to *the Music of Eternity*".

Circle of Cultivating the Gifts of an Awakened Life
(Transformative Practices)

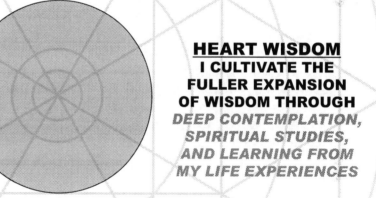

INNER FREEDOM
I CULTIVATE
INNER FREEDOM BY
EXPERIENCING
PERIODS OF SILENCE
AND ALIGNING
MY AWARENESS WITH
THE SOURCE OF LIFE

HEALTH
I CULTIVATE VIBRANT
HEALTH BY ENGAGING IN
PRACTICES LIKE YOGA,
TAI CHI & BREATHWORK
THAT SUPPORT *LIFE*
FORCE ENERGY **TO FLOW**
THROUGH MY BODY

HEART WISDOM
I CULTIVATE THE
FULLER EXPANSION
OF WISDOM THROUGH
DEEP CONTEMPLATION,
SPIRITUAL STUDIES,
AND LEARNING FROM
MY LIFE EXPERIENCES

HAPPINESS
I CULTIVATE GREATER
HAPPINESS BY
FULLY EXPERIENCING
MY EMOTIONS
IN EACH MOMENT,
AND RELEASING
MY REPRESSED FEELINGS

MIND AWARENESS

Today I consciously keep my awareness aligned with the Infinite Presence of Love.

Mind awareness is a transformative practice for heightening conscious awareness
 Which helps a person determine if their thoughts are centered in "the Light of Truth"
  Or whether they are habitually focused on "the illusions of the mind".

"The Light of Truth" is when our thoughts are aligned with *the Infinite Presence of Love*,
 And "illusion" is when we believe we're separate from *Life's Unbounded Ocean of Love*.

For every experience we have, our thoughts and emotions are linked together and integrated,
 So our thinking process is always intimately connected with our basic emotional needs,
  The primary needs we hold for **safety**, **love**, **empowerment**, and **connection**.

Each of us has a natural desire to feel safe and protected, so as a transformative practice,
 Occasionally take time to stop for a moment to be aware **if you feel safe**,
  Or whether your thoughts may be unconsciously focused on some aspect of fear.

The feeling of safety is always present and anchored within our heart and mind
 When we're genuinely aligned with *the Infinite Presence of Love*.

As you take time during the day to observe the constant flow of your thoughts,
 Practice being mindful **if you feel loved** (by other people, by *Life*, by God),
  Or whether you are habitually focused on a feeling of judgment.

The feeling of profoundly experiencing the *Limitless Love* of the Universe
 Comes from a realization of being part of *Perfect Wholeness (the Unity within everything)*.

Then throughout the day, practice being aware of what thoughts are flowing through your mind
 And notice **if you feel empowered** (by others, by *Life*, by God)
  Or whether you have a thought that is unknowingly focused on a feeling of lack.

When we truly feel one with *the Ocean of Being*, there is a dynamic sense of empowerment
 That naturally streams into our world based on a conscious alignment with *Life*.

Also before going to sleep, practice being mindful of the significant activities of your day,
 And **if, during the day, you felt connected to *the Infinite Source of Life*,**
  Or whether you felt a sense of separation from others - or from *Life*.

If we desire to change the focus of our thinking from a dysfunctional to a constructive mode,
 We don't need to force or coerce our mind into thinking in any particular manner.

Yet what we can do is *gently and consciously bring awareness to our mind*
 And notice the kind of choices we're making by the quality of the thoughts we choose,
  And then through this simple act of mindfulness
   Our thinking will be adjusted naturally in a more life-affirming way.

Could it simply be a matter of being present to the natural flow of *Love* coursing through us
 That allows *the Source of Life* to be the gentle sculptor of our ever-blossoming mind?

Circle of Mind Awareness
(A Transformative Practice)

CONNECTION
TAKE A MOMENT TO
BE AWARE IF YOU FEEL
CONNECTED TO
THE SOURCE OF LIFE,
OR WHETHER YOU FEEL
A SENSE OF SEPARATION
FROM OTHERS

SAFETY
TAKE A MOMENT
TO BE AWARE
IF YOU FEEL SAFE,
OR WHETHER YOU HAVE
A THOUGHT THAT IS
UNCONSCIOUSLY
FOCUSED ON FEAR

EMPOWERMENT
TAKE A MOMENT
TO BE AWARE IF
YOU FEEL EMPOWERED,
OR WHETHER YOU HAVE
A THOUGHT THAT IS
UNKNOWINGLY FOCUSED
ON A FEELING OF LACK

LOVE
TAKE A MOMENT
TO BE AWARE
IF YOU FEEL LOVED,
OR WHETHER YOU HAVE
A THOUGHT THAT IS
HABITUALLY FOCUSED
ON JUDGMENT

VIII

ARCHETYPES
OF LIFE
MASTERY

EVOLUTION OF *THE SPIRITUAL JOURNEY*

I am awakening to my destiny of loving all people and all expressions of life unconditionally.

In our evolutionary past when humans began to form small villages for agricultural purposes,
  A primary need arose to establish a greater sense of civil order
    Which required more progressive kinds of social agreements.

In order to create more order, village elders asked the question of how to improve their society,
  And devise better, more productive ways to live together harmoniously.

Because of their social improvements, some groups began to have additional time
  To explore their own individual creative yearnings, and fulfilled those longings
    With the development of their unique personal creativity and artistic expressions.

Over eons of time, the egoic drive that was based on personal self-oriented needs intensified
  And started to focus on fulfilling individual urges, rather than the needs of the collective.

Today for many, there is a natural inward yearning to balance these two primary impulses,
  Learning to weigh the essential needs of the individual with the needs of the collective.

Eventually, as we gain more inclusive perspectives of life and learn to live with greater compassion,
  We can, more responsibly, make conscious choices that balance these vital impulses.

In relation to our personal *journey of awakening* that we as spiritual seekers ultimately travel,
  The evolution of our *spiritual journey* directly parallels **the development of culture**.

Similar to the first small agricultural villages needing to discover ways to improve their society,
  For many of us *the spiritual journey* begins when we attempt to rid ourselves of suffering
    By seeking **self-improvement** - and by asking "the deeper existential questions".

Next, as certain levels of balance are achieved, we are driven to seek **a self-fulfilling desire**
  That attempts to attain for ourselves, what we personally believe spiritual freedom is
    Based on our limited concept of what we think it means to be spiritually liberated.

As we consciously evolve and expand our awareness using transformative practice,
  We learn to balance our personal needs with a desire to be **in service to others**.

Then from intentionally aligning our awareness with *the Natural Intelligence of Life* each day
  Joined with the daily transformative practices that help cultivate "our inner garden",
    We learn to relinquish all identification with our egoic persona
      And begin to authentically **awaken** to our *True Nature*.

Sometimes in a profound moment of epiphany, we suddenly let go of all thoughts of separation
  And experience a glimpse of our Oneness with *Life* - and of living a life of inner freedom.

Could it be that *the natural unfoldment of human culture* for the last many thousands of years
  And *the heroic journey of our spiritual awakening* are truly the same
    And are intimately intertwined as one evolutionary journey
      That's actually about learning to love all of life unconditionally?

Circle of the Evolution of *the Spiritual Journey*

AWAKENING
THROUGH ALIGNMENT
AND DAILY PRACTICE,
WE RELINQUISH OUR
IDENTIFICATION WITH
AN EGOIC PERSONA,
REALIZE OUR ONENESS
WITH *LIFE*, AND LIVE A
LIFE OF INNER FREEDOM

SELF-IMPROVEMENT
FOR MANY OF US,
THE SPIRITUAL JOURNEY
BEGINS WHEN WE ATTEMPT
TO RID OURSELVES OF
SUFFERING OR IMBALANCE
BY SEEKING SELF-
IMPROVEMENT AND ASKING
"THE BIG QUESTIONS"

SERVICE
AS WE CONSCIOUSLY
EVOLVE AND EXPAND
OUR AWARENESS,
WE BALANCE OUR
DESIRE TO FULFILL
OUR PERSONAL NEEDS
WITH A DESIRE TO BE
IN SERVICE TO OTHERS

SELF-FULFILLMENT
AS LEVELS OF INTERNAL
BALANCE ARE ACHIEVED,
WE NEXT SEEK AFTER A
SELF-FULFILLING DESIRE
TO ATTAIN OUR IDEA
OF SPIRITUAL FREEDOM
BASED ON OUR LIMITED
CONCEPT OF LIBERATION

ARCHETYPES OF LIFE MASTERY

Today I use the power of my unlimited imagination to help manifest the life I desire to create.

In order to learn expertise in a particular profession, such as becoming a master carpenter,
One must take the necessary time to develop the skills required,
Undergo the special training needed to hone the craft,
And be dedicated to diligently practice one's trade.

When someone desires to be a master musician,
He or she must be internally motivated and disciplined
So as to focus the appropriate time and energy
On developing the abilities to play an instrument proficiently.

The same is true for a master chess player, or for any other skill or occupation,
Because in order to master them, much disciplined practice is essential.

Likewise if we should hold an intention "to master our life", it also requires a similar commitment
Since training, discipline, and practice are central
To embody the needed qualities for developing greater conscious awareness.

Should we desire a specific quality or area of our life to develop, expand, or manifest,
We can then place our focused attention on it.

For example, if we were to watch a master carpenter build a piece of furniture
And directly observe the skills that he or she could demonstrate before us,
Then by witnessing, it would be much easier to build the same furniture.

When we listen to, and observe, a master musician play an instrument with expertise
And personally experience the exquisite melodies the musician is able to perform,
We can, more easily, imagine playing the same instrument ourselves
Because we have directly witnessed its beauty and sensed its possibilities.

In a similar way, we can also use certain archetypal templates within a transformative practice
To visualize *the expansive attributes of life mastery* we desire to embody in our life.

Utilizing these forms of visionary archetypes can help us imagine ourselves
Developing the skills of higher awareness and cultivating a compassionate heart
By envisioning those qualities we wish to master.

The energy and power of our unlimited imagination that's focused in this benevolent manner
Empowered by elevated emotions, such as joy or love for life,
Can be experienced as a meaningful daily practice
To help manifest the kind of life we desire to create.

Particular archetypes, such as **the Archetypes of Life Mastery**, are blueprints of possibilities
Which offer us the gift of accelerating our journey toward our yet unexpressed potential.

They are like strong and steady tailwinds, which are always available to fill our sails
And assist in navigating "the vessel of our heart" along the path of our *journey of self-mastery.*

Circle of Archetypes of Life Mastery

ENLIGHTENED KING OR QUEEN
IT IS THE PART OF ME THAT CULTIVATES GENEROSITY AND HEART WISDOM, LIVES MY LIFE IN SERVICE TO OTHERS, EMPOWERS ALL PEOPLE, AND TAKES ACTION WHICH IS GUIDED BY *LOVE*

PEACEFUL WARRIOR
IT IS THE PART OF ME THAT DEVELOPS EACH DAY THROUGH THE PRACTICES OF MINDFULNESS, CONSCIOUS RESPONSIBILITY, AND BY BEING OPEN TO UNLIMITED POSSIBILITY

SPIRITUAL MAGICIAN
IT IS THE PART OF ME THAT ALIGNS WITH *THE SOURCE OF LIFE*, *THE INFINITE CREATIVITY* OF THE UNIVERSE, SO AS TO MANIFEST WHAT *LIFE* INWARDLY DIRECTS ME TO ACHIEVE

MYSTICAL LOVER
IT IS THE PART OF ME THAT LIVES AUTHENTICALLY WITH A PASSION FOR LIFE, IS FLEXIBLE TO CHANGE, QUESTIONS EVERYTHING, AND CARES FOR THE WELLBEING OF OTHERS

105

SPIRITUAL MAGICIAN

Today I consciously co-create what Life has guided me to achieve that benefits the good of all.

For some people, the word "magic" conjures up exotic images
　　Of a flamboyant person making things mysteriously appear out of thin air
　　　　Or performing seemingly impossible feats with confident ease.

It may bring up mental pictures of a regally costumed magician
　　Pulling rabbits out of a hat - or causing a person to float high above the floor.

Every person on the planet (whether it's apparent to them or not) is "a magician-in-training"
　　Participating throughout his or her life with the *universal laws of creation,*
　　　　But, typically, many are not consciously aware of their inborn co-creative abilities
　　　　　　Due to their current, yet not fully developed, level of spiritual maturity.

From one way of viewing this, each of us is constantly making things "appear out of nothing"
　　Due to *the Creative Intelligence* within the Universe that responds to our every thought.

At the beginning phase of learning our co-creative skills, our awareness grows in small steps
　　Because, initially, we are generally ignorant of *the universal dynamics of creation*
　　　　And unconscious of our unlimited potential as co-creative spiritual beings.

For many people at the start of this process, manifesting can seem slow and laborious
　　For they've not yet discovered how to use, and embody in their life,
　　　　The principles of conscious co-creation - and so they manifest unconsciously
　　　　　　Since all positive and negative thoughts have power to create in one's life.

A Spiritual Magician is a person who consciously uses his or her awareness
　　To tap into the infinite creativity of the Universe in a way that benefits the good of all.

The visionary archetype of **the Spiritual Magician**
　　Is a symbolic blueprint we can use as a transformative practice
　　　　To visualize living in conscious **alignment with *the Source of Life***
　　　　　　And to attune our awareness with *the Power of Unlimited Creativity.*

As we ask *the Intelligence of Life* to provide clear guidance of all we're to do and achieve each day
　　And then turn that guidance into the unwavering certainty of our **intentions**
　　　　Which are fueled and empowered by our **elevated emotions**,
　　　　　　We willfully participate in "the unseen magic of co-creation".

A Spiritual Magician celebrates with **gratitude** for every intention held within the heart
　　And believes and acts as if it has already been manifested.

Needless to say, there are still a lot of people who experience a sense of lack or scarcity
　　And, obviously, there are many challenging problems to solve on our planet.

Imagine how the world would be - if everyone, when young, eager, and bursting with potential,
　　Was taught by their elders to be **a Spiritual Magician**, a conscious co-creator,
　　　　And was able to learn how to cause "the miraculous to appear out of thin air".

Circle of the Spiritual Magician
(An Archetype of Life Mastery)

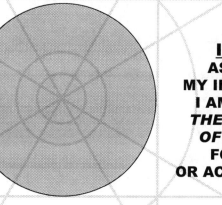

ALIGNMENT
I CONSCIOUSLY ALIGN
MY AWARENESS WITH
THE SOURCE OF LIFE
AND MAINTAIN
A HEART CONNECTION
WITH *THE POWER*
OF UNLIMITED CREATIVITY

GRATITUDE
I CELEBRATE
EACH HEARTFELT
INTENTION
WITH GRATITUDE,
AND BELIEVE AND ACT
AS IF IT HAS ALREADY
BEEN MANIFESTED

INTENTION
AS I LISTEN TO
MY INNER GUIDANCE
I AM CLEAR WHAT
THE INTELLIGENCE
OF LIFE INTENDS
FOR ME TO DO
OR ACHIEVE EACH DAY

ELEVATED EMOTION
I MANIFEST
WHAT I'M GUIDED TO DO
USING THE UNWAVERING
CERTAINTY OF INTENTION
FUELED BY MY ELEVATED
EMOTIONS, SUCH AS JOY
- OR LOVE FOR LIFE

CONSCIOUS CO-CREATION

Today I align my awareness with Infinite Intelligence - and thus miracles are natural to me.

In high school science class we learned that the interior of the Earth is made of four layers,
Starting with the *crust* as the external band at the surface, the *mantle* directly below,
Then a deeper layer called the *outer core* consisting of liquid molten lava,
And at the center the planet's *inner core* made of mostly iron.

We can use *this visual image of multiple layers* to help us understand *conscious co-creation*
Since there are multiple ways to describe *co-creation* using various layers of definition.

First and most simply, we can think of the process of *conscious co-creation*
As the merging of the creative part that we personally play
Joined with the creative part that *the Infinite Intelligence of Life* plays,
So as to **mutually manifest** a specific intention into form.

This requires that we align our individual awareness with *Universal Awareness*
To make sure, poetically speaking, "the arrow of intention from the bow of our heart
Soars in the same direction as the Arrow of the Universe".

Using the themes of **The Great Circle**, a more expansive way to define how this process works is:
Conscious co-creation is the outward manifestation which appears in the material world
As **an out-picturing of the intention** that we are inwardly guided to achieve.

Manifestation of our intention occurs through a co-creative act with *the Source of Life*
That mirrors our <u>inner</u> development and consciousness as an <u>outer</u> expression of form.

In other words - it's the co-creative process by which we manifest our heartfelt intention
Into the <u>outer</u> world of form based on the level of our <u>inner</u> awareness.

Another way to state this - is that *conscious co-creation*
Is **the external expression of our intention (empowered by our elevated emotions)**
In which the creative process is activated by *the Natural Intelligence of Life*
And brought into manifested form.

Finally, the highest definition of *conscious co-creation* can be described as being so present
And so unwaveringly aligned with *Infinite Intelligence*,
That the experience of "doing" and "not doing" become one and the same,
Making choices and experiencing choiceless awareness blend together,
Taking action and non-action eventually merge,
And with absolute certainty of the union of *Spirit* and form,
All our intentions are instantly manifested.

Living in a state of **True Presence** (an authentic alignment with *the Infinite Presence of Love*)
Is the most powerful form of *conscious co-creation*.

Could it be that an alignment with *the Source of All That Is* has been the essential key
To the "miracles" of every great spiritual master, and has been "the central core"
Of all creative power throughout the Universe since the beginning of time?

Circle of Conscious Co-Creation

MANIFESTATION
CONSCIOUS CO-CREATION
IS THE MERGING OF
THE CREATIVE PART THAT
I PLAY WITH THE CREATIVE
PART THAT *THE INTELLI-GENCE OF THE UNIVERSE*
PLAYS TO MUTUALLY
MANIFEST AN INTENTION

INTENTION
CONSCIOUS CO-CREATION
IS THE INTENTION
THAT EMERGES
INTO FORM IN WHICH
THE CREATIVE PROCESS
IS ACTIVATED
BY *THE NATURAL
INTELLIGENCE OF LIFE*

OUT-PICTURING
CONSCIOUS CO-CREATION
IS THE MANIFESTATION
WHICH APPEARS IN
THE WORLD AS AN OUT-PICTURING OF INTENTION
FROM *LIFE* MIRRORING
MY <u>INNER</u> AWARENESS AS
<u>OUTER</u> MATERIAL FORM

TRUE PRESENCE
CONSCIOUS CO-CREATION
IS A PARADOX OF "DOING"
AND "NOT DOING", TAKING
ACTION AND NON-ACTION,
AND THROUGH LIVING
IN *TRUE PRESENCE*,
ALL INTENTIONS ARE
INSTANTLY MANIFESTED

INTENTION

Today I use the power of intention to manifest the desires of my heart.

As if by the highly skilled artistic hands of some Grand Cosmic Sculptor,
  The Universe seems to be masterfully shaped by an organizing *Natural Intelligence*
    Which is intrinsically intentional - and is the very essence of unlimited creativity.

At the onset of the Universe, this *Infinite Creativity* initially directed vast sub-atomic particles
  Into massive galactic clouds of hot swirling energy
    Which, over millions of years, formed patterns within this immense sea of particles.

Galactic clouds coalesced into stars, which then exploded, creating solar systems and planets
  That were fashioned from the sculpting directive of this organizing intelligence.

Eventually on a small cooling planet we call Earth, a myriad of life forms emerged from oceans
  And were cast into millions of unique designs by chemical and biological processes.

This same *Impulse of Creativity* that sculpted the heavens, forged the geology of our planet,
  And shaped the first single-celled forms of life
    Then guided the arrival of the plant kingdom from the elemental forces of Nature.

In time, small mammals evolved and slowly developed a novel advancement called *emotion*,
  Which was another important and creative tool to help carve the next wave of evolution.

With the appearance of large mammals and hominids that developed greater brain capacities,
  The Creative Evolutionary Impulse then brought forth *rudimentary thought processes*
    Which allowed for the manifestation of more diverse forms, like the first humans.

Apparently amidst this "unfolding universal dance of creativity", a quantum leap then occurred
  As *Life* took a giant step forward, evolving primal humans into self-reflective creatures
    Which could think rationally and, finally, become aware of their own evolution.

Over eons, humanity has developed the unique ability to purposefully focus thought
  Discovering the skill to consciously direct **a creative idea** within the mind like a laser
    And learning to hone this new ability into an intrinsic power called *intention*.

Using **the power of intention** humanity could now begin to be a Cosmic Sculptor as well,
  And learn to shape into form the heartfelt desires it was inwardly guided to create.

The power of intention is to our mind
  Like *skillful inventive hands* are to a sculptor of fine art,
    For it's a sculptor's creative ideas *(desires)* that use skillful hands *(intention)*
      To shape a mound of clay into an intended piece of art *(manifested form)*.

Intention is **a crystal clear vision** of possibility we visualize to manifest our future reality,
  A single-minded inspired goal we use to realize our focused desire.

Our destiny is to learn to merge the *intentions* of the Universe with our own *intentions* of the heart
  So we can ultimately help co-create the glorious world we **imagine** is possible.

Circle of Intention

GOAL
INTENTION –
A SINGLE-MINDED
INSPIRED GOAL
WHICH I USE
TO ACTIVATE
AND REALIZE
MY FOCUSED DESIRE

CREATIVE IDEA
INTENTION –
A SPECIFIC THOUGHT
I PURPOSEFULLY
HOLD IN MY MIND
TO SHAPE
MY CREATIVE IDEA
INTO MATERIAL FORM

VISION
INTENTION –
MY CRYSTAL CLEAR
VISION OF POSSIBILITY
WHICH I FEEL
AND VISUALIZE
TO MANIFEST
MY FUTURE REALITY

IMAGINATION
INTENTION –
DIRECTING
MY IMAGINATION
IN A DELIBERATE WAY
SO AS TO ACTIVELY
UNLEASH MORE OF
MY CREATIVE POTENTIAL

BELIEFS

I am constantly re-examining my beliefs so I may learn to love all of life more fully.

When a professional contractor is commissioned to renovate a building,
    He or she aspires to have available the best and most effective tools for the job.

We all use many tools in life, yet one of the most potent "tools" we use to shape our reality
    Is the creative power of our thoughts, which are based on our existing set of beliefs.

Beliefs are simply a collection of our current thoughts or notions
    That, for a given period of time, we hold to be "true".

The beliefs we hold "true" are the mental lenses through which we presently view our world
    And are not static, permanent concepts that are meant to never change,
        But, within a healthy mind, are always adjusting and re-examining with time
            Due to one's developing awareness gained from new life experiences.

Beliefs also have a paradoxical quality about them
    Since they can be "true" in the present moment so as to help define our current reality,
        And yet they are, concurrently, "not true" because they are perpetually changing.

Our beliefs are a specific group of thoughts we use to fashion our unique personal **worldview**
    Which prominently influences how we respond or react to our various circumstances,
        Such as how we interact with our family, friends, co-workers, religion, politicians,
            And even how we relate to our physical environment.

Beliefs can be constructive or destructive, evolving or destroying, based on our awareness
    And are the powerful *inner tools* we use to help us manifest our heartfelt desires.

If the current beliefs we hold to be "true" are life-affirming, we can use them as **a set of ideas**
    To help us make benevolent choices which serve the constructive progression of life.

If we observe in ourselves (through self-examination and mindfulness)
    That our beliefs are not constructive - and are creating experiences of fear in our life,
        Then it's our responsibility to change those beliefs.

We can transform our loveless thinking by becoming consciously aware of our thoughts
    And catching ourselves when our thinking is focused on thoughts of fear or separation.

Over time, some beliefs become rigid, and as we change and evolve our core **convictions**
    (Because we've gained more inclusive perspectives from our various life experiences),
        We discover we can constantly change and redefine our point of view,
            That we can learn to make better choices,
                And from our healthier and more mature beliefs,
            We can help build a more peaceful world.

Should we desire "to renovate the mansion of new possibilities within our heart and mind"
    And accomplish this task in the most effective manner,
        We will need to acquire and use "the best tools" for the job.

Circle of Beliefs

TRUTH
BELIEFS –
A COLLECTION
OF THOUGHTS
OR NOTIONS
THAT, FOR A GIVEN
PERIOD OF TIME,
I HOLD TO BE TRUE

CONVICTION
BELIEFS –
THE CONCEPTS
OR CONVICTIONS
THAT HELP ME
MANIFEST
AND SHAPE MY
HEARTFELT DESIRES

SET OF IDEAS
BELIEFS –
A SET OF EVER-
CHANGING IDEAS
FROM WHICH
I DETERMINE HOW
TO MAKE THE MOST
BENEVOLENT CHOICES

WORLDVIEW
BELIEFS –
A PARTICULAR
POINT OF VIEW
FROM WHICH
I CREATE MY UNIQUE
PERSPECTIVE
OF THE WORLD

MODES OF BELIEF

My empowering beliefs help me develop my potential - and become the person I desire to be.

During the steady course of evolution, our human mind has acquired the capacity
    To experience different kinds of thoughts we hold to be true, or **modes of belief**,
        That can be stated as conscious, sub-conscious, and super-conscious beliefs,
            And each *mode of belief* has its own functional objectives,
                Such as daily needs, emotional balance, or developing potential.

Our **conscious beliefs** are those beliefs we are mindfully aware of in our everyday life,
    Which are the principal beliefs we use to make conscious choices
        And to interpret and identify who we believe we are.

There are many types of conscious beliefs (like the following defining and categorizing beliefs):
    I am a man or a woman - I am American or Chinese - I am a Christian or a Muslim
    I am a democrat or a republican - I am a musician or a doctor.

They can also take the form of deeply emotional and personality-shaping beliefs, for example:
    I can't do this - I feel really good about this - I will get through this challenge
    I cannot accept this experience - I am grateful for this.

These beliefs are the ones we're knowingly aware of, that rise above "the surface of the mind",
    And are like the white tips of floating icebergs which are visible above the ocean waves.

But below our conscious awareness, concealed deep beneath "the surface of our mind",
    Is a group of unconscious, habitual, and sometimes dysfunctional beliefs
        That are hidden or veiled from our daily awareness in our *shadow world*,
            Much like the hidden ice of icebergs that is out-of-sight
                Buried below the surface of the ocean.

These **sub-conscious beliefs** are held unaware in the shrouded caverns of our mind,
    Yet once enabled our emotional body to cope with past traumatic events, and look like:
        I am not enough - I do not feel safe - I am not ok the way I am,
        Or beliefs that help us habitually function, like - *I know how to drive a car.*

There is also a powerful *field of transcendent mind energy* called **super-conscious beliefs**,
    Which are the subtle life-empowering beliefs within the template of our higher potential
    And exist as the future possibilities of who we envision we can be.

We can imagine that these expansive visionary beliefs are like translucent vaporous clouds
    Hanging in "the sky of mind" above the ocean, hovering high over the floating icebergs.

Super-conscious beliefs are the life-affirming beliefs of our future potential that we access
    In order to plant the mental seeds of possibility into "the fertile garden of our life"
        That, with enough attention, will eventually "blossom into our greater flowering".

Life is always inviting us to boldly take a further step on our *journey of awakening*
    By bringing any hidden or habitual beliefs to the surface of our mind to be transformed
        So we can fully embrace the next possibility of our unlimited potential.

Circle of the Modes of Belief

ABSOLUTE REALM OF NO BELIEFS
THE TRANSCENDENT REALM OF PURE AWARENESS AND ABSOLUTE ONENESS, WHERE BELIEFS DO NOT EXIST

CONSCIOUS BELIEFS
THE EVERYDAY BELIEFS THAT I AM MINDFULLY AWARE OF, WHICH I USE TO MAKE CONSCIOUS CHOICES

SUPER-CONSCIOUS BELIEFS
THE LIFE-AFFIRMING BELIEFS REGARDING MY HIGHER POTENTIAL DIRECTED TOWARD FUTURE POSSIBILITIES OF WHO I DESIRE TO BE

SUB-CONSCIOUS BELIEFS
THE HABITUAL BELIEFS I HAVE ADOPTED OVER TIME THAT ARE HIDDEN OR BURIED BELOW MY CONSCIOUS AWARENESS

IX

MIND AWARENESS PRACTICES

RELEASE

Today I am mindful to release any disturbing emotions that arise in my awareness.

Imagine that you are holding in your hand a small number of inflated helium balloons
    And sense that each balloon represents to you a *disturbing emotion* that you're feeling.

Each single balloon has "a subtle tug" that's pulling the balloon skyward due to the helium gas
    As you recognize this upward force is "the ever-present tug of *Life"*
        Inviting you to courageously release your hold on these troubling emotions.

Yet like a young child, you experience a strong grip of attachment to your "cherished balloons",
    For at some previous time, you made a decision based on fear that it was difficult to let them go.

Releasing disturbing emotions that we've experienced
    Can be challenging when we have enmeshed ourselves in habitual patterns
        Of loveless choices and behavior for a very long time,
            But eventually - every child grows up, and must learn, one day,
                To release their habitual hold on their "coveted balloons".

In the process of *letting go of disturbing emotions* that negatively affect our life,
    There are, fundamentally, four stages of awareness we can utilize:
        1) acknowledgment, 2) willingness, 3) identification, and **4) release**.

And to assist us in this process, we can use a specific series of powerful expansive questions
    To bring greater awareness to each of the four stages.

For example, if you have a desire to let go of a disturbing emotion, such as anger,
    You could ask yourself the following set of questions (also listed on the next page).

First, open your heart and align your awareness with *the Source of Life (the Presence of Love)*
    While you ask, *"Can I admit to myself that I am feeling <u>angry,</u>*
        Which is causing me an experience of being emotionally triggered?",
            And if you can honestly answer *"yes"* to this question,
                Then acknowledge to yourself, *"What is true - is that I feel <u>angry".</u>*

Next ask the question, *"Could I be willing to accept this <u>anger</u> simply as an experience*
    In the present moment just as it is, without needing to judge it or fix it?"

Then ask, *"Can I identify who I am as the Eternal Unbounded Presence that does not change,*
    Rather than this passing experience of <u>anger</u> which comes and goes?"

Finally, ask, *"Would I, right now, fully release any attachment or negative charge*
    I have held onto concerning this <u>anger,</u> and simply let it go?"

At times, we may feel we can't let go (like a child who timidly holds onto his or her balloons),
    Habitually believing these "emotional balloons" are somehow who we really are.

Until one day through the gift of grace, we realize we can just open our grip - and let them go,
    And say *"yes to Life"* as they effortlessly float away into infinite spaciousness.

Circle of Release
(A Transformative Practice)

RELEASE
WOULD I, RIGHT NOW,
FULLY RELEASE
ANY ATTACHMENT
OR NEGATIVE CHARGE
I HAVE HELD ONTO
CONCERNING THIS
DISTURBING EMOTION,
AND SIMPLY LET IT GO?

ACKNOWLEDGMENT
CAN I ADMIT TO MYSELF
THAT I AM FEELING
A DISTURBING EMOTION,
(E.G. - ANGER, SADNESS)
WHICH IS CAUSING ME
AN EXPERIENCE
OF BEING EMOTIONALLY
TRIGGERED?

IDENTIFICATION
CAN I IDENTIFY
WHO I AM
AS THE ETERNAL
UNBOUNDED PRESENCE
THAT DOES NOT CHANGE,
RATHER THAN
THIS PASSING EMOTION
WHICH COMES AND GOES?

WILLINGNESS
COULD I BE WILLING
TO ACCEPT THIS
EMOTION SIMPLY
AS AN EXPERIENCE
IN THE PRESENT MOMENT
JUST AS IT IS,
WITHOUT NEEDING
TO JUDGE IT OR FIX IT?

CULTIVATING CONSCIOUS CO-CREATION

I cultivate the power of intention as a conscious co-creator with the Natural Intelligence of Life.

When we go for a walk, such as strolling to the grocery store, or hiking through the woods,
Every individual step we take gets us one step closer to our intended destination.

If we desire to take another kind of journey, a journey of **cultivating conscious co-creation**,
We can think of this endeavor as a series of steps that we are to learn
So we may achieve our intended goal which we're inwardly guided to manifest.

The series of steps can be easily remembered with the following key words:
Step 1 – **Co-Creative Intention**
Step 2 – **Elevated Emotion**
Step 3 – **Surrender to a Greater Power**
Step 4 – **Grateful Certainty**

First, devote some time to expand your understanding
Of *the Natural Intelligence* of the Cosmos - through study, inquiry, or contemplation
And align your awareness with *the Limitless Creative Power* of the Universe.

Then spend a moment asking what it is that *the Infinite Intelligence of Life (Source, God)*
Wants to create through you using your unique creative gifts and talents.

As it becomes intuitively clear what intention *Life* wants to manifest through you,
Draw on **the power of your co-creative intention** using your vibrant imagination,
For we all use internal pictures to communicate with our *super-conscious mind*
As a means to develop and transform ourselves,
And as an inherent force to help shape our future.

The next step is to empower your intention with an elevated emotion, such as joy - or love for life
For **strong elevated emotions** are "the fertile nutrients" and "the inner fuel"
That supports the seeds of desire in the garden of your life.

Then as you envision your intention in your mind's eye,
Surrender it to a Greater Power *(the Natural Intelligence of the Universe),*
So as to create the best outcome for all concerned.

The vast creative power of the Cosmos that knows how to do and create all things
Also knows how to bring your intention into manifestation in the most perfect way.

Finally, anchor this heartfelt intention into the world of material form
By feeling **absolute certainty and celebrating with gratitude**,
Believing and acting as if your intention has already manifested.

Be a *spiritual scientist*, experiment with your life, and find out for yourself whether or not
That as you maintain an alignment with *Infinite Intelligence*
And practice these steps on a consistent basis,
You are able to harvest the bounty of what *Life* desires to create through you
And get a step closer to being a true co-creator with *the Source of All That Is*.

Circle of Cultivating Conscious Co-Creation
(The Mastery of *Becoming*)

CO-CREATIVE INTENTION
STEP 1: I MINDFULLY USE MY CREATIVE IMAGINATION TO FOCUS A CLEAR INTENTION THAT I HAVE BEEN INWARDLY GUIDED TO CO-CREATE WITH *LIFE*

ELEVATED EMOTION
STEP 2: I EMPOWER THIS INTENTION WITH AN ELEVATED EMOTION USING "THE INNER FUEL" OF A FEELING SUCH AS JOY - OR LOVE FOR LIFE

SURRENDER TO *A GREATER POWER*
STEP 3: I SURRENDER THIS INTENTION TO *A GREATER POWER, THE POWER OF THE UNIVERSE THAT KNOWS HOW TO DO AND CREATE ALL THINGS*

GRATEFUL CERTAINTY
STEP 4: I FEEL ABSOLUTE CERTAINTY, CELEBRATING WITH GRATITUDE, AND BELIEVING THAT THIS INTENTION HAS ALREADY MANIFESTED

MAY 9
AFFIRMATIONS FOR CO-CREATING INTENTIONS

Aligning with the Source of Life is key to co-creating the intentions I've been guided to manifest.

If you expect the vegetables you've planted in your garden to flourish abundantly,
    You know that you must keep them nourished with adequate water and proper nutrients.

Some people even say that vegetables growing in a garden will thrive a bit more plentifully
    When we literally speak to them with heartfelt feeling,
        For it's believed that plants will benevolently respond to our elevated emotions.

Similarly, an *affirmation* is a certain declaration we speak out loud, or silently within us,
    That can deliberately be used to nourish "the seeds of our inner garden"
        By aligning our mind's intentions and our heart's emotions
            With an exalted vision of possibility.

We can use affirmations as transformative practices to remind us what really matters
    And to help us maintain an alignment with *the Source of Life*.

Within this alignment, we merge our personal consciousness
    With the *Universal Consciousness* that animates and shapes the entire Cosmos.

Affirmations can support us in aligning our awareness with *the Field of Limitless Creativity*
    So we may be a co-creator with *the Natural Intelligence* of the Universe.

If we then amplify the inherent power of affirmations
    By using them in a certain sequential pattern
        That includes **the Pillars of Awakening** (see April 8th)
            (The qualities of **gratitude, surrender, acceptance,** and **Oneness**),
            And also includes the three **Fields of Creation** (see June 16th)
                (**The Fields of *Light*, *Love*,** and ***Power*)**,
            We can activate within us a powerful flow of energy.

I am <u>one</u> with *the Source of Life*
    And a co-creator in manifesting the best intentions for all concerned.

I <u>accept</u> that *the Eternal Light of the Universe*
    Is co-creating with me the intentions I've been guided to manifest.

I <u>surrender</u> to *Limitless Love*,
    ***The Unbounded Universal Energy* that truly manifests all of my intentions.**

I am <u>grateful</u> for *the Infinite Power of Creation*
    That co-creates with me to manifest my intentions.

In order to "harvest the best fruits from our garden",
    These affirmations have true power when they're spoken out loud with sincerity.

You can practice these affirmations once a day, or as much as you like throughout the week,
    To help support the blossoming of your intentions within "the garden of your heart".

Circle of Affirmations for Co-Creating Intentions
(A Transformative Practice)

ONENESS
I AM ONE WITH
THE SOURCE OF LIFE
AND A CO-CREATOR
IN MANIFESTING
THE BEST INTENTIONS
FOR ALL CONCERNED

GRATITUDE
I AM GRATEFUL FOR
*THE INFINITE POWER
OF CREATION*
THAT CO-CREATES
WITH ME TO MANIFEST
MY INTENTIONS

ACCEPTANCE
I ACCEPT THAT
*THE ETERNAL LIGHT OF
THE UNIVERSE* IS CO-
CREATING WITH ME THE
INTENTIONS I'VE BEEN
GUIDED TO MANIFEST

SURRENDER
I SURRENDER TO
*LIMITLESS LOVE,
THE UNBOUNDED
UNIVERSAL ENERGY*
THAT TRULY MANIFESTS
ALL OF MY INTENTIONS

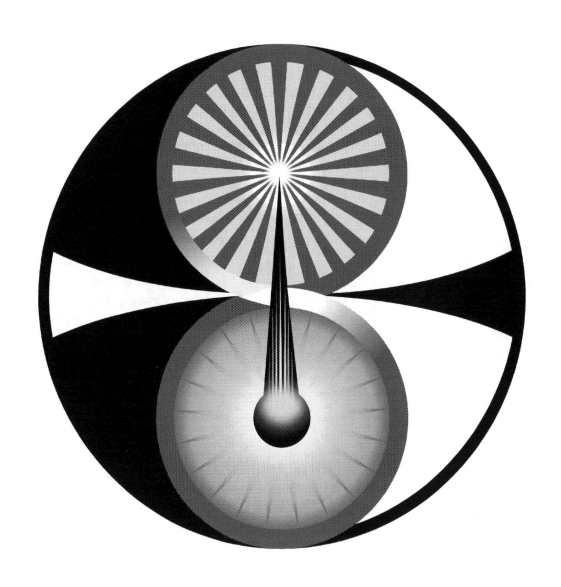

X

THE
EVOLUTIONARY
PERSPECTIVE

GIFTS FROM AN EVOLUTIONARY PERSPECTIVE

An evolutionary perspective motivates me to examine and constructively transform my life.

The last 500 years of scientific discovery have provided humanity with the laws and principles
Which enabled a range of inventions, technical breakthroughs, and "creature comforts".

For example, science has harnessed *the invisible magic of electricity* to power our homes,
Has furnished us with various appliances to make life easier and more enjoyable,
And has supplied us with an array of medical cures and surgeries
Which have aided millions of people and allowed us to live much longer.

Engineering achievements have given us all kinds of cars, trains, boats, and airplanes,
Which has made travel a lot faster - and our planet seem a lot smaller.

The marvels of science have provided us with personal computers to enhance our creativity,
And radio, TV, cell phones, and the Internet to keep us all connected with one another.

But amidst these spectacular blessings, two of the most important inventions of science
(Which have powerfully contributed to a monumental paradigm shift for humanity),
Are the *telescope* and the *microscope*.

Modern telescopes have allowed us to investigate the immense reaches of the Cosmos,
Educate ourselves about "the heavens", unravel the mysteries of the Universe,
And have revolutionized the fundamental way we think about ourselves.

Special microscopes have shown us the magnificent and complex systems of the human body,
And how each of us, and every aspect of creation, is made of "the same stuff of life".

These two inventions, the telescope and the microscope, have deepened our comprehension
Of the illuminating revelations and integral perspectives of evolutionary science.

From this evolutionary vantage, these devices have helped us gain a new understanding
That humans, and all of Nature, are interconnected in a vast system of relationships,
And this awareness forms in us the seeds of **greater compassion for all of life**.

Biology has shown how every species on Earth responds to the basic impulses of its existence
By finding ways to expand and express new possibilities, to unleash its potential,
And these facts empower us to be **responsible and integrous** with our actions.

Human developmental studies have systematically explored and defined
The stages of inner growth we each move through during the unfolding of our life,
And this "Big Picture perspective" of our **levels of psychological development**
Provides a vision and, thus, a clear motivation
To **transform** the habitual and loveless parts of our self.

Science has given us an opportunity to open our eyes, to see **the gifts of this perspective**,
For the authors of the books on evolutionary science are writing "the modern scriptures"
Of a *new universal creation story* which has the potential and promise
To harmoniously unite, as one family, all the people of the world.

Circle of Gifts From An Evolutionary Perspective

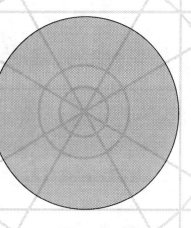

INTEGRITY
REALIZING EVERYTHING IS AN INTEGRAL PART OF A PERPETUALLY EVOLVING UNIVERSE EMPOWERS ME TO ALIGN WITH *LIFE* AND LIVE WITH INTEGRITY
+GIFT – CREATES A VISION OF LIVING WITH INTEGRITY

DEVELOPMENT
KNOWING THAT ALL OF EVOLVING LIFE HAS A NATURAL IMPULSE TO LEARN INSPIRES ME TO FURTHER DEVELOP MY OWN POTENTIAL
+GIFT – AWAKENS A JOY TO DEVELOP MYSELF

TRANSFORMATION
EMBRACING "THE BIG PICTURE" PROVIDES ME CLARITY CONCERNING MY THOUGHTS WHICH SUPPORT LIFE - AND THOSE WHICH DO NOT
+GIFT – MOTIVATES ME TO TRANSFORM MYSELF

COMPASSION
***THE EVOLUTIONARY PERSPECTIVE* HELPS ME FEEL EMPATHY FOR ANOTHER - AND LIVE A COMPASSIONATE LIFE THAT SERVES OTHERS**
+GIFT – CULTIVATES IN ME COMPASSIONATE SERVICE

THE DYNAMIC FORCES OF TRANFORMATION

Today I expand my awareness of what is true through the discipline of transformative practice.

We humans can be likened to a fleet of ships floating on an endless sea of transformation,
    For constant change is happening all around us - and within us in every moment.

Every form of life is being inwardly directed to develop, expand, and hence, transform itself,
    And therefore every person throughout the world
        Is continually being inwardly invited by *a Natural Creative Intelligence*
            To transform, evolve, and express him or herself in ever-new ways.

Yet at this current time in history within the perpetual evolution of humanity,
    Many people are like "unskilled ocean travelers who appear to be lost at sea",
        And rather than consciously choose to transform into more radiant beings,
            They seem to be "coerced into transformation" only in those moments
                When they are immersed in the anguish of suffering or crisis.

Suffering is what we experience when we're attached to wanting life to be different than it is,
    Yet our suffering also has the possibility to trigger and shake us to the core of our being,
        Potentially leading us from an intense breakdown to a profound breakthrough
            Where we discover from these situations the gift of higher awareness
                Which, over time, transforms the quality of our life experience.

Crisis and catastrophic events can also be powerful catalysts for constructive transformation
    When we're able to see them as the kind of challenging opportunities we can learn from,
        And when we respond to them with centeredness and heightened awareness.

Over thousands of years, sages, monks, and mystics from various religious traditions
    Have searched deep within themselves
        Learning how to transform their loveless habits and beliefs
            By cultivating greater mindfulness and awareness of what is true.

These consciousness explorers created numerous transformative practices
    That purposefully supported and enhanced their spiritual development.

It was through their dedication to daily practice that they refined their time-tested methods
    Enabling them to have sublime experiences of their *Eternal Nature*
        And to ultimately realize who they really are.

The spiritual practice of mindfully cultivating compassion
    And consciously exploring more inclusive perspectives of what our life is truly about
        Eventually leads us to make better life-affirming choices.

Each of us must confront the everyday choice of whether we want to be "a lost traveler"
    Or "a modern mystic" - on the endless ocean of life's constant changes.

We can either "swim in a sea of transformation" that's generated from **suffering** or **crisis**,
    Or we can choose to consciously transform our inner and outer worlds
        With daily transformative **practice** that ultimately expands our **awareness**.

Circle of the Dynamic Forces of Transformation

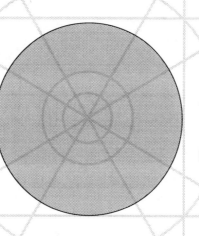

PRACTICE
TRANSFORMATION
CAN COME FROM THE
DEDICATION OF USING
TIME-TESTED PRACTICES
THAT CULTIVATE IN ME
MORE AWARENESS
OF WHAT IS TRUE

CRISIS
TRANSFORMATION
CAN COME FROM THE
MANY UNPREDICTABLE
EVENTS THAT PRODUCE
CHALLENGING
OPPORTUNITIES WHICH
I MUST RESPOND TO

AWARENESS
TRANSFORMATION CAN
COME FROM EMBRACING
INCLUSIVE
PERSPECTIVES OF WHAT
MY LIFE IS TRULY ABOUT
THAT LEAD ME TO MAKE
BETTER CHOICES

SUFFERING
TRANSFORMATION
CAN COME FROM
THE BREAKTHROUGHS
THAT OCCUR, WHICH ARE
INITIATED FROM THE
BREAKDOWNS CREATED
BY MY SUFFERING

129

THE FRACTAL NATURE OF EMERGENT EVOLUTION

It is my destiny to live an awakened life, for awakening is the natural unfolding within everything.

Fractal is a word that describes a pattern or shape which, when observed in finer detail,
    Repeats itself at smaller scales, usually with slight variations of the original pattern.

For example, the human circulatory system has evolved through a series of *fractal patterns*
    Much like the fractal patterning within the branching of a tree,
        For the main arteries that come out of the human heart are large like tree trunks,
            But the next series of general arteries that split off from the main ones
                Are much smaller in diameter - like the branches of a tree.

Tiny capillaries then extend from the general arteries,
    Which continue this repeating *fractal pattern* at smaller and smaller scales.

Throughout the Universe, groups of mammoth galaxies travel together within space
    And these galaxies orbit the central hub of what is called a *galactic super cluster*,
        Then at a smaller scale, entire solar systems make their epic cyclic journeys
            As they travel along lengthy orbits within each galaxy,
                While planets orbit their fiery suns at the core of solar systems,
                And smaller still, moons nestle into orbits around planets.

The above illustration portrays a series of *fractal patterns* that repeat at smaller scales,
    Where each similar orbiting pattern is a smaller "mirroring" of the larger previous one,
        And each pattern has some parallel characteristics of the one that came before
            Yet also creates new characteristics and functions that are unique to itself.

This ongoing repetition of *fractal patterns* is a universal principle
    And occurs throughout all of creation.

From extensive scientific observation, we find it is one of the key principles that evolution uses
    To give form to the natural world on Earth and, most likely, the same principle it uses
        To generate life on countless other planets throughout the Cosmos.

The **Earth** evolved, along with the rest of our Solar System, from a huge supernova explosion
    And gradually over time, our planet has *"awakened"*, so to speak, into a living organism
        From its four and a half billion years of geological and biological development.

Primitive humans then evolved from the continual development of biological life on Earth
    Repeating *the fractal pattern of the planet* at a much smaller scale.

The self-reflective mind developed from an earlier, primal form of human life
    Awakening into a more evolved organism, repeating this *fractal pattern* once again.

And at this current time in the ongoing developmental evolution of humanity,
    A new fractal pattern is collectively emerging across the globe
        As the self-reflective human mind is *awakening* into something ever grander,
            A deep recognition that each of us is being invited to embrace our sacred destiny
                As a fully integrated and awakened human being.

Circle of the Fractal Nature of Emergent Evolution
(In Relation to the Awakening Human)

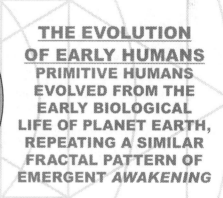

**THE EVOLUTION
OF PLANET EARTH**
THE EARTH, AS WELL AS
OUR ENTIRE SOLAR
SYSTEM, EVOLVED FROM
A MASSIVE SUPERNOVA
AND, OVER TIME,
THE EARTH *AWAKENED*
INTO A LIVING ORGANISM

**THE EVOLUTION
OF THE AWAKENED
HUMAN**
MODERN HUMANS ARE
EVOLVING TOWARD NEW
EMERGENT STAGES OF
AWAKENING, REPEATING
THE FRACTAL PATTERNS
OF ALL LIVING SYSTEMS

**THE EVOLUTION
OF EARLY HUMANS**
PRIMITIVE HUMANS
EVOLVED FROM THE
EARLY BIOLOGICAL
LIFE OF PLANET EARTH,
REPEATING A SIMILAR
FRACTAL PATTERN OF
EMERGENT *AWAKENING*

**THE EVOLUTION
OF THE SELF-
REFLECTIVE MIND**
THE HUMAN MIND
EVOLVED AND BECAME
SELF-REFLECTIVE,
AWAKENING ANOTHER
REPEATING EMERGENT
FRACTAL PATTERN

EVOLUTION OF BASIC HUMAN IMPULSES

I feel a natural yearning that constantly invites me to be aware of my Oneness with all of life.

The Great Circle is *a spiritual map of the dynamics at play within the world* which illustrates
That our experience of reality is both an inward impulse of <u>evolving consciousness</u>
(A yearning to develop our greater potential and awaken to who we really are),
And, simultaneously, a resultant outward impulse of <u>evolving creativity</u>
(A yearning to manifest new forms of creativity). (see March 28th)

Furthermore for every person on our planet, there are also two other basic impulses or drives;
1) An inherent **impulse to experience individuality**,
And 2) a natural **impulse to experience the collective**. (see October 22nd)

The impulse for individuality and the impulse for the collective are two primal instincts
That both existed as innate potentials within primitive humans,
Yet it was necessary for each of them to evolve in their own novel ways
As humanity progressed through its various stages of development.

When the first humans initially emerged as a species,
The primary drive was to survive the harsh demanding challenges of a hostile world.

After cultivating various early cognitive advances, such as the birth of symbolic language,
Humans learned to improve their primary survival skills, which allowed them additional time
To explore new possibilities - and new potential directions their lives could take.

These investigations of human expression (empowered by the emergence of rational thought)
Led to a natural longing to discover, and reap the benefits of, "an individuated self"
Which formed a level of development referred to as one's personal egoic nature.

This impulse for individuality further moved humans into a new kind of exploration of self,
A yearning to demonstrate one's own uniqueness and creatively express oneself,
Which then led to the cultural manifestations of art, science, and philosophy
But also fueled expressions of darker aspects of "the human experiment",
Such as greed, control, and personal power struggles.

Today these personal *shadow aspects* are jointly and destructively affecting our entire planet,
Yet combined with the emergence and understanding of *the evolutionary perspective,*
They are inviting us to grow to our next awareness level, awakening a core universal need
To balance our individuality with our intrinsic **impulse for the collective**.

For it's the achievement of living collectively as a conscious and compassionate global village
Guided by our *Higher Nature* and, thus, acting beyond the limitations of personal ego,
That will enable us to overcome the current enormous challenges we face.

If we're able to meet these challenges and successfully co-create a more cooperative world,
Then our innate yearning for development will continue to compel us to stretch farther
And thus will naturally lead us *to reach out and further explore the vast Cosmos*
As we, most likely, will connect with other planetary life within our galaxy
On our perpetual **journey to realize our Oneness with all of life**.

Circle of the Evolution of Basic Human Impulses
(In Relation to Evolutionary Leaps of Awareness)

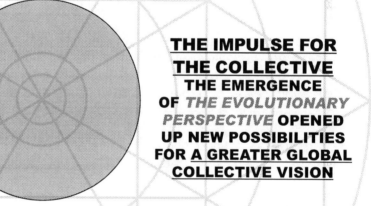

**THE IMPULSE FOR
UNITY**
THE CURRENT
WORLDWIDE EMERGENCE
OF MORE AND MORE
AWAKENED HUMANS
IS INCREASING A SPIRITUAL
AWARENESS OF ONENESS

**THE IMPULSE FOR
SURVIVAL**
THE EMERGENCE
OF SYMBOLIC LANGUAGE
WAS A POWERFUL TOOL
WHICH PROVIDED MORE
TIME TO EXPLORE MANY
NEW POSSIBILITIES

**THE IMPULSE FOR
THE COLLECTIVE**
THE EMERGENCE
OF *THE EVOLUTIONARY
PERSPECTIVE* OPENED
UP NEW POSSIBILITIES
FOR A GREATER GLOBAL
COLLECTIVE VISION

**THE IMPULSE FOR
INDIVIDUALITY**
THE EMERGENCE
OF RATIONAL THOUGHT
OPENED UP NEW
POSSIBILITIES FOR
INDIVIDUAL CREATIVE
EXPRESSION

STAGES OF DEVELOPMENTAL AWARENESS

The natural arc of my life involves cultivating an awareness of ever-greater inclusion of others.

If a lumberjack were to cut down a tall deciduous tree with a precise saw
    In such a manner that the cut was completely flat and smooth,
        One could observe the concentric rings of the tree which exist within the trunk.

These concentric rings indicate the age of a tree,
    For every year of the tree's life, it produces another outer ring of new growth
        With the inside rings showing its early years
            And the outside rings displaying its more recent annual development.

We can use this visual image to better understand how human awareness,
    As it relates to embracing and including other people, also expands over time.

As we picture the rings within the trunk of a tree in relation to developmental awareness,
    We can envision that the central ring represents a pre-human **instinctual awareness**
        Of living in the present moment that's expressed
            In the various creatures of Nature, such as all animals and early hominids.

Then as evolutionary time elapsed and the first self-reflective humans emerged on the scene,
    A personal egoic self developed from a natural survival impulse to self-individuate.

If one's *egoic self* is formed around the immature emotional development of self-centeredness,
    Then one's awareness will be focused mainly as a selfish concern for one's own needs.

This can look like a world in which people are in it for themselves, an **egocentric awareness**,
    A self-absorbed "dog-eat-dog world" that produces greed, fear, and a need to control.

Eventually, through the trials and personal growth of life experience,
    One develops an innate awareness to expand one's circle of compassion and care
        That includes a larger concern for the needs of one's family, tribe, or nation.

Throughout much of human history, the darker side of this **ethnocentric awareness**
    Has been dysfunctionally expressed as family feuds, city gang rivalries, racial battles,
        Holy wars such as the Crusades, the unrest between Israel and Palestine,
            And scenarios like the conflict between northern and southern Ireland.

Just as the circular rings within a tree trunk
    Grow larger and larger over a period of many years,
        So the stages of human awareness develop from the egocentric self
            To the ethnocentric self and, over time, arrive at the **worldcentric self**,
                The stage of human awareness where one serves the good of all.

It's up to each of us to nurture the human Tree of Life with our *awakened awareness*,
    With our daily alignment with *the Source of Life*,
        And with mindfulness that transforms our loveless habits into inner freedom,
            So "the next concentric ring of human possibility" can grow
                Into the kind of world where all people are seen as *holy and sacred*.

Circle of the Stages of Developmental Awareness
(In Relation to Embracing and Including Others)

WORLDCENTRIC
SELF
THE SOCIALLY INCLUSIVE
AWARENESS
THAT'S EXPRESSED
AS A GLOBAL CONCERN
FOR THE WELLBEING
OF ALL PEOPLE

INSTINCTUAL
SELF
A PRE-HUMAN
INSTINCTUAL AWARE-
NESS OF LIVING IN
THE PRESENT MOMENT
THAT'S EXPRESSED IN
ANIMALS AND HOMINIDS

ETHNOCENTRIC
SELF
A MORE DEVELOPED
AWARENESS
THAT'S EXPRESSED
AS A CONCERN FOR THE
NEEDS OF ONE'S FAMILY,
TRIBE, OR NATION

EGOCENTRIC
SELF
THE HUMAN AWARENESS
RELATED TO EARLY
EMOTIONAL DEVELOPMENT
THAT'S EXPRESSED
PRIMARILY AS A CONCERN
FOR ONE'S OWN NEEDS

LEAPS OF AWARENESS IN HUMAN EVOLUTION

Embracing a "Big Picture perspective of the world" helps me give deeper meaning to my life.

Science has shown us evolution does not necessarily move forward in a simple linear fashion
But regularly progresses from leaps of sudden development referred to as *emergence*.

These leaps of awareness are times of explosive creativity when something completely new
Unexpectedly appears out of the expansive growth from a prior period.

Yet even though these sudden emergent leaps seem to quickly burst into <u>outer</u> physical form,
They are produced from the slow building of <u>inner</u> awareness developing over time.

This can be visualized as similar to a teapot on a stove gradually building up pressure within
And then (when the pressure has built sufficiently) suddenly sounding its whistle.

Or a balloon that's slowly filled with air until the critical point of breaking is reached
And, thus, the balloon must now explode from the intense internal pressure.

On this planet, there are times of "extraordinary moments" in the unfolding spiral of evolution
When new expressions "explode" into existence, or abruptly emerge as a new creation.

For example, within our own human evolution many thousands of years ago,
There was the explosive leap in conscious awareness and intelligence
That resulted from the profound discovery of **symbolic language**,
And the flourishing that ensued from sharing written forms of information.

Another leap in awareness occurred when novel **philosophical concepts of governance**
And effective ways to live together were seriously debated and practically developed,
Which led to a burst of new experiments in organizing human social structures.

Obviously, the formal birth of **the sciences** allowed for monumental leaps in human unfolding
Bringing forth expanded worldviews and more comfortable lifestyles
Based on a greater understanding of the physical laws of Nature.

Today in our contemporary world, external global challenges and opportunities are heating up
Based on diverse internal pressures that are building within human consciousness,
And it feels like something totally new and innovative wants to burst forth
So it can "whistle a new emergent song of possibility".

As the many fields of science continue to unfold greater knowledge about the nature of reality
And unravel further mysteries of the ever-evolving Universe,
The evolutionary perspective is being utilized by more and more people
As a way to give deeper meaning and value to their lives
As well as to help people understand that we are one global family.

When enough people on Earth embrace *the evolutionary perspective as a scientific fact*
It has the capacity to unleash much higher levels of compassion and global cooperation
While also bringing harmony to the various ideologies and religions of the world,
Which gives us the potential to further the next great leap in human evolution.

Circle of Leaps of Awareness in Human Evolution

THE EVOLUTIONARY PERSPECTIVE
A LEAP IN PEOPLE'S COMPASSION AND GLOBAL COOPERATION RESULTING FROM CULTIVATING MORE ADVANCED PERSPECTIVES OF INCLUSION

SYMBOLIC LANGUAGE
A LEAP IN CONSCIOUS AWARENESS AND INTELLIGENCE THAT RESULTED FROM SHARING WRITTEN FORMS OF INFORMATION

THE SCIENTIFIC METHOD
A LEAP IN EXPANDED WORLDVIEWS AND LIFESTYLES BASED ON UNDERSTANDING THE PHYSICAL LAWS OF NATURE

PHILOSOPHICAL CONCEPTS
A LEAP IN EVOLVING FORMS OF GOVERNANCE AND EFFECTIVE WAYS TO LIVE TOGETHER THAT LED TO MORE DEVELOPED SOCIAL STRUCTURES

TIMELINE OF CONSCIOUSNESS

I trust that everything is unfolding perfectly in Life's perfect timing.

The visually pleasing pattern of the *spiral* is found in many of Nature's exquisite creations
   Such as the coiled shapes that numerous seashells generate on the ocean floor.

Cosmologists have found this rotating pattern in galaxies millions of light years away
   And named them *spiral galaxies* - of which our own Milky Way galaxy is one.

The spiral pattern can also be observed in various plants and flowers, such as the sunflower
   With its radial placement of seeds spinning from its midpoint.

Throughout our bodies, we have spiral patterns in our fingerprints, in the way our hearts pulse,
   And at the core of our double helix DNA.

When we look at the spiral inside of a nautilus shell that's meticulously cut in half,
   We may notice as our eyes travel inward toward its center,
      Each progressive turn of the spiral is a little smaller than its previous one.

If you imagine that the spiral within a nautilus shell was "a road heading towards a destination",
   And you visualize maintaining a constant speed on this "coiling road within the shell",
      If you start on the outside, each turn of your journey would occur faster and faster
         As you continually made your way towards the goal at the shell's center.

The spiral is also an ancient symbol that has been used to represent "the goddess",
   "Nature in continual change", and as an iconic sign for "the vast evolving Universe".

And we can even "observe" the pattern of a spiral in the **Timeline of Consciousness**
   That's seen through the evolving expressions of the Universe over very long periods.

At the start of creation (like the spiraled nautilus) "the turns of the wheel" were much longer,
   But as the Cosmos unfolded, "the turns of the wheel of time" got smaller and smaller.

In relation to our planet, the first biological life forms appeared on Earth **four billion years** ago,
   But it only took **two billion years** for simple sensations of sight and hearing to evolve,
      And then **one billion** more for complex biological impulses to develop.

Thirty thousand years ago, complex human thought produced the first languages,
   Governments formed from rational thought developed **three thousand years** ago,
      And fledgling democracies emerged only **three hundred years** ago.

In today's contemporary world, information is doubling within faster and faster periods of time
   Demonstrating that human consciousness is evolving at **quicker exponential rates**
      Expressing greater creativity and cooperation more rapidly than ever before.

When we marvel at a nautilus shell, or a spiral galaxy, or a sunflower, or a human DNA helix,
   We can use its novel pattern as a reminder that the Universe is perpetually inviting us
      To consciously and compassionately participate in the creation of its unfolding
         By contributing our creative gifts and talents to *Life's* timeless journey.

Circle of a Timeline of Consciousness
(In Relation to Planet Earth and Human Consciousness)

EXPONENTIAL GROWTH
HUMAN CONSCIOUSNESS
IS DEVELOPING
AT EXPONENTIAL RATES
THAT EXPRESS HIGHER
STAGES OF CREATIVITY
AND COOPERATION MORE
RAPIDLY THAN EVER BEFORE

SPHERE OF LIFE
(BIOSPHERE)
+ 4 BILLION YRS AGO
FIRST LIFE FORMS
+ 2 BILLION YRS AGO
SIMPLE SENSATIONS
+ 1 BILLION YRS AGO
COMPLEX BIOLOGICAL
IMPULSES

MODERN BREAKTHROUGHS
+ 200 YEARS AGO
EVOLUTION THEORY
+ 20 YEARS AGO
INFORMATION AGE
+ 2 YEARS AGO
ENDLESS ADVANCES
IN SCIENCE

SPHERE OF MIND
(NOOSPHERE)
+ 30 THOUSAND YRS AGO
LANGUAGE DEVELOPS
+ 3 THOUSAND YRS AGO
GOVERNMENTS DEVELOP
+ 3 HUNDRED YRS AGO
DEMOCRACY DEVELOPS

EVOLUTION OF SOCIAL DEVELOPMENT

The true power of my spiritual awakening is demonstrated in how I serve the wellbeing of others.

If you were to closely examine the many wondrous expressions of life on this planet
    You could observe that life is always in a perpetual process of growth and expansion.

The nature of life is to constantly find creative ways to develop something new and inventive
    Which has never been expressed before, ever exploring new pathways of possibilities.

A countless number of the unique species within Earth's long history
    Have been evolving for millions, or sometimes billions of years
        In order to produce the novel and necessary adaptations to survive and flourish.

But when early humans appeared on the evolutionary scene around two million years ago,
    Their speed of unfolding development began to increase at faster and faster rates.

In the beginning of the human evolutionary journey
    When the trials and challenges of living on a primitive Earth were consistently hostile,
        Humans, like other primates, discovered the benefits of gathering in **small clans**
            Which provided more collective resources for their groups to survive.

Primal humans then explored this stage of existence for over a million years
    Undergoing very gradual and adaptive changes.

Much later it required roughly ten thousand years (based on accepted archeological records)
    From relentless trials of conquest, power struggles, and the beginning *light of reason*,
        For humans to develop **the first centers of civilization**
            In the form of small agricultural villages, kingdoms, and the earliest cities.

Over time, humanity used these city centers to develop **various expressions of culture**
    That grew at a relatively fast tempo, especially in the last seven hundred years,
        From the personal explorations and creative investigations that took place
            Within the expanding fields of science, art, philosophy, and spirituality.

Today at this vital period in our evolution, humanity is on the brink of a new development
    In which it could possibly take less than half a century
        For *the spiritual awakenings* of many individuals to occur,
            And for awakened humans to work together to collectively develop
                The pioneering social structures of *an enlightened society*.

This natural drive to experience *the collective,*
    To yearn for greater and wider circles of cooperation, intimacy, and inclusion
        (Which is embedded in the entire fabric of the evolutionary journey for all of life),
            Expressed itself in humans by developing clans, civilization, and culture.

Yet as we continue to evolve, much of humanity is discovering that *personal enlightenment*
    (Or what has also been called *awakening*) is not primarily for the benefit of the individual,
        But the true power of *spiritual enlightenment* is in working together collectively
            To be of service - and to help consciously create *a more enlightened world*.

Circle of the Evolution of Social Development

ENLIGHTENED SOCIETY
FROM *THE PERSONAL AWAKENINGS* OF MANY PEOPLE THROUGHOUT THE WORLD, HUMANS ARE WORKING TOGETHER TO DEVELOP *A MORE ENLIGHTENED SOCIETY*

CLANS
FROM THE CHALLENGES OF LIVING DURING A PRIMITIVE TIME, EARLY HUMANS GATHERED INTO CLANS PROVIDING MORE RESOURCES TO EFFECTIVELY SURVIVE

CULTURE
HUMANS DEVELOPED CULTURE THROUGH EXPLORATIONS OF THE EXPANDING FIELDS OF SCIENCE, ART, PHILOSOPHY, AND SPIRITUALITY

CIVILIZATION
FROM THE TRIALS OF CONQUEST, POWER STRUGGLES, AND THE BEGINNING OF REASON, HUMANS DEVELOPED THE FIRST CENTERS OF CIVILIZATION

ENLIGHTENED SOCIETY

As I cultivate a more loving awareness, the world around me transforms into a more loving place.

The phrase *"an enlightened society"* can, at times, be a challenging concept to clearly define
　　Because the definition of *an enlightened society* to some people
　　　　Is only the launching pad for other individuals who have an even greater vision,
　　　　　　A more evolved picture of the potential for what human society can be.

All of life is perpetually in a natural process of evolving to the next higher stage of awareness
　　And since most people respond in some way to this innate longing to expand and learn,
　　　　Then *society* is also continuously expanding and seeking its next higher stage.

At this time in human development, there is "a center of gravity in our current social structures"
　　(Which means "the average stage of development within our current human societies")
　　　　That shares a collective vision and heartfelt desire
　　　　　　To build a more sustainable and cooperative world.

This ever-growing collective vision is attempting to picture and embody a possible future world
　　That fulfills the **primary emotional needs for all of its people**.

It is a society that creates more safety for its people, more compassionate care of others,
　　Empowers more individual and collective creative visions of what society can become,
　　　　And consciously nurtures a sense of belonging for all of its citizens.

In order to attain these lofty goals, this future society must be guided, supported, and governed
　　By **the enlightened leadership of awakened individuals**.

These are people who lead the institutions of our world from a place of *awakened awareness*,
　　And from an ongoing conscious alignment with *the Natural Intelligence of Life*.

When a society learns to live in concert with *this sacred connection to Life*,
　　Its mission becomes **consciously contributing to, and compassionately serving,**
　　　　The natural unfolding of growth and evolution for all beings on our planet.

An enlightened society is one that functions with compassion and wisdom,
　　And that uses the interplay of **multiple perspectives to improve the quality of life**.

All life on Earth, from amoebas to humans, have experiences that are both **internally driven**
　　As well as experiences that are **externally expressed**,
　　　　And **an impulse that is individually oriented** as well as **a collective impulse**.

When we learn to be aware of, and utilize within our societies, these multiple perspectives,
　　We can live our life from a place of greater wholeness, both individually and collectively.

As we cultivate these multiple perspectives while aligned with *the Natural Intelligence of Life*,
　　We will be directed to find appropriate solutions to our global challenges more easily.

We are constantly being invited by *Life* to live each day from *a more loving awareness*
　　So we can co-create with others our collective vision of *a more enlightened world*.

Circle of an Enlightened Society

SERVICE
AN ENLIGHTENED
SOCIETY CONSCIOUSLY
CONTRIBUTES TO,
AND SERVES, THE
NATURAL UNFOLDING OF
GROWTH AND EVOLUTION
FOR ALL BEINGS

LEADERSHIP
AN ENLIGHTENED
SOCIETY IS GUIDED,
SUPPORTED,
AND GOVERNED
BY THE ENLIGHTENED
LEADERSHIP
OF AWAKENED PEOPLE

PERSPECTIVES
AN ENLIGHTENED
SOCIETY FUNCTIONS
WITH COMPASSION AND
WISDOM, WHILE USING
MULTIPLE PERSPECTIVES
TO BENEFIT
THE COLLECTIVE GOOD

EMOTIONAL NEEDS
AN ENLIGHTENED SOCIETY
CREATES SAFETY,
COMPASSIONATE CARE,
EMPOWERMENT
OF OTHERS, AND
A SENSE OF BELONGING
FOR ALL OF ITS CITIZENS

XI

ARCHETYPES OF HIGHER KNOWLEDGE

ARCHETYPES OF HIGHER KNOWLEDGE

I activate the unlimited power of my creative imagination to become the person I desire to be.

The numerous evidence-based discoveries of evolutionary science have made clear
That our human species is part of a much larger animal kingdom
Which has been continually evolving on this planet for approximately a billion years.

Humans are a unique branch of a greater sub-group of animals called *mammals*
Which all share much of the same DNA.

In fact, our human DNA is over 98% identical to that of another mammal, the chimpanzee,
With only a small number of genetic variations.

Yet out of these few variations in our genome, we have evolved more highly developed brains
With the capacity to access a fuller spectrum of knowledge
And to use that knowledge to distinctively enhance our survival, think rationally,
Produce symbolic language, learn to laugh, and compose symphonies.

We humans have been on an epic quest searching for <u>truth</u>, <u>beauty</u>, and <u>goodness</u>
That has required eons of "trial and error experiences" to get us where we are today,
And to intellectually explore *the spheres of knowledge*
We refer to as **science**, **art**, **philosophy**, and **spirituality**.

As a species, we are now at an important turning point in our evolution
Where we're entering, and awakening to, *a new sphere of emergent possibility.*

We can each choose to cultivate this new possibility by using specific transformative practices
That employ primary patterns of our greater human potential called *archetypes*,
Which we will define as visionary blueprints or templates of who we can become.

The archetype of **the Awakened Scientist** invites us to dedicate our life as a living experiment
To discover greater awareness of the <u>truth</u> (what is believed to be undeniably true).

The Awakened Artist is an archetype that inspires us to cultivate abundant ways
To enjoy and experience "life as an art and as a creative expression of <u>beauty</u>".

The Awakened Philosopher can help us foster heart wisdom so we may manifest
The most harmonious, <u>good</u>, and meaningful ways to live with others.

The Awakened Mystic can empower us to use the most effective ways
To maintain an alignment with *the Source of Life* in order to truly serve others.

We can utilize these **Archetypes of Higher Knowledge** as a transformative practice
To envision ourselves expressing more of our potential, aligning with our *True Nature,*
And courageously entering a new and more expanded stage of consciousness.

In time - with enough development, we humans have the capacity to undergo *a quantum leap*
As we, ultimately, evolve into a brand new species, altering our basic DNA once again
By realizing who we really are - and that we are one with every expression of life.

Circle of the Archetypes of Higher Knowledge

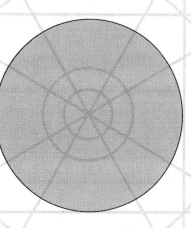

AWAKENED
MYSTIC
IT IS THE PART OF ME
THAT USES EFFECTIVE
WAYS TO MAINTAIN
AN ALIGNMENT WITH
THE SOURCE OF LIFE
SO I CAN TRULY BE
OF SERVICE TO OTHERS

AWAKENED
SCIENTIST
IT IS THE PART OF ME
THAT DEDICATES MY LIFE
AS A LIVING EXPERIMENT
SO I MAY GAIN GREATER
AWARENESS OF THE
TRUTH (WHAT IS BELIEVED
TO BE UNDENIABLY TRUE)

AWAKENED
PHILOSOPHER
IT IS THE PART OF ME
THAT FOSTERS HEART
WISDOM SO I MAY
ESTABLISH THE MOST
HARMONIOUS, *GOOD*,
AND MEANINGFUL WAYS
TO LIVE WITH OTHERS

AWAKENED
ARTIST
IT IS THE PART OF ME
THAT CULTIVATES
ABUNDANT WAYS TO
ENJOY AND EXPERIENCE
**"LIFE AS AN ART
- AND AS A CREATIVE
EXPRESSION OF *BEAUTY"***

AWAKENED PHILOSOPHER

I continually support the most moral and ethical ways to live harmoniously with others.

At the dawn of humanity's evolutionary journey
    When our ancestors lived at a primal level of mental ability,
        Primitive human thought was almost solely employed
            To sustain the everyday survival and ongoing lineage
                Of one's immediate family or local clan.

Much later on, the first clans that grasped a visionary notion to develop agriculture
    Discovered the advantages of living together with other clans and forming small villages,
        Which created greater possibilities for their survival - and for acquiring food.

Yet in order to effectively live together in this manner and for their villages to thrive,
    This new change required that the people begin to cultivate **concepts of morality**
        And more developed social structures that fostered ways to relate to one another
            Which had never been attempted before.

Then as the human species continued to evolve, further ideas of expanded social order
    (That were combined with an intrinsic drive for personal power and control over others)
        Gradually blended these small villages into kingdoms,
            Which required the cultivation of **larger perspectives of morality**
                Yielding new and better ideas of how to cooperatively live together.

Eventually, certain vanguard thinkers envisioned other stages of human expansion
    Such as strong military leaders that formed regional kingdoms into nation states
        As well as a new innovative concept of democratic rule by and for the people
            Requiring **more harmonious systems of lifestyle and governance**.

At this present time, contemporary philosophers are attempting to articulate
    The next higher level of purpose, meaning, and all that is *good* in life
        As humanity slowly takes another step in developing its social structures
            By exploring the possibility of, one day, joining our separate nation states
                Into a *unified world federation* for the benefit of every global citizen.

If we humans are to accomplish this vision, each of us must learn to change the way we live
    By personally transforming ourselves beyond our self-centered habitual desires
        (Which have imprisoned us in unconscious and dysfunctional behaviors)
            And be directed into this meaningful endeavor
                Through a sustaining alignment with *the Infinite Intelligence of All That Is.*

When we're aligned with *the Source of Life* and connected to a stream of higher knowledge,
    We will be guided to establish the best moral and ethical ways to conduct ourselves
        And create optimal systems of living harmoniously with one another
            As well as with our environment.

These concepts are a vital facet of the visionary archetype called **the Awakened Philosopher**
    And its exalted attributes live within us as *creative possibilities of who we can become*
        Eagerly waiting to be *awakened* from "a long and turbulent sleep".

Circle of the Awakened Philosopher
(An Archetype of Higher Knowledge)

GOODNESS
I CHOOSE TO
EXPRESS IN MY LIFE
MY HIGHEST PURPOSE,
MEANING, MISSION,
AND ALL THAT
IS *GOOD* IN LIFE

HARMONY
I CHOOSE TO
ENGAGE IN THE MOST
HARMONIOUS
AND ENLIGHTENED
FORMS OF LIFESTYLE
AND GOVERNANCE

INCLUSION
I CHOOSE TO
EXPAND
MY AWARENESS
SO I MAY CULTIVATE
MORE INCLUSIVE
PERSPECTIVES OF LIFE

HIGH MORALITY
I CHOOSE TO
LIVE MY LIFE
IN THE MOST MORAL
AND ETHICAL WAYS
SO AS TO COOPERATE AND
CO-CREATE WITH OTHERS

EVOLUTION OF THE MEANING OF LIFE

The meaning of my life in this moment comes from whatever meaning I currently choose to give it.

As far as we know, humans are the only creatures on Earth
    That have an inherent need to seek for *meaning.*

Meaning arises from a person who has become self-reflective and self-examining,
    And attempts to find value in, interpret, or make sense of life
        Concerning his or her relationship with one's environment - or with the entire Universe.

The physical development of the human brain and its vast mental and emotional capacities
    Has provided humanity *the ability to question,* which in turn has generated a basic need
        To find value regarding one's personal experiences of life.

Meaning is something we give to ourselves that's an interpretation of our primary values,
    And that emerges from our current level of psychological and emotional development.

As humans have evolved over time, **the meaning that was given to life evolved as well**,
    So this statement reminds us - "there is no one absolute meaning of life for everyone".

The interpretation of the meaning of life can be quite different for a given group of people
    Depending on their particular stage of consciousness - or level of development.

For early humans, the meaning of life was simply to **survive**, to feel safe, to be protected,
    And arose from their primary <u>physical</u> needs to propagate the species.

Over time as humans developed further, meaning began to be derived from experiences
    Which were based on their new evolving levels of limited <u>emotional</u> awareness.

Meaning of life for them was to be powerful, to control, to defend their views, to gain pleasure,
    And these impulses generated a long period of forming *an individuated egoic self*
        In which one focused on the acquisition of various **personal desires**.

As evolution progressed, meaning was given to life based on the development of the <u>mind</u>,
    And was expressed as a psychological need and quest for **individual creativity**.

Today, humanity is sensing an innate longing to blossom into *a new stage of awakened living*
    Where the meaning of life is based on conscious and compassionate awareness,
        And is outwardly expressed as **serving the wellbeing of others**.

For at this stage, the spiritual focus of one's life is to discover ways
    To consciously support the progression of the evolution of all life.

Sometimes from "out-of-the-blue", *the mystery of grace* gifts us with a sublime epiphany,
    An extraordinary moment of Perfect Unity in which we're aware of our Oneness with life.

During these profound moments of *grace*, there appears to be "no meaning of life at all",
    For within the actual experience of Oneness, the need for meaning simply vanishes -
        Like an early misty fog disappears in the soft morning wind.

Circle of the Evolution of the Meaning of Life
(Possible Stages of Meaning)

SERVICE
IN A MORE AWAKENED STAGE, THE MEANING OF LIFE IS BASED ON ONE'S COMPASSIONATE AWARENESS
+ VALUE COMES FROM OFFERING SERVICE TO OTHERS

SURVIVAL
IN THE EARLY STAGES OF LIFE, THE MEANING OF LIFE IS BASED ON ONE'S PRIMARY PHYSICAL NEEDS TO SURVIVE AND BE SAFE
+ VALUE COMES FROM SURVIVAL

CREATIVITY
IN A FURTHER STAGE, THE MEANING OF LIFE IS BASED ON ONE'S CREATIVE DEVELOPMENT OF THE MIND
+ VALUE COMES FROM INDIVIDUAL CREATIVITY

PERSONAL DESIRES
IN FOLLOWING STAGES, THE MEANING OF LIFE IS BASED ON ONE'S LIMITED EMOTIONAL AWARENESS
+ VALUE COMES FROM ACQUIRING SELF-ORIENTED DESIRES

HIGH MORALITY

Today I align my awareness with the Source of Life in order to make the highest moral choices.

During the last three thousand years of exploring diverse pursuits of philosophical thought
Various forward-thinking individuals have been searching for, and debating,
The most effective ways to live harmoniously with others,
As well as the best ethical forms of human conduct.

This existential search for *the right versus wrong way* (the accepted standards of conduct)
For people to most skillfully live together has been guided by the quality of *morality*.

Throughout human history, the definition of morality has slowly expanded
In a manner that's similar to the visual image of *a set of concentric circles*,
Such as the concentric circles of the planetary orbits within our Solar System.

Concentric circles are a series of different circles which all have a common midpoint,
And each circle is larger as you gain more distance from the center.

In relationship to this *model of morality*, the innermost and smallest circle at the very core
Represents an individual's self-oriented concerns for their own personal wellbeing.

Continuing with this image of concentric circles, the next outward - or slightly larger circle -
Symbolizes a person's noble concern for the wellbeing of *one's family or clan*.

And thus, each progressive circle as you move farther away from the center
Embraces and includes the wellbeing of more and more people,
Such as *the next larger circle which represents a village or local community*,
Then *the circle of the state, the circle of the nation*,
And finally the largest, *the circle that signifies the entire world*.

High morality is a phrase that refers to the outermost circle in this model,
Which embraces the compassionate concern for all people in every nation of the world.

It is choosing to take responsible action that creates **safety and protection for all creatures
And all ecosystems of the planet.**

High morality can be thought of as consciously choosing to take action
That fosters **unconditional care and compassion for all beings**,
And that **empowers people** by helping them reach their creative potential.

It's also consciously choosing to take action based on **an alignment with *the Source of Life***
And from the inner guidance we receive based on this alignment
In order to most effectively contribute to, and serve,
The wellbeing and natural progression of all life on Earth.

Our *journey of awakening* is a creative ever-unfolding process
Of learning how "to dance in bigger and bigger circles",
Always trying to hear, and be in harmony with, "the Music of the largest circle",
At least the largest circle of morality we're currently aware of.

Circle of High Morality

ALIGNMENT
HIGH MORALITY –
MY CONSCIOUS CHOICE
TO TAKE ACTION BASED
ON MY ALIGNMENT WITH
THE SOURCE OF LIFE THAT
SUPPORTS THE WELLBING
OF ALL LIFE ON EARTH

SAFETY
HIGH MORALITY –
MY CONSCIOUS CHOICE
TO TAKE ACTION THAT
HELPS CREATE SAFETY
AND PROTECTION
FOR ALL CREATURES
AND ECOSYSTEMS

EMPOWERMENT
HIGH MORALITY –
MY CONSCIOUS CHOICE
TO TAKE ACTION
THAT EMPOWERS
PEOPLE SO THEY MAY
DEVELOP THEIR
CREATIVE POTENTIAL

LOVE
HIGH MORALITY –
MY CONSCIOUS CHOICE
TO TAKE ACTION
THAT FOSTERS
UNCONDITIONAL CARE
AND COMPASSION
FOR ALL BEINGS

EVOLUTION OF GOVERNANCE

Today I help create a more enlightened world by consciously transforming my own inner being.

Modern science has shown us that everything within the four corners of the Universe,
Each individual facet of creation, from the very smallest to the most massive
(Which includes our human development), is constantly evolving.

Some developmental aspects of evolution take millions, or even billions of years to unfold,
While others seem to change within our lifetime.

One of the most evident developmental changes we can witness from human history
Is the constant **evolution of our systems of government**.

Recorded history has enabled us to observe that governance has been gradually evolving,
From primitive structures of authority to ever-more advanced systems,
For more than five thousand years.

Historians describe how these systems have slowly transformed over long periods of time,
From the first types of **governance based simply on a group's strongest warriors**
Who controlled others with mere physical power and might,
To **governance in the form of kingdoms, dynasties, and monarchies**.

Some monarchial kingdoms were based on royal authoritative rulers who dominated others
With might linked to *Divine Power* - in other words, to their belief in *an all-powerful god*.

Then, over time, this structure eventually gave way to a more innovative breakthrough
Which emerged as a **new paradigm of democratic governance**
Based on a rational system of checks and balances
Monitored by the will and vote of the people.

The actual outer expression of governance (like all evolving cultural aspects of human society)
Is a direct reflection and out-picturing of the people's internal collective consciousness,
And is an external mirror of their current stage of human development.

If we desire to create *a more enlightened society* for our future,
Then we must have more *awakened people* working together within our society today.

From comprehensively examining the unfolding of current global events and trends,
Humanity seems to be slowly headed toward an **integral form of world governance**
Based on an inclusive global institution and international agreements
That collectively support multi-culturalism and national identity.

If we want to help co-create *a more awakened world*,
Then we can participate in its creation by becoming more consciously awake ourselves.

Could it be that in order to truly develop awakened governance,
We must each responsibly look into "the mirror of our own awareness"
So we can support, and contribute to, the creation of a more cooperative world
By courageously making transformative changes within ourselves?

Circle of the Evolution of Governance

GLOBAL FORUM
GOVERNANCE BASED ON
A GLOBAL INSTITUTION
AND INTERNATIONAL
AGREEMENTS THAT
COLLECTIVELY SUPPORT
MULTI-CULTURALISM
(INTEGRAL STAGE)

WARRIOR POWER
GOVERNANCE BASED ON
THE STRONGEST
WARRIORS - THOSE WHO
CONTROL OTHERS
WITH PHYSICAL POWER
AND MIGHT
(ARCHAIC STAGE)

DEMOCRACIES
GOVERNANCE BASED ON
A DEMOCRATIC SYSTEM
OF CHECKS
AND BALANCES THAT'S
MONITORED BY THE WILL
AND VOTE OF THE PEOPLE
(RATIONAL STAGE)

MONARCHIES
GOVERNANCE BASED ON
KINGDOMS, DYNASTIES,
AND MONARCHIES
THAT DOMINATE OTHERS
WITH MIGHT LINKED
TO *DIVINE POWER*
(MYTHIC STAGE)

XII

MIND AWARENESS PRACTICES

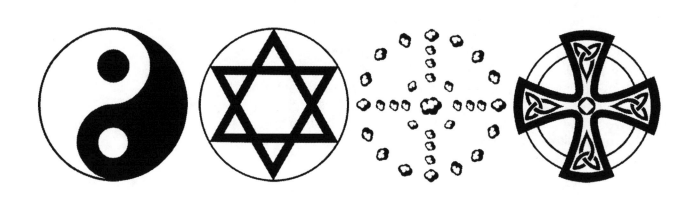

CREATIVE POWER IN RELATION TO TIME

The thoughts I consciously choose to hold in my mind have creative power to shape my future.

In India, there's a longstanding spiritual proverb that states,
"If you want to know what your thoughts were in the <u>past</u>,
Take a look at your <u>present</u> reality,
And if you want to know what your <u>future</u> will be like,
Take a look at the thoughts you are thinking <u>today</u>".

The thoughts we hold within our mind each day are full of creative possibility
And can be used to focus a natural **creative power that shapes our future reality**.

This intrinsic creative potential is available to be accessed in the present moment,
For *the eternal now* is all that's real
And is the only moment in which *true creative power* exists.

In relation to the concept of linear time, **our past thoughts are simply memories,**
And their potent creative power has been utilized to shape our present reality.

Our so-called "past moments" used this same dynamic power of creative thought
To help bring into form, the current manifestations that have appeared in our life today.

When we intend to clearly communicate the subject of "time" to another person,
We typically use the words "past" and "future" in our language to convey to them
Certain linear aspects of our "present" understanding of time.

For example, **to shape our future, we must choose our thoughts in the present moment**
That will support and empower the heartfelt intentions we hold right now.

For whatever we choose to think in this moment has the innate *creative power*
To manifest our desires in "the present moments of our tomorrows".

If we desire beautiful flowers to bloom in our gardens,
Then we will need to plant the appropriate seeds that will manifest our intended vision,
As well as be aware not to allow weeds to overtake the garden.

When we notice that "weeds of the mind" are beginning to sprout,
We must, with awareness, immediately "clear our garden of them"
So they cannot overwhelm or dominate "our future harvest".

Today let us practice being ever more aware of "the kind of seeds"
Which we are planting each moment in "the garden of our mind".

Let us be mindful "to nurture our garden" with the creative thoughts of focused intention
And consciously pluck out "the weeds of loveless thinking" we do not want.

We are living in **a garden sanctuary of infinite possibilities**
Where "the ground of limitless *Creative Power*" (the Power of Love)
Is constantly eager to receive the fertile seeds of our most heartfelt desires.

Circle of Creative Power In Relation to Time
(A Transformative Practice)

ETERNITY
I MAINTAIN
AN ALIGNMENT WITH
*THE INFINITE PRESENCE
OF LOVE*, FOR ALL TRUE
CREATIVE POWER
IS ESSENTIALLY
*THE LIMITLESS
POWER OF LOVE*

PAST
I AM AWARE THAT
MY PAST THOUGHTS
ARE SIMPLY MEMORIES,
AND I RECOGNIZE THEIR
CREATIVE POWER
HAS ALREADY BEEN
UTILIZED TO SHAPE
MY PRESENT REALITY

FUTURE
I AM AWARE
THAT THE THOUGHTS
I CONSCIOUSLY CHOOSE
TO HOLD IN MY MIND
TODAY HAVE POTENT
CREATIVE POWER
TO SHAPE
MY FUTURE

PRESENT
I AM AWARE OF
THE CREATIVE POTENTIAL
OF MY THOUGHTS,
FOR THE *ETERNAL PRESENT*
IS THE ONLY MOMENT
IN WHICH TRUE
CREATIVE POWER
EXISTS

BEING PRESENT

I recognize that the unlimited creative power of Life is always available in the present moment.

The power of conscious co-creation that's perpetually available to each of us
Cannot be fully accessed from our fear-based ego (our self-oriented nature)
But can always be accessed from an authentic experience of our *True Nature*,
The Limitless Essence within us which is eternal and unbounded.

Every time we expand our awareness - or open our heart,
We are given another opportunity to learn about living our life from this abiding *presence*
And embodying the unlimited creative power that exists in each moment.

Whenever we are blessed with a direct spiritual experience of our *True Eternal Nature*,
It aids us in developing greater awareness of *the eternal present*.

There are countless individuals who have discovered how to *consciously co-create*,
Who have learned to be *the hands and hearts that help shape a better world*,
And who naturally live in *the present* while sustaining an alignment with *Life*.

So in order to align our awareness with *the Source of All That Is*
And learn to abide more deeply in *the eternal present*,
We must be willing to let go of resentments of the past and fears of the future.

As a transformative exercise, practice **being aware and discerning** throughout the day
Of the quality and content of your thoughts so you may let go of any loveless thinking
And consciously choose your most benevolent life-affirming beliefs.

Mindfulness experienced in *the present moment* allows you to focus thought like a laser beam
Without the distractions of judgments and comparisons that would disperse its radiance.

Also practice being aware of the various **emotions** that constantly arise during the day
So you may completely feel each emotion without judgment or resistance,
For fully experiencing your emotions enables you to empower your intentions
With the fuel of *radiant joy* that's always available in *the present moment*.

And occasionally, practice being aware of your body as it moves through space
Becoming aware of the diverse bodily sensations you feel within your environment.

The conscious awareness of your body helps you experience *a deeper sense of gratitude*
As a pulsating *sensation of aliveness* that radiates in every cell of your physical body.

And as a final point, practice being aware of your **breath** and the natural flow of your breathing
Which immediately makes you mindful of, and aligns you with, *the present moment*,
For the breath can "open the door to inspired possibilities"
By bringing you to the *present* where all true creativity resides.

Being present can be thought of as our experience of "abiding at the center of the Cosmos"
And aligning with *the Source of Life* so completely that when we are truly *present*,
We, so to speak, become *the loving hands and hearts of the entire Universe*.

Circle of Being Present
(Transformative Practices)

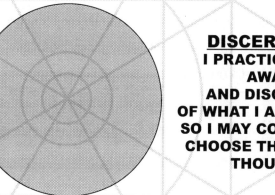

BREATH
I PRACTICE BEING
AWARE OF THE FLOW
WITHIN MY BREATH
WHICH IMMEDIATELY
MAKES ME MINDFUL OF,
AND ALIGNS ME WITH,
THE PRESENT MOMENT

BODY AWARENESS
I PRACTICE BEING
AWARE OF MY BODY
AS IT MOVES
THROUGH SPACE
WHILE MINDFUL OF ALL
THE DIVERSE BODILY
SENSATIONS I FEEL

DISCERNMENT
I PRACTICE BEING
AWARE
AND DISCERNING
OF WHAT I AM THINKING
SO I MAY CONSCIOUSLY
CHOOSE THE HIGHEST
THOUGHTS

EMOTIONS
I PRACTICE BEING
AWARE OF THE MANY
EMOTIONS THAT
CONSTANTLY ARISE
DURING THE DAY
WHILE EXPERIENCING THEM
WITHOUT JUDGMENT

FEELING GOOD

I feel good about my life - because I consciously choose to feel good.

For many people who live in our western culture, there is a common belief
    That a person's internal experience of *being happy*, or of *feeling good*,
        Is externally generated from the various outside influences of one's life.

Some beliefs about *feeling good* are based on the kind of material possessions one acquires,
    Or "the lucky breaks" in one's life that happen - or don't happen,
        Or the particular way in which someone was raised when they were children,
            Or the positive or negative environment they happen to live in,
                Or can even be thought to be dependent on one's biological genes.

All of these externally oriented forces can definitely influence our life to some extent,
    Yet, ultimately, **feeling good comes from the type of thoughts we choose**,
        And our thoughts can be consciously cultivated through daily mindful practice.

We can use the Contemplative Circle of Foundational Transformative Practices (see July 6th)
    To create greater awareness of how to increase this feeling in specific areas of our life
        By frequently practicing these four primary transformative exercises,
            Which are prayer, appreciation, contemplation and meditation.

One way to intentionally enhance our internal experience of *feeling good*
    Is **by praying for - and being in service to - the wellbeing of others**.

When we contribute to the lives of others through our prayers and compassionate service,
    Life Force energy circulates more freely throughout our body, heart, and mind,
        Which amplifies a benevolent feeling of wellbeing within us.

We can experiment in our life to see if this is true by being mindful throughout the day
    Regarding ways that we serve another's needs and notice how we feel from our actions.

We can also expand our experience of *feeling good*
    By consciously deepening our appreciation for everything going on in our life,
        As well as appreciating ourselves for who we are.

When we're focused on being grateful - or acknowledging and honoring someone,
    Our entire being is nourished with increased energy and vitality.

We can *feel good* **by contemplating and expressing the many ways of being creative,**
    For example - through music, dance, art, or journal writing,
        Or by playing fun games, which can help us rejuvenate our heart and mind.

And we can *feel good* **by simply experiencing moments of sacred silence**,
    Such as by being alone in the majesty of Nature, or through the practice of **meditation**.

The key to consciously manifesting our desires is empowering them with our heartfelt feelings,
    And if we're using "a good map of the territory", then it's always our personal choice
        To decide which road we choose to travel to get us to where we truly want to go.

Circle of Feeling Good
(In Relation to Foundational Transformative Practices)

MEDITATION
TODAY I FEEL GOOD
AS I EXPERIENCE
SUBLIME MOMENTS
OF SACRED SILENCE
+ PERIODS OF QUIET
+ NATURE TIME
+ SITTING MEDITATION

PRAYER
TODAY I FEEL GOOD
AS I PRAY FOR
AND SERVE THE
WELLBEING OF OTHERS
+ GENEROSITY
+ COMPASSION
+ CARE

CONTEMPLATION
TODAY I FEEL GOOD
AS I CONTEMPLATE
LIFE AND EXPRESS
MY CREATIVITY
+ CREATIVE ARTS
+ JOURNAL WRITING
+ GAMES OF FUN

APPRECIATION
TODAY I FEEL GOOD
AS I DEEPEN
MY APPRECIATION FOR
THE BLESSINGS IN MY LIFE
+ GRATITUDE
+ ACKNOWLEDGEMENT
+ HONORING

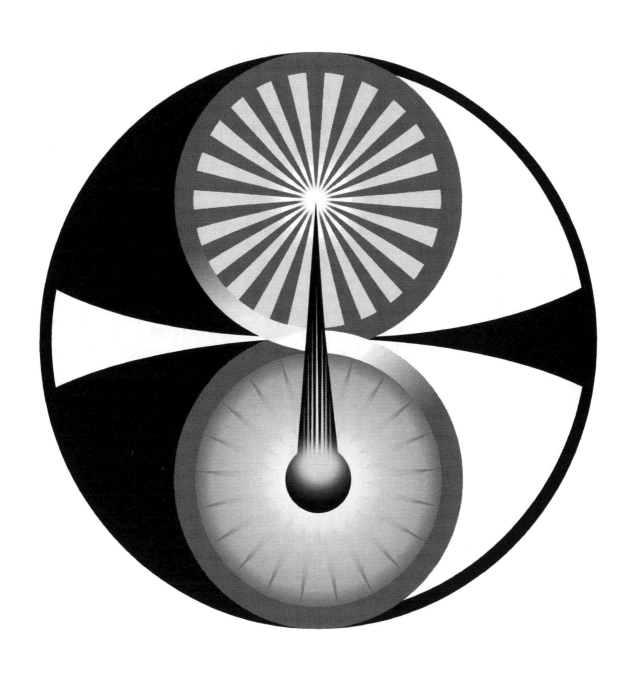

XIII

ARCHETYPES
OF SPIRITUAL
AWAKENING

ARCHETYPES OF SPIRITUAL AWAKENING

My life is a journey of discovery - a spiritual journey - a journey of awakening.

If you are driving a car on a long road in order to get somewhere you want to go,
　　It usually will be of benefit to read the numerous signposts you find along the way.

On most cross-country roads, there are specific signposts that tell us where we currently are
　　And others that point us in the direction of where we intend to go.

These signposts were strategically placed next to the road
　　By the people who have already traveled the path
　　　　So it would be easier for others to more effectively find their way to their destination.

Having signposts along the highway doesn't make the distance we need to travel any shorter,
　　But it does assist us in keeping ourselves on track - and may help us from getting lost.

Signposts can benefit the traveler by creating greater awareness of the territory
　　And greater awareness usually allows the overall journey to flow more effortlessly.

The contemplative circle on the following page portrays a series of "symbolic signposts"
　　On a road of spiritual discovery we're all destined to travel - *the journey of awakening.*

The signposts listed in this circle can serve us by creating heightened awareness
　　Of both where we currently stand on our journey, as well as where we are headed.

Each of **the Archetypes of Spiritual Awakening** is "a signpost of awareness", so to speak,
　　Along our ever-unfolding path of personal transformation.

The Young Awakening Self is an archetype referring to a point along our *journey of discovery*
　　In which we are primarily focused on our emotional survival and self-oriented needs.

"Further down life's highway" we, over time, cultivate and embody **the Compassionate Heart,**
　　An awareness of being grateful for what we're learning from every experience of our life,
　　　　Feeling an authentic compassion for others, and serving the good of all people.

Infinite Presence is a phrase that refers to *the Source of Life, "The One",*
　　The Infinite Intelligence of the Universe, and is also our *Eternal Nature.*

"The last signpost" points us to the **Master of Freedom** (one who lives a life of inner freedom
　　By serving the wellbeing of others and loving all of life unconditionally),
　　　　Which is the sublime merging of our Compassionate Heart with *Infinite Presence.*

These archetypal signposts can help us cultivate greater awareness of "where we're headed",
　　Yet as we embrace that life is full of paradox - and as our spiritual awareness expands,
　　　　We realize that we're already free, for we travel "a journey without distance".

As the transcendent desire to reach an absolute state of personal *enlightenment* fades away,
　　In its place emerges "an inner knowing" that *true enlightenment* is about serving others
　　　　By consciously contributing to, and joyously serving, *the sacred journey of life.*

Circle of Archetypes of Spiritual Awakening
(My Spiritual Journey of Personal Transformation)

**MASTER
OF FREEDOM**
MY AWARENESS AS I LIVE
AN AWAKENED LIFE
OF INNER FREEDOM - AND
LOVE UNCONDITIONALLY
+ MY COMPASSIONATE
HEART FULLY MERGED
WITH *INFINITE PRESENCE*

**YOUNG
AWAKENING SELF**
THIS IS MY LEVEL
OF AWARENESS WHEN
I AM SELF-CENTERED,
FOCUSED ON APPROVAL,
ATTACHMENT, CONTROL,
SELF-POWER, OR FEAR,
YET YEARN TO AWAKEN

*INFINITE
PRESENCE*
*"THE ONE", THE SOURCE
OF LIFE, UNIVERSAL
CONSCIOUSNESS, GOD,
INFINITE INTELLIGENCE,
LIMITLESS LOVE, THE
TRANSCENDENT SELF,
MY ETERNAL NATURE*

**COMPASSIONATE
HEART**
MY LEVEL OF AWARENESS
AS I CONSCIOUSLY LIVE
A WORLD-CENTERED LIFE
THAT IS COMPASSIONATE,
CARING, GRATEFUL
FOR LIFE, AND IN SERVICE
TO THE GOOD OF ALL

INFINITE PRESENCE

The Transcendent Self - my True Nature, which is eternal and unbounded, is who I really am.

Today within many of the mystical traditions of the world
  The devoted students of these spiritual disciplines are taught how to realize
    A direct experience of *the Transcendent Self.*

The material world we perceive with our five senses is in constant change and renewal,
  And, each day, we continually encounter a host of mutable forms that come and go.

The outer physical world we experience every moment "appears" to be solid and stable,
  Yet beyond our perception of reality, quantum physics has revealed that our world
    Is a perpetual flow of changing energy forms in a limitless field of infinite space.

Yet there have always been mystics throughout the world who've searched within themselves
  For *the Transcendent Essence of Life* which does not change,
    In other words - for that which is eternal, unbounded, infinite, and timeless.

These pioneering mystics have constantly sought for **the Source of Life, "The One",**
  Or what is also called *God, Universal Consciousness, the Unbounded Ocean of Being.*

This universal animating presence of **Limitless Love** within all of life is our *True Nature,*
  The Sublime Essence of who we really are.

As a metaphor, each of us is like an individual billowy cloud gently floating in the sky above,
  In which our **physical reality** is represented by "a passing cloud" in constant change
    And our **Eternal Reality** is symbolized by *the vast blue sky* that never changes.

Furthermore, we can be likened to an oak tree growing in a forest
  In which the part of us that is our **relative nature** is portrayed by "the maturing tree"
    Which changes and develops with each passing season,
      And the part of us that is our **Absolute Nature** is depicted by *the ground*
        Which can be thought of as ever present and unchanging.

So in order to bring clarity and understanding to the natural unfolding of our *spiritual journey,*
  We can think of this *Ground of Being* as **Infinite Presence, the Infinite Presence of Love**
    (**The Infinite Intelligence of the Universe** that transcends our personal mind).

We are like the passing images of a movie film that is projected on a blank screen
  In which our *Compassionate Heart* is "the moving images", ever shifting and changing,
    And **Infinite Presence** is *the eternal screen*, which always remains unchanged.

As we continue to expand our awareness through our many life experiences,
  We ultimately at one point along our ever-unfolding journey, become *modern mystics,*
    In other words - we learn to be modern spiritual explorers who yearn to discover
      The Eternal Changeless Essence of who we really are.

Life is constantly inviting us, day by day, to consciously embrace our *journey of discovery,*
  To recognize *the Screen*, to awake to *the Ground*, and to soar through *the Endless Sky.*

Circle of _Infinite Presence_
(The Transcendent Self - My True Eternal Nature)

"THE ONE"
"THE ONE" SOURCE
OF ALL THAT IS
+ + +
UNIVERSAL
CONSCIOUSNESS

TRUE ETERNAL
SELF
THE UNBOUNDED
OCEAN OF BEING
+ + +
THE TRANSCENDENT
SELF

THE SOURCE
OF LIFE
THE CREATIVE IMPULSE
WITHIN THE WORLD
+ + +
INFINITE
INTELLIGENCE

LIMITLESS LOVE
THE ANIMATING
PRESENCE WITHIN LIFE
+ + +
THE PRESENCE
OF PERFECT LOVE

MANY NAMES FOR *THE SOURCE OF ALL THAT IS*

I am one with the Source of All That Is - from which everything in the world has been created.

Everything we see - and touch - and sense - in the phenomenal world of Nature
  Has a source where it originates, a location where it begins, a place where it is birthed.

Many majestic rivers with their unbridled currents that snake across the Earth
  Have their source in the alpine glaciers of tall mountains.

The refreshing spatter of falling rain has its origin
  In the vaporous clouds that hang high in the sky.

A towering oak tree experiences its humble beginnings
  Within a tiny seed burrowed in moist fertile soil.

And of course, our own physical bodies were birthed into the world
  From the nurturing wombs of our mothers.

All of the above, as well as everything else in the Cosmos, emerged from an *Ultimate Source*,
  Which, through the ages, has been referred to as *Ultimate Reality*, or more simply, God,
    But is actually something that's completely and unfathomably "indefinable".

For this *Ultimate Source* is *the Origin of Everything*,
  Yet, simultaneously, it is *No-thing*.

It is *the Initial Cause of All That Changes*,
  Yet, simultaneously, it is *Formless and Unchanging*.

It is *the Fount of All Knowledge*,
  Yet, simultaneously, it is *The Great Mystery*.

Life seems to have planted into the heart of every one of us
  An innate yearning that urges us to dive into the core of this paradox,
    To courageously investigate this mystery,
      To leap off the precipice of certainty and fall into the vast unknown,
        Where we, through *grace*, may directly experience this *Source*.

This paradox proclaims that **the Source of All That Is** is the invisible **Transcendent Realm**
  From which all realms of the visible phenomenal world have been created,
    It is the timeless dimensionless **Unified Field**
      From which all sub-atomic particles have emerged,
        And it is the **Infinite Intelligence** of the Universe
          From which each form in the Cosmos has been manifested.

The Source of All That Is can also be thought of as **the Eternal Womb of Limitless Love**
  From which you and I, and every facet of creation has been birthed.

Yet to truly know this mystery, it must be directly experienced at the core of our being
  For all words and names can merely point us in the direction of its sublime majesty.

<u>Circle of Many Names for *the Source* of All That Is</u>
(Various Ways to Describe *Ultimate Reality*, or God)

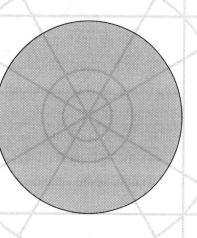

THE TRANSCENDENT
THE SOURCE
OF ALL THAT IS –
THE INVISIBLE
TRANSCENDENT REALM
FROM WHICH ALL REALMS
OF THE VISIBLE PHENOMENAL
WORLD ARE CREATED

LIMITLESS LOVE
THE SOURCE
OF ALL THAT IS –
THE ETERNAL WOMB
OF LIMITLESS LOVE
FROM WHICH EVERY
FACET OF CREATION
HAS BEEN BIRTHED

THE UNIFIED FIELD
THE SOURCE
OF ALL THAT IS –
THE TIMELESS
DIMENSIONLESS
UNIFIED FIELD FROM
WHICH ALL SUB-ATOMIC
PARTICLES EMERGE

INFINITE
INTELLIGENCE
THE SOURCE
OF ALL THAT IS –
THE INFINITE INTELLIGENCE
FROM WHICH EACH NOVEL
FORM IN THE UNIVERSE
HAS BEEN MANIFESTED

QUALITIES OF GOD

Today I am aligned with the Source of Life - and thus, I humbly embody the qualities of God.

The sacred scriptures of the Bible, the Torah, and the Koran
    Each state poetically that we humans have been made
        "In the image and likeness of God, of Yahweh, and of Allah", respectively.

And yet with the limited mental capacities of our current human brain,
    "God" is a concept that's truly incomprehensible from a purely rational perspective.

Still we continue our valiant attempts to understand the infinite vastness of *the divine mystery*
    As religious intellectuals constantly debate and strive to articulately describe
        Four fundamental **qualities of God:**
            Omnipresence, **omnipotence**, **omniscience**, and **Oneness**.

A contemporary way to understand that God expresses the quality of **omnipresence**,
    Or *that which is everywhere present*, is that God can be seen as *the Essence of <u>Divine Love</u>*
        (Also referred to as *the Impulse of Infinite Creativity,* or *the Evolutionary Impulse*)
        Which is present within, and constantly animating, everything in the Universe.

Omnipotence, or *that which is all-powerful*, is the quality of God that can be expressed
    As *limitless <u>Divine Power</u> (the Supreme Source of Life)*,
        Which is *the Sublime Creativity* that brings every facet of the Cosmos into form.

A modern evolutionary interpretation of **omniscience**, or *that which is all-knowing*,
    Is that God is *Infinite Intelligence (Universal Mind, the <u>Divine Light</u> existing in all things)*
        Creating order, novelty, diversity, and directing life toward greater cooperation
            Within all manifested forms of the natural world.

Oneness, of course, is the divine quality stating that "God *is* all" (that everything *is* God)
    And which can also be expressed as *the Totality and Perfect Unity of All That Is*.

The world's mystical traditions teach us to seek, and then become one with, *the Transcendent*,
    In other words - to have a direct personal experience of God, *the Source of everything*.

As we attune ourselves with these divine qualities of God within the sanctuary of inner silence,
    We align with **the Evolutionary Impulse** that's present everywhere
        And is constantly inviting us to manifest new horizons of possibility,
            We merge with **the Unlimited Creative Power** that fashions all of life
            And is always supporting us to express our full potential,
                We listen to **the Infinite Intelligence** that's continually guiding us,
                And we humbly surrender everything in our lives to **"The One"**.

The more we're aligned each day with *the Source of Life (the Divine Transcendent),*
    The more we begin to "vibrate", so to speak, with the same essential sacred qualities
        Which, for thousands of years, the world's religions have described as "God".

Many of the world's scriptures say we are made "in the image and likeness of God",
    So could it be that every person on our tiny planet is actually "a God-in-training"?

Circle of the Qualities of God

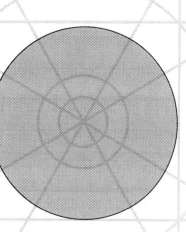

ONENESS
(ALL IS ONE)
THE QUALITY OF GOD EXPRESSED AS
ONENESS
- THE TOTALITY
AND
PERFECT UNITY
OF ALL THAT IS

OMNIPOTENCE
(ALL-POWERFUL)
THE QUALITY OF GOD EXPRESSED AS
UNLIMITED CREATIVE POWER
THAT INTELLIGENTLY BRINGS EVERYTHING INTO FORM

OMNISCIENCE
(ALL-KNOWING)
THE QUALITY OF GOD EXPRESSED AS
INFINITE INTELLIGENCE
THAT CREATES GREATER ORDER, DIVERSITY, AND COOPERATION WITHIN ALL MANIFESTED FORMS

OMNIPRESENCE
(EVERYWHERE PRESENT)
THE QUALITY OF GOD EXPRESSED AS
THE EVOLUTIONARY IMPULSE
- THE IMPULSE OF *SUBLIME CREATIVITY* **THAT'S PRESENT EVERYWHERE**

MAY 31
THE EVOLUTION OF GOD

As I cultivate my awareness and spiritually evolve, my understanding of God evolves as well.

For over 5,000 years of human history, the notion of "God" has been an adaptive concept
That has changed and modified as cognitive development evolved over time.

As human consciousness gradually progressed through numerous stages of awareness
And as humans began to experience various forms of "worldly authority figures",
The perception of "a Supreme Divine Authority" also changed and modified,
For as humanity evolves over time, so does its understanding of God.

This expanded understanding is like climbing a ladder representing the development of a child,
For during a child's life, his or her awareness matures through ascending stages of growth.

When children are growing up, they perceive the world with "magical eyes" - for example,
They look up at the sky and are mesmerized by the "magic" of sunsets and rainbows,
Yet are also terrified by "the invisible forces" behind violent storms and thunder.

As they acquire more life experience, children learn how storms and rainbows actually work,
Which transforms their previous magical thoughts into basic scientific understanding.

Later on, they learn about the social needs and benefits of becoming part of a community
And how to abide by the laws and agreements of a higher designated authority.

With time and maturity, they also learn how to follow the guidance within their own hearts,
How to live in harmony with others, and how to contribute to their society.

We humans experience similar stages of growth with **the evolution of our concept of God**,
For when humanity was young and in its primal stages of development,
It conjured up "a magical relationship" regarding its understanding of God.

Out of the worry of God's retribution, early humans paid homage to a fearful, wrathful God
With the hope that their **God would "magically" provide them divine protection**
Which could help them survive the perils of the world and continue their lineage.

As humans evolved - and as some began to live in large kingdoms with powerful ruler kings,
They let go of earlier "magical images" and replaced them with **a lawmaker God**.

Humans then tried to uphold what they believed were "the divine laws of a Supreme Being"
So they could live with their image of "God the King" in an eternal heaven after death.

Today as this image changes, many perceive **God as *an Infinite Creative Intelligence***
And are learning to live their lives in accordance with natural evolutionary principles
Which has the promise of creating a world of greater harmony and cooperation.

No one knows how this continuous "evolution of God" is going to be articulated in the future,
But from viewing the past, we can project that our concept of the divine is like an arrow
Which is constantly heading for "a cosmic target", where **Oneness of *All That Is***
(The realization that "everything is one expression of Unity") is "the bull's eye".

Circle of the Evolution of God

GOD AS ABSOLUTE ONENESS
AS HUMANS CONTINUE TO EVOLVE, IT IS ULTIMATELY REALIZED THAT EVERYTHING WITHIN CREATION IS "ONE INTERWOVEN EXPRESSION OF UNITY"

GOD AS PROTECTOR
EARLY HUMANS PAID HOMAGE TO "A MAGICAL GOD" OUT OF FEAR OF PHYSICAL DEATH AND HOPE OF DIVINE PROTECTION TO HELP THEM SURVIVE

GOD AS INFINITE INTELLIGENCE
HUMANS LEARN TO LIVE IN ACCORD WITH "NATURAL EVOLUTIONARY PRINCIPLES", SO AS TO CREATE A WORLD OF GREATER HARMONY

GOD AS LAWMAKER
LATER ON, HUMANS TRIED TO UPHOLD "THE LAWS OF GOD", SO AS TO GAIN THE REWARD OF BEING WITH GOD IN AN ETERNAL HEAVEN DURING THE AFTERLIFE

XIV

MIND AWARENESS PRACTICES

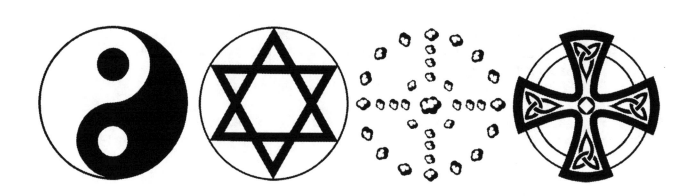

AFFIRMATIONS FOR CREATING TRANSFORMATION

I am aware of my constant flow of blessings and grace.

In general terms, *the mission of one's life* can be defined as "to create, to express one's talents,
To contribute to the natural progression of evolving life by offering one's creative gifts".

Fulfilling this mission usually requires personal growth and attaining greater conscious awareness
And many progressive thinkers have identified this growth process as *transformation*.

Our "spiritual toolkit" (in other words - developmental tools available to help us grow spiritually)
Has many diverse practices we can use for cultivating transformation.

For example, certain *affirmations* are transformative tools we can use as daily exercises
To remind us of ways to stay mindful regarding our life's mission.

The following page has a series of *four affirmations* we can declare (either silently or out loud)
That can help us maintain this form of mindfulness.

The first affirmation - *"I am aligned with the Source of Life
And aware of my constant flow of blessings and grace",*
Invokes both *a field of grace* and the awakening quality of **Oneness**
Which helps us remember to align our awareness with *Life*
And be mindful of the many gifts that appear each day.

The second - *"I cultivate spiritual freedom every time I fully feel and embrace my emotions",*
Invokes *a field of freedom* as well as the awakening quality of **acceptance**,
Proclaiming there's an inner freedom we experience
When we're able to allow our emotions to simply pass through us
Without attachment or judgment.

The next - *"I live in the present moment and let go of any attachments to my desires",*
Invokes *a field of presence* and the quality of **surrender**,
And reminds us that *the aliveness of life* and our ability to live authentically
Is deeply felt and embodied by living in the eternal now
Fully embracing our experiences of life just as they are.

The last affirmation invokes both *a field of awareness* and the quality of **gratitude**,
And is - *"I am grateful for the conscious awareness to courageously question my beliefs".*

Beliefs can be empowering or extremely constrictive - depending on our current awareness,
And our beliefs are constantly in a process of changing and refining over time.

Actually, the first statement is all we really need because when we're truly aligned with *Life*,
We are directed to live in a way that's full of freedom, presence, and awareness,
And yet the other three affirmations can help us maintain the balance required
To sustain an ongoing connection with *the Infinite Presence of Love*.

Affirmations for cultivating personal transformation are like "interim training wheels for awakening"
Until we learn "to ride *The Great Wheel of Life*" with the grace of loving unconditionally.

Circle of Affirmations for Creating Transformation
(A Transformative Practice)

GRACE
I AM ALIGNED WITH
THE SOURCE OF LIFE
AND AWARE
OF MY CONSTANT FLOW
OF BLESSINGS AND GRACE
(ONENESS)

AWARENESS
I AM GRATEFUL
FOR THE CONSCIOUS
AWARENESS
TO COURAGEOUSLY
QUESTION MY BELIEFS
(GRATITUDE)

FREEDOM
I CULTIVATE
SPIRITUAL FREEDOM
EVERY TIME I FULLY
FEEL AND EMBRACE
MY EMOTIONS
(ACCEPTANCE)

PRESENCE
I LIVE IN
THE PRESENT MOMENT
AND LET GO
OF ANY ATTACHMENTS
TO MY DESIRES
(SURRENDER)

QUESTIONS SEEKING OPPORTUNITIES

Accepting what is enables me to receive the blessings and gifts that come from my challenges.

Imagine you are traveling down a highway through a beautiful rural countryside
    Where you notice there are occasional side roads that turn off to the left or right
        Leading to unknown places you have never explored.

Since you've never driven down any of these side roads - and if you are without a map,
    Then you don't know where these roads will take you - or what adventures might unfold.

At times, our life may feel that we're *traveling a road heading towards an intended destination*
    And then we come upon what seems to be "a giant boulder in the center of the road",
        Some shocking crisis or surprising challenge that doesn't allow us
            To continue going down the same life path we originally planned to take.

In order to continue our "journey to our destination", we must decide to take another road,
    One of the side roads that branch off from the main highway.

This unexplored path has new and distinct opportunities the previous road did not have,
    But if we're *in shock from the crisis* (which can sometimes close down our heart),
        We may not be able to see these new opportunities clearly.

So for us to notice the opportunities along this different path,
    We must find ways to open our eyes and heart to the fresh potential that's there for us.

Should we be "traveling down a highway" in which crisis or chaos strikes from "out-of-the-blue",
    We can more easily maintain our alignment with *Life* by using a transformative practice
        That takes the form of asking ourselves the following questions.

What blessings or gifts might come from this challenge?

Ripe fruit may be hanging from the trees alongside the road we travel,
    But if our awareness is shut down to seeing it, the fruit will pass by unnoticed.

What could I learn about myself or about life from this experience?

The journey of life involves a continual process of consciously learning and developing,
    And we will benefit from being mindful to learn from every experience we encounter.

Is there some good that could now happen which would not have happened before?

"The many side roads of life" are full of rich adventures and possibilities,
    But we must choose to remain open and receptive so we can truly let them in.

What new opportunities might unfold from this difficult situation?

The evolution of the Earth, which includes all humans, is in a process of constant development
    Based on adapting to crisis and chaos so as to find better ways to survive and thrive,
        For *Life* always invites us "to travel new highways that lead to greater horizons".

Circle of Questions Seeking Opportunities
(A Transformative Practice – "When challenges arise, ask …")

BLESSINGS
+ + +
WHAT BLESSINGS
OR GIFTS
MIGHT COME
FROM THIS
CHALLENGE?

OPPORTUNITY
+ + +
WHAT NEW
OPPORTUNITIES
MIGHT UNFOLD
FROM THIS DIFFICULT
SITUATION?

LEARNING
+ + +
WHAT COULD
I LEARN
ABOUT MYSELF
OR ABOUT LIFE FROM
THIS EXPERIENCE?

GOOD
+ + +
IS THERE SOME
GOOD THAT COULD
NOW HAPPEN WHICH
WOULD NOT HAVE
HAPPENED BEFORE?

DIVINE PARADOX PRAYER

I embrace life's existential paradoxes, which open my heart to the gifts of spiritual freedom.

A tall thick forest on a moonless night can be so black, you cannot even see your own hands
Until you decide to turn on a flashlight which fills your surroundings with luminance.

Walking into a windowless garage late at night usually provides zero visibility,
Until you flip the power switch which illuminates the electric light on the ceiling.

A meditation room at midnight can be completely void of any light,
Until a candle is lit which sparkles the room with radiance.

Using these three examples, in one moment *darkness* is all that exists within the space
And then the simple action of bringing *light* into the area
Creates a new reality in which *darkness* is no longer present.

The experiences of life show us both *light* and *darkness* exist in our everyday world of duality,
Yet the fact is we can only encounter one or the other, at any particular moment in time.

Many of the mystical traditions from around the world attempt to teach us
That **our *True Nature* (our *Eternal Self*) is formless *Non-Existence*,**
And yet, simultaneously, we exist in a unique form as our body and mind
(In other words - we are both eternal and human at the same time).

Other eastern religious sects use different phrases and state the same thing in this way:
Our *True Nature* is *Pure Emptiness*,
(Referring to *the Mind of God*, *the Infinite Presence of Love*, *the Ocean of Being*),
And yet, simultaneously, we are expressions of *the Fullness of Life*.

These are two statements of a transformative practice called **the Divine Paradox Prayer**
Which can inwardly point us to the realization
That two contradictory yet complimentary facets of our life exist at the same time.

There are generally three basic levels, or modes of prayer:
1) *Petitioning prayer* used by one who makes personal requests of *the Divine*,
2) *Affirmative-creation prayer* used by one who is a co-creator with *the Divine*,
Who affirms one's vision of life while acting as if it has already happened,
3) *Acknowledgement prayer* used by one who consciously knows the highest truth.

To shift our identity from who we think we are as a separate body to our *True Eternal Nature*,
We can *acknowledge a higher truth* using the prayer statements on the following page.

Similar to shining a flashlight, which brings luminance to a dark forest at midnight,
These prayer statements help us perceive and accept our heart's deeper knowing
That the life we live is essentially full of spiritual paradox and divine mystery.

And so in order to further develop into our next stage of awakened awareness
As we reach toward greater horizons of our ever-unfolding *spiritual journey*,
It appears we must learn to embrace more and more of life's many paradoxes.

Circle of the Divine Paradox Prayer
(A Transformative Practice)

I AM GRATEFUL
TO BE AWARE THAT
MY *TRUE NATURE* IS
*THE UNBOUNDED
OCEAN OF BEING,*
AND YET
SIMULTANEOUSLY,
I AM AN INDIVIDUAL
WAVE IN *THE OCEAN*

I AM GRATEFUL
TO BE AWARE THAT
MY *TRUE NATURE* IS
FORMLESS
NON-EXISTENCE,
AND YET
SIMULTANEOUSLY,
I EXIST AS A
UNIQUE HUMAN FORM

I AM GRATEFUL
TO BE AWARE THAT
MY *TRUE NATURE* IS
ABSOLUTE ONENESS,
"THE ONE",
AND YET
SIMULTANEOUSLY,
I AM A NOVEL FACET
OF *"THE MANY"*

I AM GRATEFUL
TO BE AWARE THAT
MY *TRUE NATURE* IS
PURE EMPTINESS,
AND YET
SIMULTANEOUSLY,
I AM AN EXPRESSION
OF *THE FULLNESS
OF LIFE*

XV

NAVIGATING THE JOURNEY OF *THE GREAT CIRCLE*

PARADOX

Opening my heart to life's existential paradoxes helps me to realize my True Eternal Nature.

Since, in general, the human mind is naturally attracted to explore the many mysteries of life
And to constantly delve into the conundrums of the nature of existence,
Humanity is perpetually coming face to face with the concept of *paradox*.

**Paradox is the perception that two discrete realities which contradict each other
Both exist at the same time**.

It is **the notion that two expressions of reality which are complete polar opposites
Can both mysteriously take place at once.**

As physicists began to experiment with *light*, they discovered it had a paradoxical quality
Since *light* exhibits properties of both a <u>particle</u> and a <u>wave</u> at the same time.

Whether a photon of *light* expresses itself as a *particle* or a *wave* in any distinct moment
Depends on the observer of the *light* - and the process of observation.

Through one process of observation, *light* will express the solidity and physicality of a <u>particle</u>,
Yet through another process, it will take on the non-physical characteristics
Of a *field of energy*, or <u>*a wave of potential*</u>.

Scientists have learned that in order to embrace the contradictory properties of *light*
(And many other quantum properties within our Universe), they must live with *paradox*
And with the understanding that **two diametrically opposed concepts of reality
Can both exist in the same moment**.

Albert Einstein, in his explorations of *relativity (a theory of the structure of space-time)*,
Discovered that *the dimension of time* has paradoxical qualities as well.

Normally, our perception of time is such that time is always evenly measured,
For it appears to exist in a linear manner that's static, predictable, and unchanging,
But Einstein proved that as an object accelerates to extremely fast speeds
And approaches *the speed of light*, time slows down.

If you were to travel on some future spaceship at a velocity that approached *the speed of light*,
As you cruised to another part of our galaxy - and then came back to Earth again,
The actual passage of time would be quite different for you
In relation to the time of the people you know who remained on Earth.

For example, when you returned to our planet, "hundreds of earth years" would have elapsed
And all your friends would have passed away, while only a few years elapsed for you
Because of the *paradox* regarding *"your* relative time" versus *"their* relative time".

As we continue to explore the mysteries of consciousness regarding what our life is truly about,
We seem to look straight into the eyes of the more perplexing *existential paradoxes*
Which invite us to embrace a knowing that **two different realms of our life,
"The physical"** and *"our Eternal Self",* **both occur simultaneously.**

Circle of Paradox

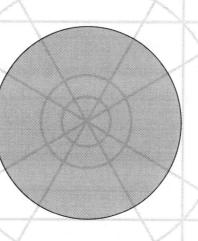

DIAMETRICALLY
OPPOSED
PARADOX –
THE UNDERSTANDING
THAT TWO DIAMETRICALLY
OPPOSED CONCEPTS
OF REALITY BOTH EXIST
IN THE SAME MOMENT

CONTRADICTION
PARADOX –
THE PERCEPTION
THAT TWO DISCRETE
REALITIES WHICH
CONTRADICT EACH
OTHER BOTH EXIST
AT THE SAME TIME

POLAR OPPOSITES
PARADOX –
THE NOTION THAT
TWO EXPRESSIONS
OF EXISTENCE WHICH
ARE COMPLETE POLAR
OPPOSITES BOTH
TAKE PLACE AT ONCE

DIFFERENT REALMS
PARADOX –
EMBRACING
THE KNOWING THAT TWO
ENTIRELY DIFFERENT
REALMS OF EXISTENCE
BOTH OCCUR
SIMULTANEOUSLY

EXISTENTIAL PARADOXES

My life is unfolding perfectly just as it is - yet I am here to help the world become more perfect.

Every person who has devoted time to deeply examine the philosophical side of life
  Has, most likely, come face to face with some of life's **existential paradoxes**.

These paradoxes, in which two completely opposing realities both exist at the same time,
  Stimulate investigations into "the Big Questions" regarding what our life is truly about.

For centuries, philosophers and clergy have explored "the eternity versus time paradox",
  Which states that from a <u>transcendent</u> perspective, **there is an eternal facet of life**,
    Yet from the perspective of the <u>material</u> world which we experience each day,
      All forms of life live in a physical body that one day will end in time.

Many traditional religions around the world have created myths
  Which attempt to give meaning and substance to this paradox,
    Yet as humanity continues to evolve,
      The meaning it gives to this mystery of life also evolves.

During the cultural expansion of the European Renaissance hundreds of years ago,
  Science emerged as the study of laws regarding how the physical world actually works.

Then with the advent of quantum physics and "the mystifying discovery" of *The Unified Field*
  (The Field from which all of creation emerges), a profound paradox was revealed.

Based on quantum mechanics, this paradox states - **all of creation is one *Unity (Oneness),***
  And yet simultaneously, the world is full of countless individual expressions of reality,
    Which you and I are obviously aware of,
      For everyday **we experience life in a body of many diverse polarities**.

Also, *evolutionary spirituality* has revealed to us that from a <u>transcendent</u> perspective *(Being)*,
  Our life is unfolding perfectly just as it is, but from a <u>material</u> perspective *(Becoming)*,
    All of life is evolving - and everything is here to help the world become more perfect.

Most people, on one occasion or another, have taken a moment in their lives
  To contemplate the paradoxical idea that relates to whether or not we have a *Soul*.

There is a paradox stating that our *Eternal and Limitless Nature*
  (In other words - **Pure Consciousness** or *Source)* is the cause of our life experience,
    Yet also states that our body, heart, and mind are the phenomenal expressions
      Which are embodied in the world (**creation**) by our *Consciousness*.

As we contemplate these **existential paradoxes**,
  They can, sometimes, shake us to our core with confusion.

Yet if we can intuit the true nature of reality by humbly opening our heart to these possibilities,
  Then these paradoxes will naturally help us embrace the supreme perfection of life
    So we may ultimately discover how to integrate *the two different sides of the coin*,
      In other words - learn to live a life of inner freedom and love unconditionally.

Circle of Existential Paradoxes
(In Relation to the Transcendent and Material Realms of Life)

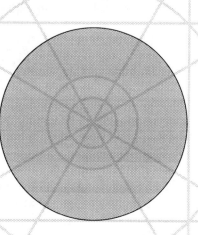

BEING /
BECOMING
TRANSCENDENT:
MY LIFE IS UNFOLDING
PERFECTLY JUST AS IT IS
+SIMULTANEOUSLY+
MATERIAL:
ALL OF LIFE IS EVOLVING
TO HELP THE WORLD
BECOME MORE PERFECT

ETERNITY /
TIME
TRANSCENDENT:
LIFE IS ETERNAL
+SIMULTANEOUSLY+
MATERIAL:
ALL FORMS OF LIFE
LIVE IN A PHYSICAL
BODY THAT ONE DAY
WILL END IN TIME

ONENESS /
DUALITY
TRANSCENDENT:
ALL OF CREATION
IS ONE UNITY
+SIMULTANEOUSLY+
MATERIAL:
LIFE IS EXPERIENCE
IN A BODY OF MANY
DIVERSE POLARITIES

PURE CONSCIOUSNESS /
CREATION
TRANSCENDENT:
PURE CONSCIOUSNESS (OR
THE SOURCE) IS THE CAUSE
OF ALL LIFE EXPERIENCE
+SIMULTANEOUSLY+
MATERIAL:
MATERIAL EXPRESSION IS
CONSCIOUSNESS IN FORM

ILLUSIONS OF THE MIND

Today I consciously focus my mind on what really matters - and let go of any loveless thoughts.

Professional magicians who perform on theatrical stages for large audiences
Call their mesmerizing magic tricks "illusions".

They are referred to as "illusions" because, for a brief moment, they seem to trick our minds
Into somehow believing that we're experiencing a spellbinding event
When, actually, something altogether different is taking place.

Numerous spiritual traditions, especially some of the Eastern religions, believe in the idea
That the material world which constantly changes is an "illusion", what they call "maya",
And that God, *the Transcendent,* is the only *True Reality* which is eternal and unchanging.

We humans, throughout the long evolutionary progression of our egoic development,
Have unconsciously convinced ourselves to view the world in certain illusory ways
Which are "tricks of the mind", because at another more expanded level of reality
Beyond what we now perceive, something quite different is taking place.

Many have called the world an "illusion", yet surely there are specific **illusions of the mind**
Which humanity has been "tricked into believing" for thousand of years
That erringly express the habitual ways we identify who we think we are.

One illusion is that **we believe we are our individual thoughts, emotions, and sensations**
Rather than experiencing our *True Nature* as an endless *River of Awareness*
Within *an Infinite Field of Oneness*.

There is a scientific set of fact-based revelations regarding quantum physics that has shown us
Everything within reality emerges out of a timeless dimensionless *Unified Field,*
Which is one unbounded *Universal Field* of pure energy.

Yet still, **most of us believe we are separate and distinct from the rest of creation,**
When according to quantum physics, at the most fundamental level of existence
"We *are* the Universe" - and we are intimately one with every facet of it.

We have also come to habitually believe that we are merely isolated physical bodies
Rather than our *True Eternal Self* which through a co-creation with *the Source of Life*
Brought these particular bodies into manifested form to learn and serve.

Plus, there is a common illusion that deals with our sense of self-worth,
In which **we sometimes believe we are inadequate and must prove our worthiness**
Rather than recognizing we are, and have always been,
The magnificence of a *Universal and Limitless Love*.

It's as if *the collective consciousness of humanity* is under the magic spell of a grand magician
In which all of life is an immense stage, and you and I have been part of the audience
Watching and "caught up in" the magician's riveting performance,
Temporarily mesmerized and believing in all of "the unreal illusions"
Which our minds, at our current awareness, have been tricked into.

Circle of Illusions of the Mind

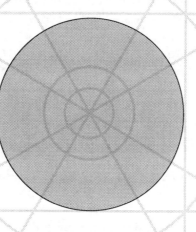

I AM MY BODY
THERE IS AN ILLUSION
IN WHICH I BELIEVE I AM
MY THOUGHTS, EMOTIONS,
AND BODILY SENSATIONS
RATHER THAN
EXPERIENCING MY *TRUE
NATURE* AS AN ENDLESS
RIVER OF AWARENESS
IN *A FIELD OF ONENESS*

I AM ISOLATED
THERE IS AN ILLUSION
IN WHICH I BELIEVE I AM
MERELY AN ISOLATED
BODY RATHER THAN MY
ETERNAL SELF WHICH,
THRU A CO-CREATION
WITH *THE SOURCE OF
LIFE,* BROUGHT MY BODY
INTO MANIFESTED FORM

I AM SEPARATE
THERE IS AN ILLUSION
IN WHICH I BELIEVE
I AM SEPARATE FROM
THE REST OF
CREATION RATHER
THAN REALIZING
"I *AM* THE UNIVERSE"
AND THAT I'M ONE WITH
EVERY FACET OF IT

I AM NOT ENOUGH
THERE IS AN ILLUSION
IN WHICH I BELIEVE I AM
A PERSON THAT'S INADE-
QUATE WHO MUST PROVE
MY WORTHINESS RATHER
THAN RECOGNIZING I AM,
AND HAVE ALWAYS BEEN,
THE MAGNIFICENCE
OF *LIMITLESS LOVE*

TRUTH

My beliefs are thoughts I currently hold to be true - yet what I believe is constantly changing.

When you listen to a symphony orchestra perform, you can hear many types of instruments
From a varied assortment of low-pitched instruments, such as basses and bassoons,
To a variety of mid-spectrum instruments, such as oboes and violas,
And at the high aural range, ones like piccolos and xylophones.

If you examined the various spans of musical notes for every instrument of the orchestra
Using a visual chart of all orchestral instruments found in a music theory textbook,
You would notice each individual instrument has a specific range of pitched tones
Which either is positioned within the lower frequencies of the orchestra
Or fits near the high frequencies, or is somewhere in between.

Hypothetically, if the only instruments you knew of were ones with low frequencies,
Then the choice of an instrument to play would be limited to just a few bass instruments,
But as you learned about additional instruments that produced higher tones,
You could then choose to play one of these higher-pitched instruments
(Since your awareness of possible choices would have expanded).

As a simple metaphor, the concept of *truth* is similar because **truth is the particular way
We understand a certain aspect of the nature of reality in any given moment**.

It's as if we're always discovering a range of higher sounding instruments (higher awareness)
That we can now choose to play within "the symphony of life",
For as our understanding of life evolves, our idea of what is true evolves as well.

Truth is the collection of thoughts we currently hold and believe are true,
And yet our *truth* constantly changes over time as we constantly expand our awareness.

Long ago people believed the Earth was flat and, during that era, this belief was common *truth*,
Until eventually it was proven the Earth is a round spherical planet
And then, after a period of time, this new revelation became common *truth*.

Over many centuries, **our interpretation of the diverse facts** of science enabled our *truth*
To change numerous times, such as from believing the Sun revolved around the Earth
To believing the Sun was the center of our Universe,
To then believing the Milky Way galaxy was the entirety of the Cosmos,
And now believing the Universe consists of billions of galaxies.

Today there are some progressive cosmologists that even believe our known Universe
Is possibly one of a billion, or maybe an infinite number, of universes in existence.

Therefore, we can see that **truth is a specific concept or idea we hold within our mind
Which, at any moment in time, we determine is real for us**.

The more we expand our comprehension of the nature of reality and widen our current perspectives,
The more we can use our "higher instruments of understanding"
To compose our ideas of what we, at least in this moment, believe to be true.

Circle of Truth
(From a Relative Point of View)

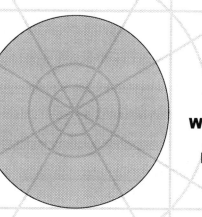

BELIEF
TRUTH –
A COLLECTION OF
THOUGHTS I CURRENTLY
BELIEVE ARE TRUE,
WHICH CAN CHANGE
OVER TIME AS I EXPAND
MY AWARENESS

UNDERSTANDING
TRUTH –
THE PARTICULAR WAY
I UNDERSTAND
A CERTAIN ASPECT
OF THE NATURE
OF REALITY
IN ANY GIVEN MOMENT

CONCEPT
TRUTH –
A SPECIFIC CONCEPT
OR IDEA I HOLD
WITHIN MY MIND WHICH,
AT THIS MOMENT
IN TIME, I DETERMINE
IS REAL FOR ME

INTERPRETATION
TRUTH –
MY UNIQUE PERSONAL
INTERPRETATION
OF THE DIVERSE FACTS
THAT I EXPERIENCE
AT THIS PRESENT
MOMENT OF MY LIFE

THE GREAT CIRCLE OF CONSCIOUSNESS AND CREATIVITY

Everything that I perceive in the world of form is created in "the womb of consciousness".

Because the instinctual movement of the breath within our bodies
    Is one of the most natural and primary impulses we experience,
        Nearly all people go about living their day-to-day lives
            Without consciously thinking that they are always breathing.

Without our need to think about it, *the Natural Intelligence of Life* is constantly directing us
    To take an <u>inhalation</u> of air, and then instinctively follow it with an <u>exhalation</u>.

Using certain spiritual practices from various religious traditions,
    The breath is internally visualized as a circle, or as an invisible wheel within one's body,
        In which the *in-breath* moves up the back of the spine
          And the *out-breath* moves down the front of the torso.

One of the fundamental dynamics of *The Great Wheel of Life*, **The Great Circle**,
    Is life's <u>inward</u> yearning to move toward greater awareness and expanded growth,
        And to constantly further its development and evolution.

There is also a fundamental <u>outward</u> drive within every phenomenal structure in the Universe
    Which is to be creative, express more diversity, contribute to its environment,
        And transform into a greater version of itself.

Physical reality is constantly evolving and changing,
    And when we look at life through the wide lens of our current scientific knowledge,
        We can observe continual development taking place all around us
            From molecules to muscle groups, from ants to the tallest trees,
                And from the tiniest flowers to human beings.

The Great Circle, which visually illustrates the never-ending unfolding
    Of the universal impulses of *evolving consciousness* and *evolving creativity*,
        Symbolically depicts these two primary dynamics of our life
          As two perpetual movements of evolution around *an eternal wheel*.

Evolving consciousness is our inward expansive impulse that can always be felt within us
    And which constantly longs for us to learn and develop, reach for what really matters,
        Move beyond limitation, and expand our awareness of **"The One"** *Source of Life*.

Evolving creativity is our outward expressive impulse that continually creates,
    In other words - it's **"The Many"** manifested forms and contributions we create each day
        Which are mirrored and expressed in our world based on our inner development.

Just like our breath must first take a new inhalation of air
    Before another exhalation can occur,
        So too does our <u>inner expansion</u> and development
            First internally expand toward greater possibilities of what we can become
                So we can then manifest our new awareness of what is true
                    As the <u>outer expressions</u> of our personal creativity.

The Great Circle of Consciousness and Creativity

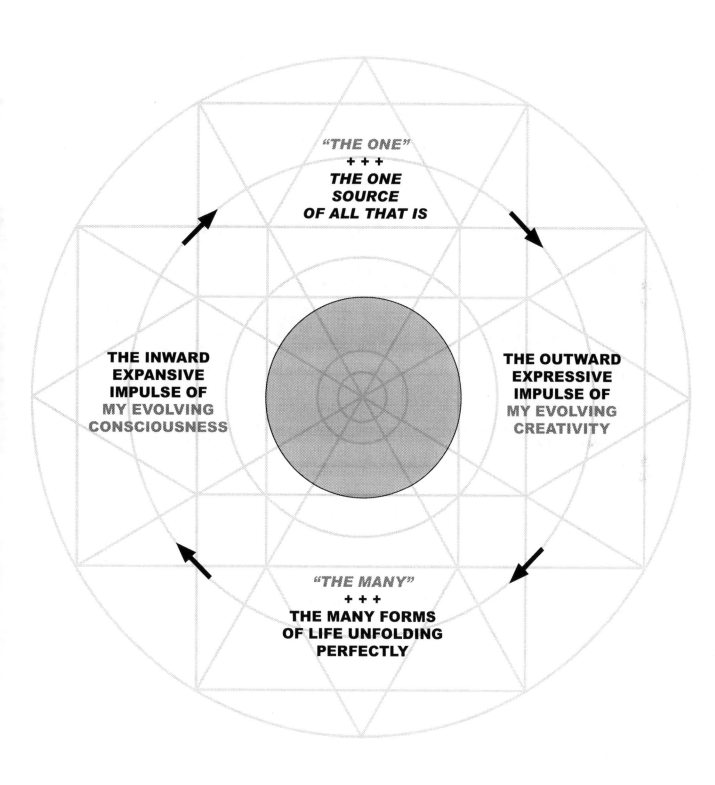

"THE ONE"
+ + +
THE ONE
SOURCE
OF ALL THAT IS

THE INWARD
EXPANSIVE
IMPULSE OF
MY EVOLVING
CONSCIOUSNESS

THE OUTWARD
EXPRESSIVE
IMPULSE OF
MY EVOLVING
CREATIVITY

"THE MANY"
+ + +
THE MANY FORMS
OF LIFE UNFOLDING
PERFECTLY

EXTERIOR EVOLUTIONARY IMPULSE

My external reality is a mirror, an out-picturing, of my consciousness and internal awareness.

If you were to examine the universal dynamics of life from a transcendent perspective,
　　In other words - from the limitless vantage of the infinite realm of *Unity Consciousness*
　　　　(Or what scientists have referred to as *The Unified Field),*
　　　　　　From this absolute reality, there is no principle of *cause and effect*
　　　　　　Because in this infinite unbounded realm, there is only Oneness.

Yet from a material perspective, viewing our world of time, space, and opposing polar forces
　　Where we experience a host of seemingly solid physical objects with our five senses,
　　　　We live in a dualistic three-dimensional reality where both *cause and effect* exist.

From basic physics class, one learns when an initiating force *(cause)* is applied to an object,
　　A corresponding force *(effect)* always takes place in response to the initial force.

From chemistry class, one discovers that when a new element *(cause)* is added to a molecule,
　　A brand new molecule *(effect)* is formed with different characteristics and properties.

In the 13.8 billion year progression of forming the evolving Universe, **cause** is consciousness
　　And its corresponding external creative expression is the **effect** which follows.

Creation *(effect)* is the outer physical structures and forms of the material Universe
　　Which directly mirror the expansion of an inner evolving consciousness **(cause)**.

For us humans, *cause* is our ever-expanding consciousness - and its *effect* is manifestation,
　　In other words - its *effect* is the external **expression** that's manifested into form
　　　　Which mirrors our current level of internal awareness of what we believe is true.

Regarding humanity's spiritual evolution which is potential within all people,
　　Cause is the consciousness of one's personal inner development and growth,
　　　　And its natural created *effect* is one's **outer transformation and healing**.

In regards to *spontaneous healing*, the miraculous *effect* of this type of healing
　　Is the seemingly instant result of a long cumulative period of inner development *(cause)*
　　　　That manifests itself as a sudden emergent shift in one's wellbeing and balance.

At this present time within the ever-expanding spiral of evolution on Earth,
　　Humanity is undergoing a kind of "birthing process", a collective spiritual awakening,
　　　　A turning point or emergence into an entirely new level of consciousness,
　　　　　　A monumental leap into a higher stage of human awareness.

Today, for many conscious people who are intentionally cultivating their inner development,
　　Cause is one's spiritual awakening and its direct *effect* is **conscious contribution**,
　　　　For contribution and compassionate service to others
　　　　　　Are the most natural expressions of a fully awakened individual.

This impulse of consciousness or *cause* can also be called *the Interior Evolutionary Impulse,*
　　And its creative *effect* can been described as ***the Exterior Evolutionary Impulse***.

Circle of *the Exterior Evolutionary Impulse*
(My Evolving Creativity)

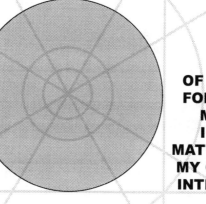

CREATION
THE IMPULSE
OF CREATION THAT FORMS
THE OUTER MATERIAL
STRUCTURES OF THE
NATURAL WORLD AS IT
MIRRORS THE EXPANSION
OF AN INNER EVOLVING
CONSCIOUSNESS

CONTRIBUTION
THE CREATIVE IMPULSE
THAT FORMS THE GIFTS,
CONTRIBUTIONS,
OR SERVICE GIVEN
TO OTHERS AS
A NATURAL EXPRESSION
OF A CONSCIOUSLY
AWAKE INDIVIDUAL

EXPRESSION
THE IMPULSE
OF EXPRESSION THAT
FORMS MY EXTERNAL
MANIFESTATIONS
IN THE REALM OF
MATTER OUT-PICTURING
MY CURRENT LEVEL OF
INTERNAL AWARENESS

**TRANSFORMATION
AND HEALING**
THE IMPULSE OF
TRANSFORMATION THAT
FORMS MY RESULTANT
WELLNESS OR HEALING
WHICH MANIFESTS IN MY
BODY-MIND MIRRORING
MY INNER DEVELOPMENT

VARIOUS MEANS OF MANIFESTATION

I use the creative power of intention to manifest the desires that I am guided by Life to achieve.

If you want to acquire a new wooden chair for your home, there are a number of creative ways
It can be manifested into reality, depending on your current level of developmental awareness.

One way that requires lots of time and energy is to trek into the forest, cut down a tree,
And saw the tree trunk into long boards so you can build your new chair from scratch,
Or - you could buy *a wooden chair kit* with the components already prepared
So all you need do is assemble it properly.

Of course, an easier means to manifest the chair would be to purchase one at a furniture store,
And - "the most magical and miraculous approach" (if you knew how to achieve it)
Would be "to make the chair appear out of thin air" like a great magician does.

Yet all people are constantly engaged in (whether they're consciously aware of it or not)
An ongoing process of manifesting their reality - through *the Power of Intention*,
For the vast creative *Power of Intention* is one of **the means of manifestation**
That's always occurring daily - whether consciously or unconsciously.

Nature's earliest *process of manifestation* relates to the innate biology within our physical bodies
Which, through a natural progression of adaptive organic evolution, instinctively knows
How to continuously manifest ever-more effective ways of thriving in this world.

At this most basic level of biology, *manifestation* develops from our **natural instinctual drives**,
Our inborn impulses that, over time, evolve superior biological systems within our body.

For most people, in order to manifest something new within the world of material form,
They usually first become mentally aware of, or observe, a specific need or desire,
And then must **physically build it - using their personal skills and efforts**.

In other words - at this fundamental level of awareness, to make things appear in one's reality,
One's needs to "work" or "put in effort" to manifest it.

Today many people are discovering **the power of intention** and *the energy of consciousness*,
And are learning to purposely use *the Field of Intention* to manifest their desires.

Much of humanity is young and inexperienced at this approach, but in time, it holds the promise
Of realizing an entirely new paradigm of consciously manifesting and co-creating reality.

This new paradigm has the potential to gift us with "the magic" of the great Spiritual Magicians,
Those spiritual sages and masters who, because of their authentic alignment with *Life*,
Have learned to co-create, so-called, "miracles" with the power of their intention.

In time, as we continually grow in spiritual awareness regarding what our life is truly about,
We climb the ladder of possible *means of manifestation* that are available for us to use.

One future day, humanity may be at a level of consciousness, a specific stage of **life mastery**,
Where a person just has to simply think of a chair - and then a chair appears.

Circle of the Various Means of Manifestation
(Diverse Ways of Expressing My Creativity)

LIFE MASTERY
MANIFESTATION COMES
FROM CULTIVATING
ADVANCED STAGES
OF MASTERY WHILE FULLY
ALIGNED WITH
THE SOURCE OF LIFE
THUS CREATING WHAT ARE
NOW CALLED "MIRACLES"

NATURAL INSTINCT
MANIFESTATION COMES
FROM MY NATURAL
INSTINCTUAL DRIVES
OR INBORN IMPULSES
THAT, OVER TIME,
EVOLVE SUPERIOR
BIOLOGICAL SYSTEMS
WITHIN MY BODY

INTENTION
MANIFESTATION COMES
FROM ALIGNING
MY INTENTION AND
PERSONAL CONSCIOUS-
NESS WITH *UNIVERSAL
CONSCIOUSNESS*
SO AS TO BECOME A
CO-CREATOR WITH *LIFE*

PHYSICAL WORK
MANIFESTATION COMES
FROM BECOMING AWARE
OF A SPECIFIC NEED
OR DESIRE,
AND THEN PHYSICALLY
BUILDING IT
USING MY PERSONAL
SKILLS AND EFFORTS

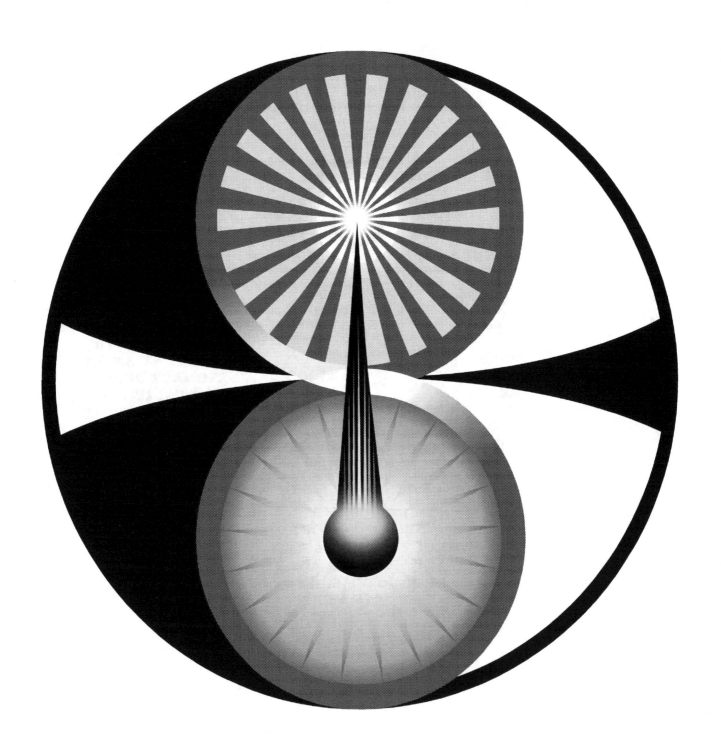

XVI

THE ART OF
TRANSFORMATION
AND HEALING

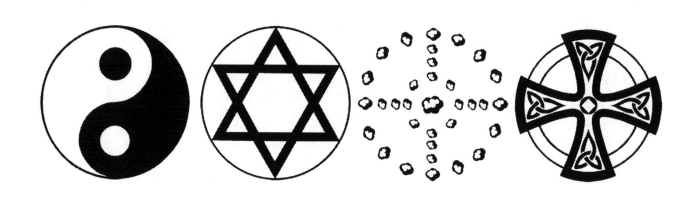

THE GREAT CIRCLE OF DEVELOPMENT AND TRANSFORMATION

As I learn to love more fully, Life then mirrors my inner development as outer transformation.

If you decide to plant seeds of corn in the fertile soil of your vegetable garden,
    You can obviously expect to harvest ears of corn in late summer.

If you want to enjoy fresh tomatoes from your garden,
    Then you must plant tomato seeds in early spring.

The same *Universal Principle of Cause and Effect* applies, as well, to the thoughts we think,
    For when we continually sow thoughts of negativity in "the garden of our mind",
        We will most likely generate experiences in our life that are not constructive,
            Whereas when we sustain thoughts of kindness and gratitude,
                We co-create with *Life* opportunities of "harvesting peace of mind".

In a similar manner, if we desire our body-mind to be transformed and healed at a core level,
    Then we must cultivate the natural expansion of our conscious awareness
        Through the discipline of daily inner development and spiritual growth.

Our life is a direct out-picturing that mirrors the consciousness of our inner world
    And, correspondingly, the creative manifestations that we express in our <u>external reality</u>
        Support opportunities for us to further the blossoming of our <u>internal awareness</u>.

If we become unconscious in our life - in other words, if we stop growing inwardly
    And remain stagnant in one particular stage of awareness because of fear or ignorance,
        Then the resultant outer expression of our life will remain stagnant as well.

Evolving creation always mirrors *evolving consciousness*
    And both are perpetually unfolding dynamics of **The Great Circle** of our life.

As we consciously plant the seeds of <u>inner</u> development in "the garden of our *heart*",
    We correspondingly support the bounty of our <u>outer</u> transformation and healing.

In the same way, the <u>outer</u> expression of our transformation and healing sets the stage
    For more seeds of <u>inner</u> growth and development to be planted within our being
        As a natural progression of *The Great Wheel of Life*.

As we expand our awareness of what really matters within the endless turning of this *Wheel*,
    We are constantly being invited by *the Natural Intelligence* within us
        To embrace a higher understanding of the mystery and paradox of life.

For example, in the <u>relative</u> realm of our life (our everyday material reality),
    Both the "seed" and the "harvest" are individual expressions
        Of two distinct and separate moments in time,
            A definitive beginning and a clear ending, respectively.

Yet in the timeless <u>absolute</u> realm, the "seed" and the "harvest" are unique colors of our world
    Which are blended together into a unified whole expression within *"the Rainbow of Life"*
        As one never-ending **Great Circle**.

The Great Circle of Development and Transformation
(The Transformative Dynamics of Healing)

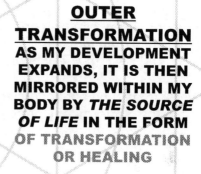

"THE ONE"
THE ONE SOURCE,
INFINITE INTELLIGENCE
+ + +
WITHIN THE REALM OF
ABSOLUTE ONENESS,
I AM ALWAYS ALIGNED
WITH THE INFINITE
PRESENCE OF LOVE

INNER
DEVELOPMENT
I CONSTANTLY EXPAND
MY AWARENESS OF WHAT
IS TRUE, LEARN TO LOVE
MORE FULLY,
AWAKEN TO WHO I AM,
AND DEVELOP MY
CREATIVE POTENTIAL

OUTER
TRANSFORMATION
AS MY DEVELOPMENT
EXPANDS, IT IS THEN
MIRRORED WITHIN MY
BODY BY THE SOURCE
OF LIFE IN THE FORM
OF TRANSFORMATION
OR HEALING

"THE MANY"
I AM A PERFECTLY
UNFOLDING EXPRESSION
OF THE MANY
UNIQUE FORMS OF LIFE
+ + +
IN THE PRESENT
MOMENT, I AM ALREADY
HEALED AND WHOLE

THE GREAT CIRCLE OF THE SPHERES OF CONSCIOUSNESS AND FIELDS OF CREATION

Consciousness and creation are merged as one endless "dance of Limitless Love" in my life.

The Great Circle can be viewed as "a spiritual map of an awakening life"
That visually illustrates the universal dynamics at play in the world - and in our life,
As one integrated flow of a unified whole system.

These primary dynamics all exist within us as one interconnected stream of our unfolding life,
And yet we can use this *circle* to understand each of these dynamics more clearly
By dividing the *circle* into four quadrants so we may investigate more closely.

At the top of the *circle*, the north quadrant signifies a transcendent power that many call "God"
*(The Infinite Intelligence of the Universe, the Source of Life, Limitless Love, **"The One"**)*
From which every material expression in the Universe emerges.

All outward manifestations are portrayed at the bottom of the *circle*, or south quadrant,
Which represents ***"The Many"*** manifest forms within the natural world and Universe
That, in the present moment, are unfolding perfectly.

There are also two fundamental *evolutionary impulses* illustrated in this *circle*
Which are *the impulse of* **evolving consciousness** depicted in the left quadrant
And *the impulse of* **evolving creativity** shown in the right quadrant.

In order to deepen our understanding of *evolving consciousness*, it can be further divided
Into **the Spheres of Consciousness** which point us to the natural emergence
Of three *spheres of consciousness* that have appeared within the Universe over time.

They are as follows: **the Sphere of Matter** - the universal consciousness that first gave shape
To the physical realm of the Cosmos, and is expressed within humans as the <u>physical body</u>,
The Sphere of Life - the next level of universal consciousness that gave shape
To the emotional realm in myriad life forms, and is expressed as the <u>human heart</u>,
And **the Sphere of Mind** - the most recent level of evolving consciousness
That has given shape to the realm of intelligent thought in certain life forms,
And is expressed within humans as the <u>self-reflective mind</u>.

The impulse of evolving creativity represented on the right side of the *circle*
Can also be further sub-divided into **the Fields of Creation**
In order to expand our understanding of the various *dynamics of manifestation*.

The three distinctions within **the Fields of Creation** can be conveyed as:
The Field of Light, or the quantum reality - the unlimited potential of what is possible,
The Field of Love, or *Infinite Intelligence* - the supreme force of transformation,
And **the Field of Power**, or the many manifested forms of the material world.

One of the numerous mysteries of evolving life - as well as a conundrum of **The Great Circle**
Is that all four of these individual key dynamics,
<u>*"The One"*</u>, <u>*"The Many"*</u>, <u>consciousness</u>, and <u>creativity</u>, are all unfolding
As one unified "dance of *Limitless Love*" in every moment of our life.

The Great Circle of the Spheres of Consciousness and Fields of Creation

"THE ONE"
EVOLVING CONSCIOUS-
NESS IS OUTWARDLY
MIRRORED BY *"THE ONE"*,
THE SOURCE OF LIFE,
AND IS EXPRESSED INTO
THE WORLD OF FORM
(EVOLVING CREATION)

**THE SPHERES
OF CONSCIOUSNESS**
REALM OF THOUGHT
SPHERE OF MIND
EMOTIONAL REALM
SPHERE OF LIFE
PHYSICAL REALM
SPHERE OF MATTER

**THE FIELDS
OF CREATION**
UNLIMITED POTENTIAL
FIELD OF LIGHT
INFINITE CREATIVITY
FIELD OF LOVE
THE WORLD OF FORM
FIELD OF POWER

"THE MANY"
THE MANY MANIFEST
FORMS OF LIFE WITHIN
THE WORLD ARE
UNFOLDING PERFECTLY
- AND THEREFORE, IN
THE PRESENT MOMENT,
ARE WHOLE AND HEALED

THE FIELD OF LIGHT

Everything I perceive has been created from a limitless ocean of pure universal energy.

If you were to spend a few moments pondering the word "light"
    You might first think of the endless rays of energy streaming into the Earth
        From the nearby fiery star we call the Sun,
            Or you might reflect on the gradual illumination of the dawn
                After a lingering night of darkness,
                    Or the radiance of a lit candle
                        That fills a small room with brilliance.

Yet there's also a more esoteric and fundamental meaning for the word "light"
    That points us to what some metaphysicians call **the Field of Light**
        (Or in religious language, *"the Light of God"*),
            Referring to *Light* as the pure universal energy within all of existence
            From which the building blocks of everything within reality is made.

The Field of Light is an unfathomable mystery of the Cosmos,
    And yet from modern physics we can think of this *Field* as the infinite array of quantum particles
        That appear out of nothing, emerging from and disappearing back into
            The formlessness of, what many scientists call, *The Unified Field*.

In other words - *the Field of Light* is **the limitless ocean of universal energy**
    That emerges into the natural world from the unbounded *Unified Field*.

It is **the ceaseless flow of radiant sub-atomic particles referred to as the quantum realm**
    Appearing in material reality which are birthed from *an Infinite Void*.

The Field of Light also refers to *the causal realm of all possibility (the realm of Being)*,
    For it's the **pure potentiality** emerging from *the Source of All That Is*.

It is **the Field** of infinite possibilities that have the potential to manifest into form**
    Which emerge out of the unlimited spaciousness of *Unity Consciousness*.

These primary building blocks of universal energy which make up *the Field of Light*
    Can be thought of poetically as infinite grains of sand that form a never-ending shoreline
        From which *the Ultimate Power of Life* sculpts its many "sand castles",
            Its majestic mountains and fertile valleys, its tall trees and ornate flowers,
                As well as all the myriad creatures on Earth.

From this "Big Picture perspective", not only what we typically think of as "light"
    (For example - the rays of the Sun, the illumination of the dawn, or the radiance of a candle)
        Is shaped into form from the sub-atomic particles of this *Field of Light,*
            But so is each and every unique phenomenal expression of reality.

So next time you feel inspired to ponder the word "light",
    You can use your vivid imagination to help you understand
        That everything you see, hear, and touch in your everyday world
            Has been creatively fashioned into form from this sublime **Field of Light**.

Circle of *the Field of Light*
(The Unlimited Potential Within the Quantum Realm)

UNIVERSAL ENERGY
THE FIELD OF LIGHT –
THE LIMITLESS OCEAN
OF PURE UNIVERSAL
ENERGY THAT EMERGES
INTO THE NATURAL
WORLD FROM
THE UNIFIED FIELD

THE QUANTUM REALM
THE FIELD OF LIGHT –
THE FOUNDATIONAL
BUILDING BLOCKS OF
SUB-ATOMIC PARTICLES
WHICH EMERG
INTO MATERIAL REALITY
FROM AN INFINITE VOID

INFINITE POSSIBILITIES
THE FIELD OF LIGHT –
THE INFINITE
POSSIBILITIES THAT
HAVE THE POTENTIAL
TO MANIFEST INTO FORM
WHICH EMERGE OUT OF
UNITY CONSCIOUSNESS

PURE POTENTIALITY
THE FIELD OF LIGHT –
A CONSTANT SOURCE
OF PURE POTENTIALITY
EMERGING FROM *THE
SOURCE OF ALL THAT IS,*
WHICH IS ALSO CALLED
THE CAUSAL REALM

THE FIELD OF LOVE

Everything in my life has been shaped into form by the Infinite Creativity of Limitless Love.

The word "love" is a multi-faceted expression in the English language
    That we all use in various contexts of meaning.

Yet in general, it refers to the sentimental feelings of deep connection and bonding
    That two people experience between one another
        Whether it's a lover and beloved, a parent and child, or two cherished friends.

In many of the world's religious texts, we see phrases like:
    "God is Love", "Love your neighbor as yourself", or "Love is all that's real".

These simple but profound phrases, when reflected upon more deeply,
    Point us to another more esoteric meaning of love that's universal and primary
        Which some spiritual teachers have referred to as **the Field of Love**.

They are referring to the omnipresent, all-powerful, and mysterious *Force of Life*
    That perpetually guides and fashions the fundamental components of reality
        (The foundational building blocks of pure universal energy within all of creation)
            Into the vast magnificent expressions and structures of the Cosmos.

Or another way of describing this *Transcendent Force (the Field of Love)*
    Is **the Universal Intelligence** that organizes *the Field of Light*
        (Which is a phrase that represents the vast building blocks of quantum energy)
            Into the individual and unique vibratory patterns of the natural world.

This unlimited *Field* can be thought of as **the Infinite Creativity** of the Universe
    That naturally shapes sub-atomic particles into the countless phenomenal forms of creation.

The Field of Love in religious terms has been called *"the Love of God"* or ***"Limitless Love"***,
    The Boundless Creativity that directs which one of the infinite possibilities in existence
        Will manifest into the world of form, and has also been referred to as *the Vibrational Realm*.

This *Field* can be portrayed as **the Intelligent Evolutionary Impulse of Unlimited Creativity**
    That shapes all of the atomic structures of the Cosmos into diverse material expression.

The Infinite Intelligence of the Universe can be poetically envisioned as a grand creative artist
    Who is building beautifully crafted "castles of sand" on an endless ocean shoreline
        Using the vast grains of sand that are perpetually available.

And it is like a great sculptor who skillfully carves figures of regal individuals from moist clay,
    Or a master visual artist who sketches on canvases the contours of exotic faces.

Yes, we have all heard the spiritual proclamations that *"God is Love"*
    And that *"God created everything in the Universe"*.

Another way of saying this is - *"Everything in the Cosmos is being shaped, now and forever,*
    *By the unfathomable creative artistry of the limitless **Field of Love**".*

Circle of the Field of Love
(*The Infinite Creativity* of the Universe)

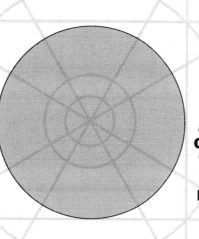

UNIVERSAL INTELLIGENCE
THE FIELD OF LOVE –
THE UNIVERSAL INTELLI-
GENCE THAT ORGANIZES
THE FIELD OF LIGHT
(UNLIMITED QUANTUM
ENERGY) INTO UNIQUE
VIBRATORY PATTERNS

INFINITE CREATIVITY
THE FIELD OF LOVE –
THE INFINITE CREATIVITY
OF THE UNIVERSE THAT
SHAPES SUB-ATOMIC
PARTICLES INTO
THE MYRIAD MATERIAL
FORMS OF CREATION

THE EVOLUTIONARY IMPULSE
THE FIELD OF LOVE –
THE INTELLIGENT
EVOLUTIONARY IMPULSE
OF UNLIMITED CREATIVITY
THAT FASHIONS ALL THE
ATOMS OF THE COSMOS
INTO SOLID EXPRESSIONS

LIMITLESS LOVE
THE FIELD OF LOVE –
THE BOUNDLESS *ENERGY*
OF CREATION THAT
DIRECTS WHICH ONE
OF THE INFINITE
POSSIBILITIES WILL
MANIFEST INTO FORM
-*THE VIBRATIONAL REALM*

THE FIELD OF POWER

All I perceive is made of pure Light organized into form by the creative artistry of Limitless Love.

One of the multiple meanings of the word "power" refers to the notion of control over others,
    Such as the intentional control of people by their government
        Which can be either democratically civil or ruthlessly unjust.

In science, "power" also refers to the concentration of potential energy within a container
    That can produce a specific force or action,
        Such as the contained electrical charge within a battery,
            The forward momentum of a motorized vehicle,
                The captured radioactive energy stored in a nuclear reactor,
                    Or the colossal heat within the fiery furnace of the Sun.

Every microscopic atom holds an immense amount of potential energy
    Which has been demonstrated many times in the massive explosions of nuclear bombs.

All physical forms and structures within the Universe are made of sub-atomic particles
    That consist of immense quantities of tightly-fused stored power.

The Field of Power is a phrase that can be used to describe physical expressions of form
    Since all material objects in the Cosmos are manifestations of vast stores of energy.

It also points to the scientific evidence (based on the discoveries of quantum physics)
    That all structural forms which exist in the Universe take on the appearance of solidity
        And yet, in actuality, they are essentially pure energy in constant motion *(Light)*
            Which creates, within our mind, the perception of being "solid".

The Field of Power is - *the Field of Light (in other words - the limitless potential of pure Light)*
    Coalesced into **the many physical forms of the natural world**
        By the creative organizing force of *the Field of Love (Infinite Intelligence)*.

In religious terms - it is *"the Power of God"*, **the myriad manifestations of the Universe**
    That have been creatively fashioned into form by *the Infinite Intelligence* of the Cosmos.

The Field of Power can be seen as **the phenomenal expressions of the material realm**
    Which are formed by *the Source of Life* from an infinite number of potential possibilities.

It can also be thought of as **the basic building blocks of quantum energy**
    Shaped into "the solid patterns" of manifest creation by *Natural Intelligence*.

Using the metaphor of "a cosmic shoreline with an unlimited number of grains of sand",
    The Field of Power is like many different "sand castles" that might be built on shore
        Each one made from the same fundamental components of sand,
            Yet manifested in unique forms (like stars, planets, oceans, rocks,
                Or the numerous organisms of life that have evolved on Earth).

Each material phenomenon is like "a novel sand castle on the infinite shoreline of the Cosmos"
    Cast into physical form by a focused intention from *the creative artistry of Limitless Love.*

Circle of *the Field of Power*
(The Myriad Manifestations of Form in the World and Universe)

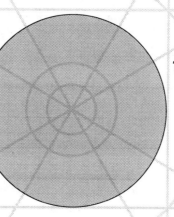

CREATION
THE FIELD OF POWER –
THE BUILDING BLOCKS
OF QUANTUM ENERGY
THAT ARE SHAPED INTO
"THE SOLID PATTERNS"
OF CREATION BY
NATURAL INTELLIGENCE

MANIFESTATIONS
THE FIELD OF POWER –
THE MYRIAD MANIFESTA-
TIONS OF THE UNIVERSE
THAT HAVE BEEN
CREATIVELY FASHIONED
INTO FORM BY
INFINITE INTELLIGENCE

"THE MANY" FORMS
THE FIELD OF POWER – PURE
LIGHT COALESCED
INTO THE MANY FORMS
OF THE NATURAL WORLD
BY THE CREATIVE
ORGANIZING POWER
OF *THE FIELD OF LOVE*

MATERIAL REALM
THE FIELD OF POWER –
THE PHENOMENAL
EXPRESSIONS OF THE
MATERIAL REALM THAT
HAVE BEEN FORMED BY
THE SOURCE OF LIFE FROM
INFINITE POSSIBILITIES

FIELDS OF CREATION

I manifest my love-centered intentions by consciously co-creating with the Source of All That Is.

Since the dawn of time the same underlying dynamics of manifestation have been taking place
Throughout the Universe, producing a range of massive galaxies to microscopic bacteria.

Consciousness, together with the dynamics of creation, constantly spins the wheel of evolution
And equally these dynamics maintain the movement of development and transformation
For all of the myriad phenomenal forms of expression within the Cosmos.

The elegance of creation is a perpetual process of ever-unfolding manifestation
That occurs naturally within the Universe as part of one whole unified system.

Yet in order to understand the various dynamics of manifestation more clearly,
We can observe and investigate its distinct individual components
And describe the totality of these individual aspects as the **Fields of Creation**.

The first and primary dynamic of this infinitely creative process is **The Unified Field**,
Or in religious language it has been called *"the Unity of God"*, or more simply "God",
The Source of All That Is (Unbounded Consciousness, The Transcendent)
From which every myriad form of creation emerges into manifestation.

From the Womb of this formless eternal *Source*, pure universal *Light* is birthed,
Which is described as **the Field of Light**, or in religious language, *"the Light of God"*,
The unlimited ocean of quantum energy
That constantly emerges into existence from *The Unified Field*.

It is from these basic building blocks of energy, these quantum particles of pure potentiality,
From which all expressions of the Universe are creatively formed and shaped
By **the Field of Love** *(also referred to as Limitless Love, Infinite Intelligence)*
That organizes *the Field of Light* into localized vibratory patterns.

The Infinite Intelligence of the Universe (also referred to as *the Evolutionary Impulse)*
Has unlimited organizing power to creatively fashion the raw energy of the Cosmos
Into specific mental structures - as well as unique configurations of physical form.

The Field of Power is a metaphysical phrase portraying all material structures and patterns
Which make up the natural world (and the evolving Universe),
And which consist of pure *Light* shaped into the apparent "solid" forms of creation
By *the Natural Intelligence* of *the Field of Love*.

The Field of Power is another way of describing tightly fused patterns of stored energy
Organized into countless forms - like majestic mountains that tower toward the heavens,
The transformation of a caterpillar into a butterfly,
Or the healing that takes place in sentient creatures like you and me.

All of these so-called individual **Fields of Light, Love,** and **Power,** plus **The Unified Field,**
Are happening as one dynamic process of manifestation, transformation, or healing,
And can be displayed in a totality that is recognized as **the Fields of Creation**.

Circle of the Fields of Creation
(The Universal Dynamics of Manifestation and Transformation)

THE UNIFIED FIELD
(THE TRANSCENDENT)
THE SOURCE OF ALL
THAT IS - FROM WHICH
EVERY MYRIAD FORM
OF CREATION EMERGES
INTO MANIFESTATION
+UNBOUNDED
    CONSCIOUSNESS
+THE UNITY OF GOD

FIELD OF POWER
(MANIFESTED FORMS)
PURE *LIGHT* SHAPED
INTO THE "SOLID" FORMS
OF CREATION BY *THE*
INFINITE INTELLIGENCE
OF *THE FIELD OF LOVE*
+THE MANY FORMS OF
    THE NATURAL WORLD
+THE EVOLVING UNIVERSE

FIELD OF LIGHT
(INFINITE POTENTIAL)
THE UNLIMITED OCEAN
OF QUANTUM ENERGY
THAT CONSTANTLY
EMERGES INTO
EXISTENCE FROM
THE UNIFIED FIELD
+PURE POTENTIALITY
+THE QUANTUM REALM

FIELD OF LOVE
(LIMITLESS LOVE)
THE INFINITE INTELLI-
GENCE OF THE UNIVERSE
THAT ORGANIZES
THE FIELD OF LIGHT
INTO LOCALIZED
VIBRATORY PATTERNS
+INFINITE CREATIVITY
+EVOLUTIONARY IMPULSE

UNIVERSAL DYNAMICS OF EMERGENT HEALING

My true healing is about using the challenging events of my life to learn to love unconditionally.

From a familiar point of view, one might look at what's going on within the world today
And be overwhelmed with distress by the range of humanity's massive global problems:
Famine, war, ecological devastation, injustice, and terrorism - to name just a few.

Yet if the same person could simply shift their focus to that of an astronaut orbiting the globe
And then look down at the spinning Earth from his or her vista far out in space,
They would see one harmonious expression of evolving life on a beautiful world.

From this perspective, where one can observe our blue sphere from a much larger viewpoint,
The world's challenges seem to mingle with the magnificence of the rest of the planet,
For the Earth's problems have, from this greater vantage, all merged as part
Of a larger unified matrix of growth, creativity, transformation, and healing.

Similarly a shift can occur for each of us as we embrace a bigger perspective regarding our life
In which we recognize that true healing is not just about fixing "our so-called problems",
But really is about using difficult life situations that are currently happening to us
To discover new creative ways to fully accept our life just as it is,
As well as learn to love all people and all of life - unconditionally.

From a limited and narrow perception of our self-oriented nature,
What we've called "our problems" can seem huge and, sometimes, overwhelming to us,
And we may, therefore, vehemently resist these challenging experiences of life.

Yet from a spiritually awakened perspective in which we perceive "a Bigger Picture of life"
Where we are an integral part of an ever-evolving Universe, we can redefine *healing*
As a natural *Transcendent Impulse* within us that yearns for higher stages of awareness,
As well as view crisis and challenge as key parts of this *healing process*.

Universal Intelligence is continually surrounding each of us with waves of pure potential energy
(Or quantum particles of **Light**) which are unlimited possibilities available for us to experience
And which directly respond to our love-centered intentions and growing awareness.

As we consciously remove any stress or blockages to the natural flow of this universal energy
And expand our awareness, this **Light** responds to, and mirrors, our higher awareness.

Furthermore, as we realize an expansive leap in the evolution of our consciousness,
The Field of Love then reorganizes the wave patterns of universal **Light** within us
Producing *an emergent shift* that, in turn, naturally balances our *subtle energy body*.

This reorganization **(Love)** of our *subtle energy body* **(Light)** into greater order and balance
Is manifested within us as *healing* **(Power as form)** in our physical, emotional, or mental body.

Healing is always occurring as a vital facet of Nature, for <u>healing</u> and <u>creation</u> are intertwined
Because every part of creation constantly seeks higher stages of order and awareness -
Thus *healing* is a natural manifestation of perpetual evolution within the Universe
Which, at certain times, yields a sudden, emergent, and miraculous form of expression.

Circle of the Universal Dynamics of Emergent Healing
(Healing In Relation to the Fields of Creation)

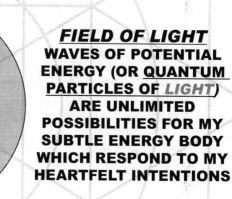

THE UNIFIED FIELD
+ *INFINITE INTELLIGENCE*
+ *THE SOURCE OF ALL
   THAT IS*
+ *UNBOUNDED
   CONSCIOUSNESS*
+ *PERFECT WHOLENESS*
+ *INFINITE PRESENCE*
+ *GOD*

FIELD OF POWER
THE REORGANIZATION
(LOVE) OF MY SUBTLE
ENERGY BODY *(LIGHT)*
INTO GREATER ORDER
AND BALANCE IS THEN
SUDDENLY MANIFESTED
AS *EMERGENT HEALING*
(<u>INNER</u> *POWER* AS FORM)

FIELD OF LIGHT
WAVES OF POTENTIAL
ENERGY (OR <u>QUANTUM
PARTICLES OF</u> *LIGHT*)
ARE UNLIMITED
POSSIBILITIES FOR MY
SUBTLE ENERGY BODY
WHICH RESPOND TO MY
HEARTFELT INTENTIONS

FIELD OF LOVE
AS I REMOVE ANY STRESS
OR BLOCKAGES AND
EXPAND MY AWARENESS,
THE FIELD OF LOVE THEN
REORGANIZES THE WAVE
PATTERNS OF *LIGHT*
WITHIN ME INTO GREATER
ORDER AND BALANCE

THE GREAT CIRCLE OF AWAKENING AND EMERGENT HEALING

I claim the holiness and magnificence of who I am - and feel unconditionally loved by all of creation.

The Great Circle, as "a spiritual map of an awakening life", illustrates that our internal awareness
Creatively **shapes** the way our external reality is expressed and experienced within our daily life.

Equally, what we create and experience in our external reality then **informs** our internal awareness,
For example new areas of healing or transformation initiate new areas of our inner development.

From the perspective of *evolutionary spirituality,* true healing is perceiving each challenge as a *gift*
Which we use to cultivate and deepen a love-centered heart that serves the wellbeing of others,
While we expand our awareness so as to better contribute to the beneficent evolution of life.

Using this perspective to understand what true healing is, **an awakening healer** can be thought of
As a person who is consciously developing spiritual awareness, the inward expansion of self,
And one's **healing or transformation** is the outward expression of wellbeing that results.

Every time we experience pain, illness, or affliction (opportunities in our life to foster inner freedom)
We can use our pain to help us heal at the core of our being (i.e. we learn to become *the healer*
As well as the person receiving *the healing*) by actualizing six powerful *evolutionary keys.*

The first three keys develop our internal awareness (our evolving consciousness - the left quadrant)
Which are the spiritual realizations that we, as **an awakening healer,** cultivate within our heart,
And keys 4, 5 and 6 transform our external reality (our evolving creation - the right quadrant)
Which are sacred gifts that *the Infinite Intelligence of Life* manifests in us as **healing.**

1) I align with *Infinite Intelligence* as I set an intention to live a life of serving the common good of all
And learning to awaken to a higher consciousness that creates emergent transformation in me.

2) I am grateful for everything I'm learning in my life, I surrender all attachments to my intentions,
I accept that my life is unfolding perfectly just as it is, and I am aware of my Oneness with all life.

3) I claim the holiness and magnificence of who I am, I feel unconditionally loved by all of creation,
And I witness the realization of my *True Eternal Nature* awaken within my human experience.

- - - - -   - - - - -   - - - - -   - - - - -   - - - - -   - - - - -   - - - - -   - - - - -

4) My healing exists in the quantum field as a latent possibility that mirrors my inner development
And yearns for my body, heart, and mind to express the sacred gift within this quantum potential.

5) *The Omniscient Intelligence of Limitless Love* then shapes within me this one quantum possibility
As my body's etheric energy field reorganizes into the gift of a vibratory pattern of perfect health.

6) My *awakening* to a sphere of higher consciousness creates within me the gift of physical rebirth
That manifests as *emergent healing,* the miraculous transformation of my body, heart, and mind.

Our personal quest for *emergent healing* is not only about alleviating our pain, illness, or affliction
But is really about awakening to who we truly are, our *True Nature,* as we serve the good of all.

Knowing our *True Nature* enables us to embody our sacred destiny of living a life of inner freedom,
Loving all of life unconditionally, and contributing our gifts and talents to others and the world.

The Great Circle of Awakening and Emergent Healing
(Evolutionary Keys For Creating a Miraculous Transformation)

PERFECT LOVE
INFINITE INTELLIGENCE
(UNBOUNDED CONSCIOUS-
NESS, LIMITLESS LOVE,
GOD, THE SOURCE OF LIFE)
MIRRORS MY INNER
DEVELOPMENT WITHIN
MY BODY OR MIND AS AN
EXPRESSION OF HEALING
("THE ONE" SOURCE)

THE AWAKENING HEALER
(INTERNAL AWARENESS)
1 MATTER - I ALIGN WITH
INFINITE INTELLIGENCE
AS I SET MY INTENTION
2 LIFE - I ACCEPT MY LIFE
IS UNFOLDING PERFECTLY
3 MIND - I AWAKEN TO
THE REALIZATION OF MY
TRUE ETERNAL NATURE
(CONSCIOUSNESS)

HEALING OR TRANSFORMATION
(EXTERNAL REALITY)
4 LIGHT – HEALING AS
QUANTUM POTENTIAL
5 LOVE - LIMITLESS LOVE
REORGANIZES MY BODY
INTO PERFECT HEALTH
6 POWER - MY AWAKENING
TO HIGHER AWARENESS
MANIFESTS AS HEALING
(CREATION)

PERFECT FORM
IN EVERY MOMENT
MY CURRENT LEVEL OF
AWARENESS IS ALWAYS
PERFECTLY MIRRORED
AND EXPRESSED
INTO FORM AS HEALING
OR TRANSFORMATION IN
MY BODY, HEART OR MIND
("THE MANY" FORMS)

XVII

CONCLUSION - SACRED DESTINY

THE GREAT CIRCLE OF MAINTAINING INNER FREEDOM

Each day I learn new ways to expand my awareness, help create a better world, and serve others.

There are many different types of aircraft that have been invented
    Such as propeller driven planes, jets, cargo planes, bi-planes, etc.

And even though these various aircraft have diverse kinds of mechanisms,
    They all fly through the air due to a few basic and essential components.

First, each aircraft must have wings that are aerodynamically designed
    To create what is called "lift" - so the plane will ascend into the air properly.

Then the aircraft must have a propulsion system (e.g. motor-driven propeller, jet engine)
    That will thrust the plane up into the sky and keep it airborne,
        And as well, must contain a mechanism for steering the aircraft.

Finally, each aircraft must have an experienced pilot
    To navigate the journey and respond to any course corrections or emergencies.

All of the different aircraft listed above also have many other important features,
    But they must at least have these four basic components in order to fly.

Similarly, you and I can read many books about spirituality, attend numerous self-help workshops,
    And learn scores of techniques regarding inner freedom,
        Yet **maintaining inner freedom** seems to come down to a few basic principles.

The Great Circle (a spiritual map of the universal dynamics at play in the world and in our life)
    Reveals that we can maintain our inner freedom each day by fostering a key awareness
        Expressed in the four words: 1) **learning**, 2) **aligning**, 3) **creating**, and 4) **serving**.

Inner freedom is the conscious realization that our life is unfolding perfectly just as it is -
    And the heart-centered awareness that we embody when we love all of life unconditionally.

It is a conscious life of developing our unlimited potential, correcting any unloving thoughts,
    Learning what really matters, expanding awareness of what our life is truly about,
        And thus awakening our consciousness to the realization of who we really are.

Inner freedom is also authentically **aligning** our awareness with *the Source of All That Is,*
    And sustaining this sublime alignment by mindfully living our life in the present moment.

As our spiritual development unfolds, we can choose to devote our growth and transformation
    To finding meaningful ways to contribute our gifts and talents to help **create** a better world.

Furthermore inner freedom is compassionately loving ourselves and all expressions of life fully,
    As well as following our natural and noble impulse to **serve** and be kind to others.

So to maintain a radiant life as we "soar through the limitless skies of authentic inner freedom",
    We can keep asking the perennial "Big Questions": **Who am I? - Why am I here?**
        What really matters? - What is my life truly about?

The Great Circle of Maintaining Inner Freedom
(Four Key Words to Deepen My Awareness of What Is True)

ALIGNING
I CONTINUE TO ASK
"WHO AM I?" AND "WHAT
IS MY *TRUE NATURE?*"
- AS I AM CONSTANTLY
ALIGNING
MY AWARENESS WITH
THE SOURCE OF ALL THAT IS

LEARNING
I CONTINUE TO ASK
"WHAT IS MY LIFE
TRULY ABOUT?" AND
"WHAT IS MY PURPOSE?"
- AS I AM CONSTANTLY
LEARNING HOW TO
EXPAND MY AWARENESS

CREATING
I CONTINUE TO ASK
"WHY AM I HERE?"
AND "WHAT IS
MY LIFE'S MISSION?"
- AS I AM CONSTANTLY
CREATING
A BETTER WORLD

SERVING
I CONTINUE TO ASK
"WHAT REALLY MATTERS?"
AND "WHAT IS THE MEANING
OF MY LIFE?"
- AS I AM CONSTANTLY
FINDING MEANINGFUL WAYS
OF **SERVING** OTHERS

This series of Contemplative Practices continues in

The Summer Volume: June 20 – September 21

The Autumn Volume: September 22 – December 20

The Winter Volume: December 21 – March 18

The Great Circle Mantra

My life is unfolding perfectly
Just the way it is
Because all that truly exists
Is *Perfect Love*
Yet I am here
To help the world become more perfect
By living my life
Perfectly guided by *Love*

Introduction To The Poem - *A Wizard of Words*

This poem was written to symbolize the *epic evolutionary journey of global awakening* that's taking place right now on our planet within the hearts and minds of every individual.

The simple mythic story told within the poem depicts a collective *journey of discovery, a journey of self-mastery* that every person upon the Earth is embarked on (whether he or she is consciously aware of it or not). This universal archetypal story is symbolically illustrated in the Contemplation Circle called the Archetypes of Spiritual Awakening.

The menacing fire dragon represents the dysfunctional self-oriented nature within every individual that must eventually be healed and transformed. The young awakening goddess symbolizes the inner growth unfolding within each person who is dedicated to personal development and cultivating inner freedom. This awakening process is displayed in the Contemplation Circle as the healing and transformation of the archetype of the **Young Awakening Self** which, through time and much life experience, eventually evolves into the **Compassionate Heart**.

The goddess within us all is overtaken for a time by the dark power of the dragon (the unloving and dysfunctional self that's unconscious within every person), but then, through conscious dedication and inner revelation, is transformed and awakened. *"The One"* god who abides on the throne of stars represents the archetype of *Infinite Presence*, in other words - *the Transcendent Nature of Life*.

When these two aspects of our inner being are merged as one (the joining together of the **Compassionate Heart** with the *Transcendent*, the union of the "Servant of Love" with the *"Mind of God"*), then this sublime merging is the ultimate realization of the Fully Awakened Self, the **Master of Freedom**, that is destined to be embodied and fully lived within each one of us.

—*Oman Ken*

This poem is an excerpt from Oman Ken's poetry book entitled
"Infinite Awakenings – Philosophical Story Poems Envisioning A More Glorious World".

A Wizard of Words

They all marched through the night to a rattle of crickets
    Half asleep as if ambling in a dream
        Lumbering through the dark pine forest
            Their throbbing hearts longing to be awake

From the four winds - they were each drawn in
    Like hypnotized moths magnetized to flame
        Captured by a spellbound gravity
            Seized by a circle of mesmerizing radiance
                Until all stood waiting in the open clearing
                    Where a raging bonfire blazed
                        Reaching for the canopy of starlight

Dancing flames dashed wide illuminating the superior form of a man
    As he poured his gaze into each heart
        While pacing around the warm glowing circle
        Among this eager assemblage of listeners

He was a wizard of words
    A magician of spoken language with a timeless story on his tongue
        Arranging tonal images in perfect sequence
            Like polychrome beaded necklaces artfully crafted
                Or patterned rows of flowers within a regal garden
                    Stretching their vivid petals toward the sun

Each mind was locked on his words
    As an epic saga began to unfurl
        An iconic tale of a menacing dragon breathing fire
            Living its sordid days near the kingdom
                Terrorizing those who dwelt upon this fragile world
                    With malicious chains of suffering
                    The shackles of ruthless control
                        Coercing the air into a dungeon of fear and death

Then - over the turns of time the dragon applied its cleverness
    To capture the greatest jewel within the kingdom
        The young awakening goddess
            Whose very essence inhabited the heart of every village dweller

The goddess was overtaken - intoxicated by the dragon's elixir of dark magic
　　Entranced by its glamorous illusions
　　　　Dazed into submission by its hypnotic induction
　　　　　　Yet at the same time she could hear the chant of an incessant voice
　　　　　　　　Intoning *an intimate love song* that beckoned from somewhere within

The dragon's manacles held the goddess captive
　　Hopelessly imprisoned in her solitary tower
　　　　Chained to an ancient wall of ignorance
　　　　　　Bound by blind self-delusion
　　　　　　　　Wings clipped and broken - unable to soar

Yet all the while *"The One"* who is eternal and benevolent
　　Who everlastingly abides on the throne of stars
　　　　Who perpetually invokes the natural longings within every god and goddess
　　　　　　Waited patiently for her with his hallowed offerings
　　　　　　　　Invisible - translucent in his dominion of seeming paradoxes
　　　　　　　　　　Witnessing the ceaseless play of light and darkness
　　　　　　　　　　　　The unfolding spiral of body and *Soul*
　　　　　　　　　　　　　　Within *"The Many"* forms of the world
　　　　　　　　　　　　　　　　The constant wheel of seasons

The storyteller's words became the pages of the night
　　Like a book illustrating life's visions of tomorrow's potential
　　　　Displaying celestial possibilities for all children of the kingdom
　　　　　　And awakening the passion for liberty
　　　　　　　　In each listener's heart

The wizard's words chronicled a turning point - revolving around her inner revelation
　　A profound epiphany - a leap of awareness that transformed everything
　　　　As she unreservedly embraced the transcendent offerings of *"The One"*
　　　　　　And unrestrainedly dove into his *Ocean* amid the throne of stars

Through reams of quaking inquiry from her questioning heart
　　The goddess cultivated waves of surrender - a blanket of acceptance
　　　　And gratitude wildly rippling within her core
　　　　　　Which all gently merged into a sea of Oneness
　　　　　　　　Until she and *the Translucent One* were utterly fused
　　　　　　　　　　As droplets from his *Ocean* baptized her crown
　　　　　　　　　　　　Unfurled her wings - she began to free herself
　　　　　　　　　　　　　　Shaking the entire Universe into a new pattern of possibility

And now a once sleeping goddess
Who had awakened a soaring desire within her *Soul*
Through her communion of becoming one with his *Eternal Gift*
Miraculously dispatched her prayer
Carried by a messenger angel
On a brazen arrow flung by her supple bow
Perfectly arriving at its destined target
Burying itself deep into the bones of the dragon
Until its terrorizing fire and fear
Were extinguished

All of its dragonfire melted into a hallowed song
For without its deceptive mask and trickery
The dragon was truly seen
Beyond its scales of illusion
To be the gift of *Light*
At the center of every living form
And was revealed to be an immortal friend
That was forever avidly alert within the kingdom
To ward off any future threat of foe or malice

The holy song revealed a new heaven and a new earth
In such a way that god and goddess were intimately joined
Ageless lovers in blissful communion
A miracle of transmutation
Metamorphosis of two now one
Birthing a mastery of life
That constantly bowed to Mystery

All could hear the exalted hymn
Of two beloveds entwined in the arms of compassion
Like the mother ocean that's always caressing
Each of her untethered river children

Of twin winged lovers merged in sacred union
Birthed within the womb of creation
From which all star clusters and planets
Offer their simple melodies
In some synchronized cosmic symphony

Then - for a lingering moment
    The impresario of words was still
        Like a blue heron
            Anchored next to a forest stream
                Allowing for an ever deeper story
                    To display its heart-wisdom within the burning silence

They all closed their eyes
    As he stood firm and motionless for a very long time
        Two legs balanced
            Body and *Soul* aligned
                Both supporting his paradoxical Universe
                    The Silent Witness on one side
                        The Servant of *Love* on the other

When their eyes opened - he was gone
    So one by one
        The band of listeners re-entered the dawning light of the woods
            Carrying their new treasure with them
                As if it were precious gold upon their shoulders
                    Returning to their warm firesides
                        In homes of far off villages
                            Eager to bestow the sacred gift they received
                                To share the story from the wizard of words
                                With all of their children

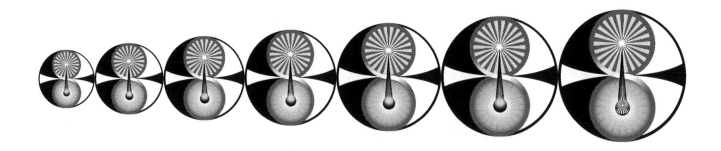

✳ JOURNEY OF *THE GREAT CIRCLE* – GLOSSARY OF TERMS ✳

Being defines the invisible and formless realm of *the Transcendent*. It is the sublime realm of existence in which all that exists is *Transcendent Oneness* - all that exists is *Absolute Perfection* - all that exists is *Unbounded Eternity* - all that exists is *Limitless Love*.

Becoming defines the natural process within any form of life that is developing its potential - which leads to manifesting more diverse creative expressions of itself or its environment. In relation to human beings, *Becoming* is one's *journey of awakening.* It is the *journey of discovery* or *spiritual journey* regarding one's inner development, the expansion of one's awareness, or one's spiritual awakening - which leads to greater contributions of one's creative gifts and talents employed in the service of others. *Becoming* can also be referred to as "one's creative actions and expressions to help make the world a better place".

Biosphere is *the Universal Consciousness* that gives shape to all biological life like microbes, plants, animals, which have evolved physical sensations and basic emotions.

Cause and Effect – The originating cause of everything within the phenomenal Universe is consciousness. The resulting effect from the creative intelligence of consciousness is the manifestations within the world of form (creation).

Consciousness is the invisible *Force of Natural Intelligence* which creates the visible world - the non-physical *Transcendent Power* which creates the physical Universe - an intangible internal *Awareness* which creates a tangible external reality. It is the invisible field of natural intelligence and information of any material or phenomenal structure that determines and gives creative shape to its visible form or pattern. Consciousness is the transcendent interiority of any structure of life which is the animating creative power that brings exterior form to its temporal body.

There is always some facet of consciousness (or natural intelligence) in every form of material expression within the Universe, such as the unique consciousness in every human being, animal, plant, micro-organism, rock, planet, star, galaxy, and beyond.

Consciousness is also the level or ability of a manifested form or structure within the Universe to be aware of, and respond to, experiences in its environment. A plant has a limited ability to respond to its environment. Whereas an animal has a greater, more developed ability. As far as is generally accepted, human beings have the greatest ability to be aware of, and respond to, experiences in their environment, and thus it is said that humans have the most evolved consciousness of all creatures on Earth.

Creation defines the phenomenal embodiment of the material realm. It is all expressions of the Universe - such as galaxies, stars, planets, microorganisms, plants, animals, and humans. Creation is also a word that represents the world of Nature.

In this book, the words Nature, Sun, Moon, Earth, Solar System, Universe, Cosmos are capitalized to represent that at a particular realm of consciousness, they are each a living entity of creation which is to be held in reverence, respect, honor, and is to be seen as sacred.

Emergent Healing is the spontaneous transformation that instantaneously happens within our body, heart, or mind when we experience a radical and profound shift in consciousness. *Emergent healing* is an extraordinary change and sudden balance that occurs in our being when we experience an internal "quantum leap" to a higher stage of awareness.

At these higher stages of awareness where we embody a greater level of wholeness, various forms of disease and imbalance, which we may have encountered previously, can no longer exist within the elevated frequency of *Limitless Love.*

Enlightenment is the sublime embodiment of inner freedom - which is living at a stage of spiritual consciousness where one abides in inner peace no matter what occurs. *Enlightenment* (from the perspective of this book) is not only about one's personal *awakening* or awareness of Oneness with God (*the Transcendent*), but that any sustained individual alignment with *Ultimate Reality* must also be embodied and grounded within one's physical body and then shared collectively through the personal actions of serving the wellbeing of others.

In some contemporary spiritual groups, the concept of *enlightenment* is now perceived as an ongoing experience of loving others and loving self unconditionally while serving the good within all of life.

Evolution is the creative and natural development within all of life. It is the response within every phenomenon to *the Natural Intelligence* of the Universe which directs each facet of existence to further develop, expand its possibilities, create diversity, and express more of its potential.

The Evolutionary Impulse is *the Natural Intelligence* within the Universe that animates every material form along a path of perpetual creative unfoldment. It is the transcendent organizing principle within all of Creation. It can be thought of as *the Infinite Creativity* within all of existence that intelligently shapes and organizes higher expressions of manifested form such as galaxies, stars, oceans, myriad life forms, and every human being.

The Evolutionary Impulse is (from a religious perspective) the same as *the Universal Force of God* that guides development and manifestation within all forms of the natural world. It is the *Force* that "attracts together" sub-atomic particles, the planets in their solar orbits, all interdependent ecosystems, as well as two lovers who experience romantic passion.

Evolutionary Perspective – see Evolutionary Spirituality

Evolutionary Spirituality is a phrase that describes a "Big Picture Perspective" way of thinking about how our lives develop and transform. Evolutionary spirituality provides us with the gifts of a much larger perspective of reality inspiring us to further develop our higher potential, to motivate us to transform our fear-based self-oriented nature, to create the seeds of greater compassion for all of life, and to take responsible conscious actions toward building a more sustainable future.

Evolutionary spirituality merges both *the Transcendent Power of Consciousness* and the myriad forms of creation. It unifies God with evolution. It is the awareness which embraces a Oneness of an *Infinite and Eternal Intelligence* with an ever-unfolding Universe.

Existence is defined as the totality of the physical and the non-physical, the visible and the invisible, the Immanent and *the Transcendent*. It is the wholeness and merging of consciousness and creation, God and the Universe, Spirit and form, *"The One"* and *"The Many"*, *Being* and *Becoming*.

Fractals are natural objects or mathematical patterns that repeat themselves at smaller scales in which a reduced-size copy of the initial pattern is formed in succeeding generations, typically producing new emergent variations within each later generation.

There is also a group of *fractal patterns* that repeat themselves identically as they get smaller, yet the vast majority of *fractals* repeat their patterns with slight variations each time generating new and novel formations at different levels of magnification.

For example, trees grow in *fractal patterns* both above and below the ground, as well as the veins and arteries within the human body. Other *fractal patterns* that occur in the natural world are not as obvious - such as the way amorphous clouds slowly accumulate and form in the sky, how the ragged rock edges of mountain ranges are structured, the manner in which the coastlines of countries take shape, and how the patterns of galaxies and solar systems are created.

God – see *the Transcendent*

The Great Circle is "a spiritual map of an awakening life" which illustrates that our internal awareness creatively shapes the way our external reality is expressed and experienced within our daily life. In other words, it portrays the universal dynamics of our inward expansion of consciousness mirrored as our outward creative expression.

There are many examples of traditional iconic images that represent *The Great Circle* - such as the Yin Yang symbol, the Star of David, the medicine wheel, and the sacred cross.

The primary function of **The Great Circle** as a transformative tool is to simply portray a useful collection of words and phrases for the purpose of deeply comprehending the nature of existence. With this awareness we can develop a greater understanding of what our life is truly about and what really matters - and thus, cultivate an unconditional love for each expression of life.

Holiness and Magnificence is another way of describing our *True Eternal Nature*, our *Transcendent Self*, who we really are. In religious language, it is our sacred divinity.

Infinite Awakenings represents the perpetual evolution and constant development that occurs in every phenomenal structure in the Universe - including galaxies, stars, planets, animals, plants, micro-organisms, and humans. "Awakening" describes a natural process of "developing to a higher level of awareness" or "expanding to a more elevated stage of consciousness" or "evolving to a new species". "Infinite" points to the awareness that *Life's* "awakenings" continue on and on without end.

Infinite Intelligence – see *The Transcendent*

The Infinite Presence of Love – see *The Transcendent*

Inner Freedom is when one consciously realizes the perfection that's always unfolding within - and within all of life. Living with this awareness allows the natural states of peace, happiness, joy and harmony to effortlessly arise. It is a life of one who has devotedly learned to love others and all of life unconditionally - and who has gained the joyful awareness of serving the wellbeing of others. In these writings, one who attains this level of mastery is referred to as a **Master of Freedom**.

Therefore, when we are aligned with *the Source of Life* - and gratefully celebrate every experience we have while fully loving and accepting ourselves, as well as every part of life - we are free.

Journey of Awakening is the natural evolutionary journey of ongoing inner development that every person in the world is constantly embarked on (whether he or she is consciously aware of it or not). Over time, this *journey of discovery* becomes conscious and intentional through a process of expanding one's awareness, transforming one's beliefs, discovering how to master a life of inner freedom, and contributing one's creative gifts and talents to the wellbeing of others. This is also referred to as the *spiritual journey* or the *journey of self-mastery*.

Life (when italicized and spelled with a capital) is a word that represents *the Transcendent, the Source of All That Is, the Infinite Intelligence* of the Universe. It is a short way of referring to *the Source of Life*. When "life" is not italicized and capitalized, it represents our human existence in the physical world.

Limitless Love – see *The Transcendent*

"The Many" can be defined in a number of ways, such as the myriad forms of life, the countless expressions of natural creativity on the Earth and throughout the Universe, all that is created, the endless manifestations of creation, etc. In relation to human beings, *"The Many"* is the totality of all humans that exist on the planet. Every person is a unique creative expression of *"The Many"*.

Master of Freedom is a visionary archetype that represents our *Fully Awakened Self,* one's *True Eternal Nature* completely experienced and lived within one's physical body. It is the embodied realization of a person who lives a life of inner freedom, loves all of life unconditionally, and serves the good of all with their creative gifts and talents. It is every person's sacred destiny to embody the *Awakened Self* and fully experience their life as a **Master of Freedom.**

Morphogenetic Field is a phrase used in developmental biology and consciousness studies that proposes there is a tangible field of energy that's generated by all things, both physical structures and even mental constructs, which serves to organize the structure's characteristics and patterns.

When we consciously align ourselves to *the morphogenetic field of a specific visionary archetype*, we begin a process of personally resonating to the archetype - and bringing into our awareness the expansive qualities and visionary characteristics which the archetype symbolizes.

Noosphere is *the Universal Consciousness* that gives shape to both the individual and collective mind, which resides within all intelligent life forms.

"The One" – see *The Transcendent*

Oneness is Ultimate Reality in which every form of creation is a unique expression of one *Unity*. It can be described as Infinite Reality in which each expression of life is an integral part of *one unfolding never-ending spiral of Consciousness*. Oneness can be thought of as Quantum Reality in which all of the manifest world of form is made of the same *universal energy (Light)* in constant motion. It can also be described as Transcendent Reality in which the Universe and everything in it is comprised of *one Universal Love*, and many people simply call this *Love* - "God".

Paradox is the perception that two discrete realities which contradict each other both exist at the same time. It is the notion that two expressions of reality which are complete polar opposites can both take place at once.

In the writings of **Journey of *The Great Circle***, embracing the existential paradoxes of life is a key to the cultivation of spiritual awakening. Embracing certain paradoxes enables us to merge consciousness with creation - God with the Universe - *Heaven* with Earth.

Physiosphere is *the Universal Consciousness* that gives shape to all material structures in the Universe - such as atoms, galaxies, stars, mountains, etc.

The Source of Life (The Source of All That Is) – see *The Transcendent*

Spiritual Journey – see *Journey of Awakening*

The Transcendent is the *Supreme Ubiquitous Intelligence* that is beyond form. It represents the invisible and formless *Natural Intelligence* throughout the Universe. *The Transcendent* is the sublime organizing principle which fashions everything in the manifested world of the material realm.

For millennia, this *Natural Intelligence* has been referred to in many ways throughout the world (The Thousand Names of the Divine) - such as *the Source of Life, Universal Consciousness, Pure Awareness, God, Allah, Tao, the Creator, the Great Spirit, the Great I Am, the Infinite Presence of Love, the Unbounded Ocean of Being, "The One", Infinite Intelligence, Limitless Love,* and so many more exquisite names for this sublime *Transcendent Power*. In many religious traditions this *Natural Intelligence* is simply referred to as "God".

(Note: Words that represent *"The Transcendent"* within **Journey of *The Great Circle*** are capitalized and italicized)

The Transcendent Impulse is defined as a constant spiritual yearning that we become aware of in our lifetime. It is the natural impulse to expand our awareness of what our life is truly about, to develop our potential, and to awaken to who we really are (an ascending impulse).

At the same time, it is the constant spiritual yearning of our expanding inner development to manifest ever-new expressions of creativity in our life (a descending impulse). This intrinsic and constant yearning (which is both the longing for spiritual awakening and for spiritual embodiment) that perpetually exists within us and within all forms of life - is called *the Transcendent Impulse*.

True Eternal Nature is the invisible transcendent consciousness of who we really are. It is the part of us that is eternal, unbounded, and limitless. Our *True Nature* is the aspect of who we are that guides and directs our life when we have learned to be aware of it.

There are numerous names for our *True Eternal Nature* - such as *the Higher Self, the Transcendent Self, the Authentic Self, the Essential Self, the Divine Self*. In many religious traditions, it is commonly referred to as the *"Soul"*. Within **Journey of *The Great Circle*** it is also called our "holiness and magnificence".

The Unbounded Ocean of Being – see *The Transcendent*

The Unified Field is a term, which comes from quantum physics, that's defined as a limitless field of all possibilities that is formless and unbounded from which everything in the entire known Universe has emerged. Many religious traditions speak of this *Field* simply as "God" - or "The Kingdom of God" - or the Divine.

Unisphere is *Universal Consciousness* - which can also be referred to as *"The One", the Oneness within all of Consciousness, the Source of All That Is, Infinite Intelligence, The Unified Field, God.*

Universal Consciousness – see *The Transcendent*

Visionary Archetypes are poetic images of our greater potential or possibility. They represent qualities and virtues on ever-higher levels of human consciousness. Visionary archetypes are symbolic templates that point us to higher stages of inner development and to the qualities and realms of creative expression we strive to achieve. They can be thought of as pictorial representations of superior moral qualities which can empower and motivate us to express something greater in ourselves, a promise of a more positive future for our life.

✳ THE STORY OF AWAKENING WITHIN THE FIRST NARRATIVES ✳

IN THE CONCEPTUAL DESIGN of **Journey of *The Great Circle***, there is a poetic interweaving of themes within the first four contemplative narratives of each volume. Together these four narratives reveal "a hidden archetypal story" about every person's *spiritual journey of discovery.*

The first four narratives of the Spring Volume are:
1) Gifts of Spring
2) Qualities Within the Seasons of Life
3) The Great Story of Awakening
4) *Journey of Awakening*

The Transcendent Gifts of the Four Seasons

The first narrative of every volume depicts the transcendent gifts of each season, such as "Gifts of Spring" in this volume. Each season has four qualities listed that describe important interior aspects of our unfolding lives. Every quality has a particular placement either in the north, east, south, or west orientation.

Qualities Within the Seasons of Life

The second narrative within each of the four volumes is called "Qualities Within the Seasons of Life". This narrative lists all the transcendent qualities from the season on the previous page as well as all four qualities from each of the other seasons from the remaining volumes. Therefore, each of the four seasons displays four essential qualities (totaling sixteen individual qualities) that relate to our human developmental journey.

The Great Story of Awakening

The third narrative of each volume is called "The Great Story of Awakening". This narrative explains how the universal archetypal story of our spiritual awakening can be derived from organizing the four transcendent qualities from each of the four seasons into four specific chapters of a "story" that we are calling "The Great Story". These four chapters are the key components of the universal story of an awakening life (The Great Story) - and are listed as:

1) *The Great Circle*
2) Pillars of Awakening
3) Master of Freedom
4) Spheres of Contribution

"The Great Story of Awakening" can be thought of as "the spiritual portrayal of an awakening life" - and is the personal story of our conscious inner development and expansion of our awareness. It is our individual *journey of awakening*, our *journey of self-mastery*, in which we learn to awaken to a higher stage of spiritual consciousness.

The First Chapter: *The Great Circle*

The first chapter of "The Great Story of Awakening" is called **The Great Circle.** This chapter is formulated by gathering the first or top quality of each season from the previous narrative entitled "Qualities Within the Seasons of Life". The chapter of **The Great Circle** includes the following four qualities:

1) From **Winter:**   Align With *"The One"*   - (renewal and alignment)
2) From **Spring:**   Outward Expression   - (creativity and contribution)
3) From **Summer:**   Serve *"The Many"*   - (service to others and cultivating self-care)
4) From **Autumn:**   Inward Expansion   - (development and expanding awareness)

As we explore the daily narratives throughout this book, we will be introduced to the various dynamics at play in the world and in our lives. The first chapter called **The Great Circle** speaks to the natural invitation from *The Transcendent Impulse of Life* to learn what our life is truly about, discover what really matters, and cultivate an awareness of how to live a life of inner freedom.

The Second Chapter: Pillars of Awakening

In the first chapter, **The Great Circle** invites us to explore the Big Questions of *Life* and what our life is truly about. The personal inner development from this pursuit provides us with insights about the next segment of our unfolding story of discovery.

The second chapter, **Pillars of Awakening**, is created by gathering the second set of transcendent qualities from the narrative "Qualities Within the Seasons of Life". This includes the four following qualities:

1) **Winter:**   Oneness
2) **Spring:**   Acceptance
3) **Summer:**   Surrender
4) **Autumn:**   Gratitude

These four qualities are actually different ways to describe self-love and unconditional love - and are the personal attributes we develop using daily transformative practice to consciously transform our suffering into a life of inner freedom.

As an *artist of life*, we practice these spiritual attributes as a way to develop our highest expression of ourselves, as a means to cultivate our creative potential, and as a vehicle to reach for the next horizon of possibility of what we can become. Through our daily practice, we learn to maintain an ongoing alignment with *the Essence of Creation, the Source of Life, the Love of God.* And we reconnect with a natural transcendent yearning within us to feel this alignment in every moment of our life.

The Third Chapter: Master of Freedom

As we develop spiritual maturity and learn to maintain an alignment with *Life*, with *the Source of All That Is* we enter into the third chapter of our *awakening journey*, **Master of Freedom**.

Master of Freedom is the visionary archetypal image of an individual who is a fully integrated awakened being - and who experiences inner freedom, consciously maintains an alignment with *the Source of All That Is,* and uses his or her unique gifts and talents to serve the good of all. The chapter **Master of Freedom** is formulated by gathering the third set of transcendent qualities from the narrative "Qualities Within the Seasons of Life". This includes the qualities:

1) **Winter:**   Awakened Presence
2) **Spring:**   Endless Creativity
3) **Summer:**   Unconditional Love
4) **Autumn:**   Limitless Development

Through dedicated daily transformative practice these four qualities empower us to integrate our inner development into our everyday life as an embodied and anchored experience. These are the qualities of consciously cultivating the mastery of living a life of inner freedom - in other words, living an awakened life. Once this level of spiritual awareness has been realized, it becomes obvious that the most important way to use our creative energy is to offer our unique mission to the world through our personal contributions. Furthermore, we recognize how natural it is to follow the inner guidance of our heart as we share our novel contributions to help create a more glorious world.

The Fourth Chapter: Spheres of Contribution

The fourth chapter of "The Great Story of Awakening" is called **Spheres of Contribution**. As we explore this chapter, we discover ever-greater ways of living in this world and offering our creative gifts and talents. The chapter **Spheres of Contribution** gathers the fourth set of transcendent qualities from the narrative "Qualities Within the Seasons of Life". These include:

1) **Winter:**   Contributions to Oneself
2) **Spring:**   Contributions to Family
3) **Summer:**   Contributions to Community
4) **Autumn:**   Contributions to the World

When we learn to maintain an experience of living our life with peace of mind and inner freedom, the next obvious and intrinsic awareness is for us to serve the wellbeing of others - and to contribute our unique creative gifts and talents.

When these four chapters, ***The Great Circle***, **Pillars of Awakening, Master of Freedom,** and **Spheres of Contribution** are placed together sequentially, they form the universal great story of our spiritual awakening, or what has been referred to in this book as **"The Great Story of Awakening".**

THE GREAT STORY
OF AWAKENING - SPRING VOLUME

Quadrant Directions	Gifts of Spring		Qualities Within the Seasons of Life		The Great Story of Awakening
NORTH Winter	**Outward Expression**	*	Align With *"The One"*		*The Great Circle*
		+	Oneness	*	Align With *"The One"*
		–	Awakened Presence	*	**Outward Expression**
		x	Contributions to Oneself	*	Serve *"The Many"*
				*	Inward Expansion
EAST Spring	**Acceptance**	*	**Outward Expression**		**Pillars of Awakening**
		+	**Acceptance**	+	Oneness
		–	**Endless Creativity**	+	**Acceptance**
		x	**Contributions to Family**	+	Surrender
				+	Gratitude
SOUTH Summer	**Endless Creativity**	*	Serve *"The Many"*		**Master of Freedom**
		+	Surrender	–	Awakened Presence
		–	Unconditional Love	–	**Endless Creativity**
		x	Contributions to Community	–	Unconditional Love
				–	Limitless Development
WEST Autumn	**Contributions to Family**	*	Inward Expansion		**Spheres of Contribution**
		+	Gratitude	x	Contributions to Oneself
		–	Limitless Development	x	**Contributions to Family**
		x	Contributions to the World	x	Contributions to Community
				x	Contributions to the World

Journey of Awakening

The fourth contemplative narrative found within each volume is entitled *"Journey of Awakening"*. It has been written as another pragmatic version and additional way of understanding the preceding narrative **"The Great Story of Awakening"**.

"Journey of Awakening", with its four stages that describe our *spiritual journey*, form the foundation for our conscious exploration and inner development of self throughout the four volumes of **Journey of *The Great Circle***. The four stages are:

1) Development = *The Great Circle*
2) Transformation = Pillars of Awakening
3) Mastery = Master of Freedom
4) Contribution = Spheres of Contribution

✳ THE DANCE, POETRY, AND SONG OF THE FRONT COVER ART ✳

THE FRONT COVER ART of **Journey of *The Great Circle*** is a visual representation of the relationship between three facets of reality: the transcendent aspect of life, one's *Eternal Nature*, and one's physical embodiment. In other words - it is a symbolic representation of the integration of *Spirit, Soul*, and body.

We are so much more than we appear to be. Our physical bodies are just a small part of the magnificent totality of who we really are. The realm of our physical body is like an iceberg that appears above the surface of the water. Yet ninety percent of the mass of an iceberg remains invisible underneath the ocean's waters. Similarly a vast part of who we really are remains invisible to our senses, yet it is present in, and determines, every aspect of our life.

Our physical body is obviously visible in the world of form, yet our *True Eternal Nature* and *the Infinite Intelligence within All That Is,* which created everything in the Cosmos, is invisible to our five senses.

The artwork of the front cover symbolically represents this awareness, and gives us a visual metaphor to use to deepen our understanding of it.

The black and white meditator represents our physical body that is embarked on a *journey of discovery* to learn to love all of life unconditionally.

The gold branches and roots of the Tree of Life represent our *True Eternal Nature,* our *Higher Self,* our *Soul,* which is eternal and unbounded - and is the consciousness that is mirrored in our physical body.

The circle around the Tree of Life, as well as the Universe of infinite stars, represent *the Transcendent, the Infinite Intelligence* of the Universe, *the Source of All That Is.*

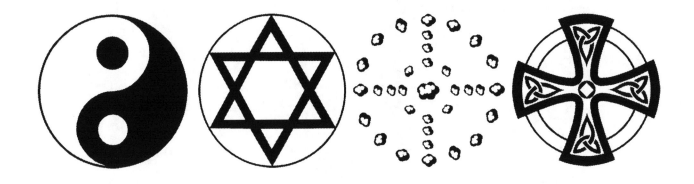

✳ RESOURCES ✳

Braden, Gregg. *The Isaiah Effect + The Divine Matrix*

Brown, Michael. *The Presence Process*

Capra, Fritjof. *The Tao of Physics*

Chopra, Deepak. *The Path of Love + The Seven Spiritual Laws of Success + How To Know God + Quantum Healing*

Cohen, Andrew. *Evolutionary Enlightenment + What Is Enlightenment Magazine*

Davies, Paul. *The Mind of God*

Dispenza, Joe. *Becoming Supernatural + Breaking the Habit of Being Yourself + You Are The Placebo*

Dowd, Michael. *Thank God For Evolution*

Green, Brian. *The Fabric of the Cosmos*

Hawkins, David. *Power Vs. Force + Discovery of the Presence of God + The Eye of the I*

Houston, Jean. *The Possible Human + Life Force + A Mythic Life*

Hubbard, Barbara Marx. *Conscious Evolution*

Katie, Byron. *Loving What Is*

Lipton, Bruce and Steve Bhaerman. *Spontaneous Evolution: Our Positive Future and a Way To Get There From Here*

Mandelbrot, Benoit. *The Fractal Geometry of Nature*

McTaggert, Lynne. *The Field*

Millman, Dan. *Way of the Peaceful Warrior*

Ming-Dao, Deng. *365 Tao Daily Meditations*

Moore, Robert and Douglas Gillette. *King, Warrior, Magician, Lover*

Morter, Sue. *The Energy Codes*

Murphy, Michael. *The Future of the Body*

Patten, Terry. *A New Republic of the Heart*

Ra, Kaia. *The Sophia Code*

Reich, Robert. *The Common Good*

Rudd, Richard. *The Gene Keys*

Swimme, Brian. *Canticle to the Cosmos*

Swimme, Brian and Thomas Berry. *The Universe Story*

Teilhard de Chardin. *The Human Phenomenon*

Tolle, Eckhart. *The Power of Now + A New Earth*

Trott, Susan. *The Holy Man*

Tzu, Lao. *The Way Of Life*

Wilbur, Ken. *The Marriage of Sense and Soul + Sex, Ecology, Spirituality - The Spirit of Evolution*

Williamson, Marianne. *A Return To Love + Enchanted Love + The Healing of America + Everyday Grace*

Yogananda, Paramahansa. *Autobiography of a Yogi*

The new creation story of *evolutionary spirituality*
merges God with evolution
- merges an *Infinite Intelligence* with an ever-unfolding Universe.
It provides us with the gifts of a much larger perspective of reality
inspiring us to further develop our unlimited potential,
to motivate us to transform our fears and limitations,
to create the seeds of greater compassion for all of life,
and to take responsible conscious actions
toward building a more sustainable future.

✳ ACKNOWLEDGEMENTS ✳

I THANK THE FOLLOWING PEOPLE for helping me bring this creative project into form.

First, I thank my dear friend, Bob Sizelove, with whom I've shared many adventurous camping trips for over a decade. During one of these camping trips at a place we call "paradise", I received my first Contemplative Circle which became the springboard for **Journey of The Great Circle**. For years, Bob and I have discussed the primary themes of this book around a blazing campfire under a star-strung sky. Bob's deep devotion to God and his commitment to ongoing self-development and service has been an inspiring aspect for me in writing this book.

Next, I thank my friend, Jo Norris, for her constant support of my writings. Jo is a progressive and creative catalyst for change and has touched so many people with her loving presence and wisdom. She has touched and inspired me profoundly. Jo has been a supportive angel at many steps during the evolution of this book.

I thank my Beloved partner, Yana DiAngelis, for her unconditional love and perpetual support of seeing the holiness and magnificence within me. Her unwavering recognition of who I really am has been a powerful testament of the unconditional love and compassion that is possible for our glorious world. Her love gave me inner strength during the completion of this project.

I thank my Soul Friend and Anum Cara, Enocha Ranjita Ryan, for years of listening to me read each morning the daily contemplative narrative. She has been such a fervent and constant support of my creativity. Her steady love and the inspiring way she lives her life was so empowering to me in bringing these writings into manifestation.

Furthermore, I thank my dear friend, Maria Cavendish, for her loving support and encouragement all the many years as I spent time contemplating at the creek to bring through this body of work.

I thank my long time friend, Shambhu, who is a masterful guitar recording artist and creative wonder. Shambhu's consistent support and encouragement of all my creative endeavors has been a blessed gift in my life.

And I thank the following editing angels: Maureen Levy for her Amazonian feats, Chaka Ken-Varley, Robert Varley, Kathleen Haverkamp, Rhianne Teija Newluhnd, and those who have given me discerning feedback and assistance in various ways toward the polishing of this work: Shanti Norman, Karl Anthony, Mia Margaret, Charley Thweatt, and Iala Jaggs for showing me a magical place at the creek where I spent over 10 years downloading the inspiration for this book.

As a final note, I thank the following inspiring teachers of philosophical and spiritual viewpoints that have pointed me to embracing larger perspectives of what I believe my life is truly about and what really matters: Marianne Williamson, Jean Houston, Barbara Marx Hubbard, Deepak Chopra, Joe Dispenza, Dr. Sue Morter, Gregg Braden, Alan Cohen, Andrew Harvey, Ken Wilber, Michael Dowd, Brian Swimme, Andrew Cohen, Kaia Ra, and Paramahansa Yogananda.

✳ ABOUT THE AUTHOR ✳

Oman Ken has devoted his life to being a multi-instrumentalist and singer. He lives in a home filled with exotic instruments from around the world, and professionally has focused his musical presentations on the harp, guitar, piano, Native American and ethnic flutes, as well as the gift of his voice. He has performed hundreds of concerts and celebrations across the United States while creating 15 professional recordings of his original vocal and instrumental music.

Oman has also composed three Ritual Theater musicals which he directed and produced in Hawaii, entitled "Genesis: A Ritual of Transformation", "Starwheel: Journey of the Sacred Circle", and "The Mask and the Sword". Furthermore, he has produced myriad multi-media Solstice and Equinox Celebrations with a troupe of 25 people in Houston, Texas and Cincinnati, Ohio.

Oman has presented his transformational workshops: "The Ceremonial Art of Celebration", "Dance Movement as Spiritual Practice", and "The Power Within the Archetypes of the King, Warrior, Magician, and Lover", in various spiritual conferences and retreats around the United States.

After a challenging physical condition made it unfeasible to continue his musical travels, Oman deepened his spiritual quest for inner freedom by spending an abundance of time in Nature contemplating what life is truly about - and what really matters.

The result of his personal investigations was a host of poetic contemplative narratives that became the foundation for this book **Journey of The Great Circle**.

Oman now lives in the majestic Red Rocks of Sedona, Arizona.   JourneyOfTheGreatCircle.com

JOURNEY OF *THE GREAT CIRCLE*
DAILY AFFIRMATION STATEMENTS FOR SPRING

(Copy - then cut along the dotted lines to carry an affirmation with you each day)

I - THE DANCE OF THE INFINITE SEASONS

MARCH 19 or 20   GIFTS OF SPRING

I have a personal mission to use my unique creative talents to help co-create a better world.

MARCH 19 or 20   QUALITIES WITHIN THE SEASONS OF LIFE

The creative impulse within me is the same Infinitely Creative Intelligence that spins the Cosmos.

MARCH 21   THE GREAT STORY OF AWAKENING

My spiritual journey is the same as my Soul's longing to learn to love all of life unconditionally.

MARCH 22   *JOURNEY OF AWAKENING*

Today I expand my awareness of what my life is truly about - and what really matters.

MARCH 23   TRANSFORMATION

I transform myself as I replace fear-based beliefs with love-centered beliefs that empower me.

MARCH 24   TRANSFORMATIVE PRACTICE

Today I use daily transformative practice as a powerful way to learn to love unconditionally.

MARCH 25   FAITH

I have unwavering faith in the Transcendent Power that's pointing me to my greater potential.

MARCH 26   INNOCENCE

Today I willingly surrender everything in my life to the Infinite Presence of Love.

MARCH 27   POLARITIES OF EXISTENCE

Universal Consciousness and my Eternal Self are one - thus the Universe and I are one.

II - <u>THE POETRY OF *THE GREAT CIRCLE*</u>

MARCH 28   *THE GREAT CIRCLE*

My inner development gives creative shape to how my external reality is experienced in my life.

MARCH 29   *THE GREAT CIRCLE* OF HEART WISDOM AND COMPASSION

Learning what my life is truly about and what really matters transforms into greater compassion.

MARCH 30   *THE GREAT CIRCLE* OF THE STAR OF DAVID

I see the world with eyes of Love, and thus all I perceive points me to my journey of self-mastery.

MARCH 31   THE PERPETUAL UNFOLDING OF *INFINITE CREATIVITY*

The Creative Intelligence of the Universe is constantly inviting me to realize my Eternal Nature.

APRIL 1   *THE LIMITLESS FIELD OF INFINITE CREATIVITY*

The Infinite Creativity of the Universe is the same limitless creativity that flows through me.

APRIL 2   GOD AS "THE CREATION"

I am in awe of the vast Intelligence that animates the countless elegant expressions of Nature.

III - <u>MIND AWARENESS PRACTICES</u>

APRIL 3   FOUNDATIONAL TRANSFORMATIVE PRACTICES
Consistent self-cultivation is the center of my spiritual development.

APRIL 4   CONTEMPLATION
I consistently cultivate an awareness of what really matters - and what my life is truly about.

APRIL 5   A CONTEMPLATION PRACTICE
I frequently quiet my mind so as to receive heart wisdom and insights from my Eternal Self.

IV - <u>THE SONG OF EMBODIED LOVE</u>

APRIL 6   THE NATURAL STATES THAT EMERGE FROM *BEING*
I nurture a quiet mind allowing the natural states of peace, happiness, joy and harmony to arise.

APRIL 7   THE NATURAL STATE OF HAPPINESS
Today I choose to be happy for the blessed gift of simply being alive.

APRIL 8   PILLARS OF AWAKENING
I accept that my life is unfolding perfectly just as it is.

APRIL 9   ACCEPTANCE
I realize that my life is unfolding perfectly just as it is - and thus, I fully accept "what is".

APRIL 10   PATIENCE
I align myself with Life - so I may be intuitively guided to take right action at the proper time.

APRIL 11   PAIN VERSUS SUFFERING

I consciously respond to each experience of pain in my life and accept it as part of "what is".

APRIL 12   PATHWAYS OF SELF-INQUIRY

Asking questions about the purpose and meaning of my life helps me cultivate peace of mind.

V - <u>MIND AWARENESS PRACTICES</u>

APRIL 13   SELF-INQUIRY

I frequently ask myself "the Big Questions of life" as a way of discovering who I really am.

APRIL 14   CULTIVATING HAPPINESS

Today I choose to be happy which serves me to effectively respond to each situation in my life.

APRIL 15   NATURAL INTERESTS

Active engagement in the interests I'm passionate about awakens a greater purpose for my life.

VI - <u>ARCHETYPES OF CONSCIOUS CONTRIBUTION</u>

APRIL 16   EVOLUTION OF PRIMARY HUMAN IMPULSES

I realize that everything I experience is in my life to help me spiritually awaken to who I really am.

APRIL 17   PRIMARY EMOTIONAL NEEDS

My longing to feel safe, loved, empowered, and connected leads me to realizing who I really am.

APRIL 18   SPHERES OF CONTRIBUTION

I feel a natural yearning in me constantly inviting me to contribute my creative gifts and talents.

APRIL 19   CONTRIBUTION TO FAMILY

I support my "loved ones" by helping each person feel safe, loved, empowered, and connected.

APRIL 20   FAMILY ARCHETYPES

Today I use the power of my imagination to envision myself expressing my creative potential.

APRIL 21   *THE GREAT CIRCLE* OF THE ARCHETYPES

I consciously use my creative imagination as a tool to help me envision all that I desire to be.

APRIL 22   ARCHETYPES OF CONSCIOUS CONTRIBUTION

Today I offer my unique gifts and talents in ways that help create a better world.

APRIL 23   VISIONARY TEACHER

I support the authentic goodness, inner beauty, and true creative potential within all people.

APRIL 24   ALIGNMENT

Today I consciously align my awareness with the Source of Life, the Infinite Presence of Love.

APRIL 25   SUPPORT

Today I support the people in my life by honoring their intrinsic holiness and magnificence.

APRIL 26   EXEMPLAR

I choose to live the greatest life I can possibly live - and be the best person I can possibly be.

VII - <u>MIND AWARENESS PRACTICES</u>

APRIL 27   WELLBEING OF THE MIND
Today I question what I believe is true - so I can be mindful to transform any loveless beliefs.

- -

APRIL 28   CULTIVATING THE GIFTS OF AN AWAKENED LIFE
Daily transformative practices help me cultivate peace of mind and a life of inner freedom.

- -

APRIL 29   MIND AWARENESS
Today I consciously keep my awareness aligned with the Infinite Presence of Love.

- -

VIII - <u>ARCHETYPES OF LIFE MASTERY</u>

APRIL 30   EVOLUTION OF *THE SPIRITUAL JOURNEY*
I am awakening to my destiny of loving all people and all expressions of life unconditionally.

- -

MAY 1   ARCHETYPES OF LIFE MASTERY
Today I use the power of my unlimited imagination to help manifest the life I desire to create.

- -

MAY 2   SPIRITUAL MAGICIAN
Today I consciously co-create what Life has guided me to achieve that benefits the good of all.

- -

MAY 3   CONSCIOUS CO-CREATION
Today I align my awareness with Infinite Intelligence - and thus miracles are natural to me.

- -

MAY 4   INTENTION
Today I use the power of intention to manifest the desires of my heart.

- -

MAY 5 BELIEFS

I am constantly re-examining my beliefs so I may learn to love all of life more fully.

MAY 6 MODES OF BELIEF

My empowering beliefs help me develop my potential - and become the person I desire to be.

IX - <u>MIND AWARENESS PRACTICES</u>

MAY 7 RELEASE

Today I am mindful to release any disturbing emotions that arise in my awareness.

MAY 8 CULTIVATING CONSCIOUS CO-CREATION

I cultivate the power of intention as a conscious co-creator with the Natural Intelligence of Life.

MAY 9 AFFIRMATIONS FOR CO-CREATING INTENTION

Aligning with the Source of Life is key to co-creating the intentions I've been guided to manifest.

X - <u>THE EVOLUTIONARY PERSPECTIVE</u>

MAY 10 GIFTS FROM AN EVOLUTIONARY PERSPECTIVE

An evolutionary perspective motivates me to examine and constructively transform my life.

MAY 11 THE DYNAMIC FORCES OF TRANSFORMATION

Today I expand my awareness of what is true through the discipline of transformative practice.

MAY 12 THE FRACTAL NATURE OF EMERGENT EVOLUTION

It is my destiny to live an awakened life, for awakening is the natural unfolding within everything.

MAY 13   EVOLUTION OF BASIC HUMAN IMPULSES

I feel a natural yearning that constantly invites me to be aware of my Oneness with all of life.

MAY 14   STAGES OF DEVELOPMENTAL AWARENESS

The natural arc of my life involves cultivating an awareness of ever-greater inclusion of others.

MAY 15   LEAPS OF AWARENESS IN HUMAN EVOLUTION

Embracing a "Big Picture perspective of the world" helps me give deeper meaning to my life.

MAY 16   TIMELINE OF CONSCIOUSNESS

I trust that everything is unfolding perfectly in Life's perfect timing.

MAY 17   EVOLUTION OF SOCIAL DEVELOPMENT

The true power of my spiritual awakening is demonstrated in how I serve the wellbeing of others.

MAY 18   ENLIGHTENED SOCIETY

As I cultivate a more loving awareness, the world around me transforms into a more loving place.

XI - ARCHETYPES OF HIGHER KNOWLEDGE

MAY 19   ARCHETYPES OF HIGHER KNOWLEDGE

I activate the unlimited power of my creative imagination to become the person I desire to be.

MAY 20   AWAKENED PHILOSOPHER

I continually support the most moral and ethical ways to live harmoniously with others.

MAY 21 EVOLUTION OF THE MEANING OF LIFE

The meaning of my life in this moment comes from whatever meaning I currently choose to give it.

MAY 22 HIGH MORALITY

Today I align my awareness with the Source of Life in order to make the highest moral choices.

MAY 23 EVOLUTION OF GOVERNANCE

Today I help create a more enlightened world by consciously transforming my own inner being.

XII - MIND AWARENESS PRACTICES

MAY 24 CREATIVE POWER IN RELATION TO TIME

The thoughts I consciously choose to hold in my mind have creative power to shape my future.

MAY 25 BEING PRESENT

I recognize that the unlimited creative power of Life is always available in the present moment.

MAY 26 FEELING GOOD

I feel good about my life - because I consciously choose to feel good.

XIII - ARCHETYPES OF SPIRITUAL AWAKENING

MAY 27 ARCHETYPES OF SPIRITUAL AWAKENING

My life is a journey of discovery - a spiritual journey - a journey of awakening.

MAY 28 *INFINITE PRESENCE*

The Transcendent Self - my True Nature, which is eternal and unbounded, is who I really am.

MAY 29   MANY NAMES FOR *THE SOURCE OF ALL THAT IS*

I am one with the Source of All That Is - from which everything in the world has been created.

MAY 30   QUALITIES OF GOD

Today I am aligned with the Source of Life - and thus, I humbly embody the qualities of God.

MAY 31   THE EVOLUTION OF GOD

As I cultivate my awareness and spiritually evolve, my understanding of God evolves as well.

XIV - MIND AWARENESS PRACTICES

JUNE 1   AFFIRMATIONS FOR CREATING TRANSFORMATION

I am aware of my constant flow of blessings and grace.

JUNE 2   QUESTIONS SEEKING OPPORTUNITIES

Accepting what is enables me to receive the blessings and gifts that come from my challenges.

JUNE 3   DIVINE PARADOX PRAYER

I embrace life's existential paradoxes, which open my heart to the gifts of spiritual freedom.

XV - NAVIGATING THE JOURNEY OF *THE GREAT CIRCLE*

JUNE 4   PARADOX

Opening my heart to life's existential paradoxes helps me to realize my True Eternal Nature.

JUNE 5   EXISTENTIAL PARADOXES

My life is unfolding perfectly just as it is - yet I am here to help the world become more perfect.

JUNE 6 ILLUSIONS OF THE MIND

Today I consciously focus my mind on what really matters - and let go of any loveless thoughts.

JUNE 7 TRUTH

My beliefs are thoughts I currently hold to be true - yet what I believe is constantly changing.

JUNE 8 *THE GREAT CIRCLE* OF CONSCIOUSNESS AND CREATIVITY

Everything that I perceive in the world of form is created in "the womb of consciousness".

JUNE 9 *EXTERIOR EVOLUTIONARY IMPULSE*

My external reality is a mirror, an out-picturing, of my consciousness and internal awareness.

JUNE 10 VARIOUS MEANS OF MANIFESTATION

I use the creative power of intention to manifest the desires that I am guided by Life to achieve.

XVI - THE ART OF TRANSFORMATION AND HEALING

JUNE 11 *THE GREAT CIRCLE* OF DEVELOPMENT AND TRANSFORMATION

As I learn to love more fully, Life then mirrors my inner development as outer transformation.

JUNE 12 *THE GREAT CIRCLE* OF THE SPHERES OF CONSCIOUSNESS AND FIELDS OF CREATION

Consciousness and creation are merged as one endless "dance of Limitless Love" in my life.

JUNE 13 *THE FIELD OF LIGHT*

Everything I perceive has been created from a limitless ocean of pure universal energy.

JUNE 14   *THE FIELD OF LOVE*

Everything in my life has been shaped into form by the Infinite Creativity of Limitless Love.

- -

JUNE 15   *THE FIELD OF POWER*

All I perceive is made of pure Light organized into form by the creative artistry of Limitless Love.

- -

JUNE 16   FIELDS OF CREATION

I manifest my love-centered intentions by consciously co-creating with the Source of All That Is.

- -

JUNE 17   UNIVERSAL DYNAMICS OF EMERGENT HEALING

My true healing is about using the challenging events of my life to learn to love unconditionally.

- -

JUNE 18   *THE GREAT CIRCLE* OF AWAKENING AND
                   EMERGENT HEALING

I claim the holiness and magnificence of who I am and feel unconditionally loved by all of creation.

- -

XVII - <u>CONCLUSION – SACRED DESTINY</u>

JUNE 19   *THE GREAT CIRCLE* OF MAINTAINING INNER FREEDOM

Each day I learn new ways to expand my awareness, help create a better world and serve others.

- -

Printed in the United States
by Baker & Taylor Publisher Services